Nature Education with Young Children

Now in a fully updated second edition, *Nature Education and Young Children* remains a thoughtful, sophisticated teacher resource that blends theory and practice on nature education, children's inquiry-based learning, and reflective teaching.

Reorganized to enhance its intuitive flow, this edition features a Foreword by David Sobel and three wholly new chapters examining nature and literacy in kindergarten, outdoor play and children's agency in a forest school, and the power of nature inquiry for dual language learners. Revised to reflect the latest research and guidelines, this book offers a seamless integration of science concepts into the daily intellectual and social investigations that occur in early childhood.

With a fresh framing of nature exploration in the context of our current educational landscape, this text is a comprehensive guide for educators and students looking to introduce and deepen connections between nature education and teacher inquiry and reflection.

Daniel R. Meier is Professor of Elementary Education at San Francisco State University, USA.

Stephanie Sisk-Hilton is Professor of Elementary Education at San Francisco State University, USA.

Nature Education with Young Children

Integrating Inquiry and Practice

Second Edition

EDITORS

Daniel R. Meier and Stephanie Sisk-Hilton

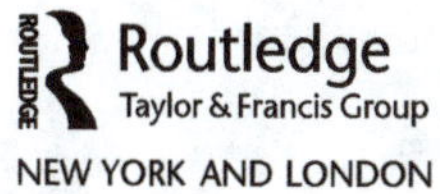

NEW YORK AND LONDON

Second edition published 2020
by Routledge
52 Vanderbilt Avenue, New York, NY 10017

and by Routledge
2 Park Square, Milton Park, Abingdon, Oxon, OX14 4RN

Routledge is an imprint of the Taylor & Francis Group, an informa business

First edition published by Routledge 2013

Library of Congress Cataloging-in-Publication Data
Names: Meier, Daniel R, editor. | Sisk-Hilton, Stephanie, editor.
Title: Nature education with young children : integrating inquiry and practice / edited by Daniel R. Meier and Stephanie Sisk-Hilton.
Description: 2nd edition. | New York, NY : Routledge, 2020. | Includes bibliographical references and index.
Identifiers: LCCN 2019044050 (print) | LCCN 2019044051 (ebook) | ISBN 9780367138530 (hardback) | ISBN 9780367138547 (paperback) | ISBN 9780429028885 (ebook)
Subjects: LCSH: Nature study. | Education, Preschool. | Inquiry-based learning. | Reflective teaching.
Classification: LCC LB1140.5.S34 N38 2020 (print) | LCC LB1140.5.S34 (ebook) | DDC 372.35/7–dc23
LC record available at https://lccn.loc.gov/2019044050
LC ebook record available at https://lccn.loc.gov/2019044051

ISBN: 978-0-367-13853-0 (hbk)
ISBN: 978-0-367-13854-7 (pbk)
ISBN: 978-0-429-02888-5 (ebk)

Typeset in Minion Pro
by Wearset Ltd, Boldon, Tyne and Wear

In memory of my father, who loved the beach and the water and the salt air

— Daniel R. Meier

to Maxwell and Juliet, whose love of nature, science, and life fuels my own

— Stephanie Sisk-Hilton

CONTENTS

FIGURES

CONTRIBUTOR BIOGRAPHIES

Alicia Alvarez was born in Jalisco, Mexico. She has been working at Las Americas Early Education School as a paraprofessional for the last six years. She is currently taking courses at City College of San Francisco to complete her AA degree in early childhood education. She enjoys working with children in the schoolyard garden, observing how they interact with nature and take care of plants. She finds delight in listening to children's ideas and uses her observations to write Learning Stories, which she shares with families and also with colleagues in monthly teacher inquiry meetings. She has attended ecology and nature-based workshops offered by the school district. Although she grew up in a big city, she remembers spending fun summers as a child in her grandma's house in a small agricultural community where she played in the local river with her siblings. She would like the young children under her care to also find enjoyment in nature-based activities as part of their preschool experience.

Darcy Campbell has over 30 years of experience working with teachers, families, and children in the San Francisco Bay Area. She has taught and learned from children three months to 12 years old. She has taught early childhood education courses at San Francisco State University for 16 years. She conducts early childhood training and consultations with families, schools, and educational organizations internationally, and is the Director of Cow Hollow School, a magical inquiry-based school in the Presidio. She is a strong advocate for children and specializes in reflective, responsive, collaborative teaching and parenting practices and is the founder of R.E.A.L. Parenting and Teaching, co-founder of Keep It Real, two seminar platforms for responsive parenting and teaching practices, and founder of the Cow Hollow School The Collabatory, a social responsibility seminar series for parents and teachers.

Camille T. Dungy is the author of the poetry collections *Trophic Cascade* (Wesleyan University Press, 2017), *Smith Blue* (Southern Illinois University Press, 2011), *Suck on the Marrow* (Red Hen Press, 2010), and *What to Eat, What to Drink, What to Leave for Poison* (Red Hen Press, 2006). She has also written a collection of personal essays, *Guidebook to Relative Strangers: Journeys into Race, Motherhood and History* (W.W. Norton, 2017). She is the editor of *Black Nature: Four Centuries of African American Nature Poetry* (UGA, 2009), coeditor of *From the Fishouse: An Anthology of Poems that Sing, Rhyme, Resound, Syncopate, Alliterate, and Just Plain Sound Great* (Persea, 2009), and assistant editor of *Gathering Ground: A Reader Celebrating Cave Canem's First Decade* (University of Michigan Press, 2006). Her poems and essays appear widely in anthologies, print journals, and online. Her numerous honors and awards include fellowships from the Guggenheim Foundation, the National Endowment for the Arts, Cave Canem, and the Sustainable Arts Foundation, as well as an American Book Award, two Northern California Book Awards, a Silver Medal Winner in the California Book Award, and two NAACP Image Award nominations. Dungy is a Professor in the English Department at Colorado State University.

Isauro M. Escamilla is an early childhood educator at Las Americas Early Education School, a dual language preschool of the San Francisco Unified School District. He has authored a number of articles and book chapters on teacher inquiry and documentation in early childhood education. He was elected to serve a four-year-term as a member of the National Association for the Education of Young Children (NAEYC) Governing Board in 2016. He has taught undergraduate courses and is currently a doctoral student in the Educational Leadership EdD program at San Francisco State University. He considers the school garden and nature-based activities integral components of the children's preschool education. He believes that these early experiences will help children develop a sense of place and stewardship to protect plants, animals, and our natural environments. He believes that the process of reflection is better performed in community with other teachers and instructional coaches. He proposes writing Learning Stories to capture children's theories, emotions, knowledge, and skills from a strength-based pedagogical perspective.

Anna Golden is an artist and teacher in Richmond, Virginia. She is Atelierista at Sabot at Stony Point School, a preschool through eighth grade independent school that is influenced by the Reggio Emilia approach. In this capacity, she helps children test hypotheses and to make their ideas visible. She writes about and presents stories from her teacher-research at conferences in the United States and abroad. You can find her blog, Atelierista, at atelierista-anna.blogspot.com.

Sahara Gonzalez-Garcia has been working at Las Americas Early Education School for 13 years as a paraprofessional. She was born in Guadalajara Jalisco, Mexico. As a young child growing up in a small town in Mexico she recalls playing in her grandmother's orchard. Among plum, mango, orange, and lemon trees, together with her siblings and cousins, she created forts with fabrics hanging from tree branches and made pretend foods with leaves, flowers, pebbles, and mud. Her early childhood memories have influenced her pedagogical stance and she would like her young students to include natural elements in their daily play since nature-based games and activities help children to soothe themselves and have fun while learning and playing. She is pursuing an AA degree in early childhood education at City College of San Francisco. She loves working with children in the garden and writing Learning Stories in Spanish and English. She believes that writing Learning Stories based on daily occurrences and sharing them with other teachers has helped her to become a better observer and writer.

Marty Gravett is Director of Early Childhood Education and Outreach at Sabot at Stony Point an independent, Reggio-inspired social constructivist school – preschool through eighth grade in Richmond, Virginia. In the field for almost 40 years – teaching in both early childhood and university settings, mentoring, administrating, and consulting – she has thrice visited the schools of Reggio Emilia, and presents nationally and internationally on the work of Sabot at Stony Point. She writes about her practice with young children.

Kelsey Henning grew up in a small central coast town in California and spent a majority of her childhood in the outdoors – camping, hiking, and exploring. Her deep connection to nature and passion with working with young children both began at a young age and has continued and strengthened throughout her adulthood. After attending San Francisco State University and earning her BA in Child and Adolescent Development, she began working as a preschool teacher and eventually an education coordinator at a school located in the Presidio in San Francisco. Within her various roles in the field of early childhood education, her passion for connecting children with nature has never faltered. She enjoys watching how young children use their imaginations to discover the world around them and is constantly fascinated with the way children investigate, connect, and construct meaning around the natural environment. She currently works at Cow Hollow School in the Presidio as a teacher of three to five year olds and after ten years of working with young children she has become even more enthusiastic, passionate, and curious about the way in which children identify themselves in the world.

Gita Jayewardene was born and raised in Sri Lanka where she learned to appreciate nature as a young child. She holds an MA in early childhood education from San Francisco State University, and her MA field study focused on promoting nature education for toddlers. She is a long-time and experienced early childhood educator, and has worked for a number of years at the University Child Care Center of the University of California, San Francisco. She particularly enjoys working with toddlers, and exploring nature found in an urban area.

Lilian G. Katz is Professor Emerita of Early Childhood Education at the University of Illinois (Urbana-Champaign) where she is on the staff of the Clearinghouse on Early Education and Parenting (CEEP). She is a Past President of the National Association for the Education of Young Children, and the first President of the Illinois Association for the Education of Young Children. She is currently editor of the first online peer-reviewed *trilingual* early childhood journal, *Early Childhood Research & Practice (English, Spanish & Chinese).* She is the author of more than 100 publications including articles, chapters, books, pamphlets, etc., about early childhood education, teacher education, child development, and parenting of young children. She was founding editor of the *Early Childhood Research Quarterly.* Her most recent book (co-authored with J. H. Helm) is *Young Investigators: The Project Approach in the Early Years* (3rd edition, Praeger, 2014). In 2000 she published the second edition of *Engaging Children's Minds: The Project Approach* (3rd edition, Teachers College Press, 2016), co-authored with S. C. Chard. It has been translated into several languages, as have many of her other works.

Daniel R. Meier is Professor of Elementary Education at San Francisco State University where he teaches at the credential, MA, and

EdD levels in reading/language arts, narrative inquiry, qualitative research, international education, multilingualism and literacy, and families and communities. He has written numerous articles and books on teaching and learning, language and literacy, and reflective practice and teacher research. His most recent publications include the co-authored *Documentation and Inquiry in the Early Childhood Classroom* (Routledge, 2017), the co-authored *Narrative Inquiry in Early Childhood and Elementary School* (Routledge, 2016), and the forthcoming *Supporting Literacies for Children of Color – A Strength-Based Approach to Preschool Literacy Education* (Routledge, 2019). His current school-based work focuses on early childhood inquiry groups in the San Francisco Bay area and preschool early literacy development.

Jean A. Mendoza grew up exploring the outdoors and has advocated outdoor experiences for children all of her professional life. She holds a master's degree in early childhood education (University of Illinois Chicago), a master's in counseling psychology (Adler School of Professional Psychology), and a PhD in curriculum and instruction (early childhood) from University of Illinois at Urbana-Champaign. She has worked as a child care provider, a counselor of children and families, a child protection worker, an early childhood classroom teacher, a university faculty member, and a writer and editor of academic and professional materials in early care and education. An avid birder, she enjoys getting her grandchildren "out into nature."

Stephanie Sisk-Hilton is Professor of Elementary Education at San Francisco State University. Her teaching and research focus on the intersections of children's science learning, child development, and collaborative teacher learning. She received a PhD in Cognition and Development from The University of California, Berkeley, a Masters Degree in Education Policy and Administration from Stanford University, and a BA in Cognitive Science from Johns Hopkins University. She has taught elementary and middle school in Prince George's County, MD, Atlanta, GA, Brooklyn, NY, and Oakland and Berkeley, CA. She has also worked extensively as a teacher professional developer in school-wide curriculum reform and with science curriculum and pedagogy. She is the author of *Teaching and Learning in Public: Professional Development Through Shared Inquiry* (Teachers College Press, 2009) and co-author of *Narrative Inquiry in Early Childhood and Elementary School: Learning to Teach, Teaching Well* (Routledge, 2016).

Patricia Sullivan holds an MA and EdD in early childhood education. She is also the owner and director of Baby Steps, a home-based child-care program in San Francisco. She is a veteran early childhood educator, highly experienced with inquiry and nature education. Her school abuts a large, beautiful park in San Francisco, and her school makes ample and daily use of the park for play, science learning, nature exploration, and cross-age interactions and discoveries. She is also a passionate proponent of equity and social justice in early childhood education, her dissertation focused on the challenges and supports for African American early childhood students in higher education.

Heather B. Taylor has taught exclusively in the outdoors since 2007 at Berkeley Forest School, Duck's Nest Preschool, and an afternoon program she designed for elementary students, Outside School. She is reopening Outside School as an alternative to indoor education for children of kindergarten age and older in the East Bay, California. She also produces movies with her husband, became a Nationally Registered Emergency Medical Technician in 2018, and works on the Fire/Safety Team at Sonoma Raceway. You can reach her at teachoutside@gmail.com, view information about Outside School at www.outside.school, and connect to outdoor education resources at www.teachoutside.org.

Shawna Thompson is a lifelong educator and learner, and believes that emotional wellbeing and cognitive development are very much intertwined with our physical health. Social–emotional connectivity is also at the heart of her work. She is committed to advocating for the rights of children. She had the honor of being a founding teacher at a handful of excellent and innovative schools in San Francisco. In 2016 she became a mother and now has two little girls. Watching her babies grow and learn has deepened and intensified her progressive educational philosophy, dedication to learning in nature, and following the child's lead. On or off the job, she loves being in the outdoors; relaxing at the beach, going hiking, and camping are among her favorite activities. She also spends a lot of time in the kitchen and at farmers' markets, because she believes that home-cooked food from fresh ingredients is an essential building block of a happy life.

Jana Walsh is a native San Franciscan and attended City College of San Francisco and San Francisco State University, where she received her Master of Arts in Education: Concentration in Language and Literacy. A 20-year kindergarten teacher, she is passionate about incorporating science, literacy, and inquiry into her practice. She has attended teaching training workshops at Teachers College, Academy of Sciences, the SF Botanical Gardens, and the Exploratorium. She enjoys crossword puzzles, quilting, cooking, and watching movies. You can often find her walking in Golden Gate Park or Ocean Beach with her family and her Welsh Corgi, Buster.

Mabel Young has a Bachelors of Science in Human Development from University of California Davis and a minor in Education. She received her Masters in Early Childhood Education and has taught since 1987. Taking long daily hikes on and off trails and exploring the outdoor environment of land and sea with children keep her connected to the smallest creatures and the vast open space.

FOREWORD

David Sobel

What a joy to see that nature-based early childhood is starting to grow up and be respected by school administrators, parents, and teacher education faculty. The second volume of *Nature Education with Young Children: Integrating Inquiry and Practice* edited by Daniel R. Meier and Stephanie Sisk-Hilton represents the coming of age of this movement toward "naturalizing" early childhood education. No longer hidden in the closet or lost in the weeds, nature-based early childhood programs, like the ones illustrated in the diverse essays in this book, are getting the respect they deserve. Along with physicians who are writing prescriptions for more nature time for children and families, the authors of the provocative essays here are providing children with a healthy daily dose of spider webs, banana slugs, eucalyptus groves, marsh grasses, and jellyfish in the nearby natural world.

The nature preschool and forest kindergarten movement, which took hold in Europe about 60 years ago, adopted a very different approach toward early childhood education. Instead of only focusing on early literacy and numeracy skills, nature preschool and forest kindergarten educators aspired to developing social competence, individual resilience, and a readiness to learn in young children. There are more than 1000 forest kindergartens in Germany and there are programs throughout Scandinavia, the UK, Japan, and Australia. There's even an association of forest kindergartens in Korea. The conviction of these educators is that real natural world experience provides the confidence, resilience, and perseverance that are the foundation for increased motivation and improved academic performance in young students. The movement has been growing quickly in the United States over the past 20 years and there are now probably more that 500 early childhood programs which embrace a nature-based approach.

In the beginning these programs cropped up at nature centers in leafy suburbs or in rural areas. But then everyone realized that urban children probably needed a daily dose of nature more than rural children. Heart-of-the-city nature preschools then took root in Boston, Washington, DC, New York City, Atlanta, and Miami, followed by the innovative Tiny Trees program that spread across eight different urban parks in Seattle.

A number of these urban endeavors currently flourish in the community gardens, urban greenspace, and national parks in and around San Francisco. This is where much (but not all) of the inspired practice described in this book takes place. We're led into the hidden corners amid the urban bustle by teachers who appreciate the virtue of observing children's bewonderment with the natural world. As one author says, "It feels good to slow down a little, to walk together, hand in hand." Each of these authors takes you by the hand for a quiet walk with their children.

There are at least four different unique elements that weave through all of these essays:

TEACHERS DRAW INSPIRATION FROM THEIR OWN CHILDHOOD NATURE EXPERIENCES

Many of these teachers clearly articulate their own early experiences with nature and recognize these as a source of their commitment to providing similar experiences to urban children. Gita Jayewardene, who grew up in Sri Lanka, recalls "looking for gecko's eggs behind my father's bookshelves (their favorite place to lay eggs) and placing them in empty match-boxes lined with cotton wool." And her students are entranced with her stories of "*how I caught dragonflies, grasshoppers, worms, frogs and other creatures and about my pet fox, peacocks, squirrels and porcupine among others.*" Similarly, Heather B. Taylor recounts how her skills,

> as a natural scientist were developed by collecting insects, fish, polliwogs, and rocks, climbing trees, digging in dirt, sliding down hills, and splashing in twaterways, along with all the time in the world. A rusty coffee can was a place to store random treasures on my bedroom shelf. My family embraced the sciences and I was allowed to keep small animals for a week before returning them to their natural homes.

And Jana Walsh recalls her mother's richly timbred voice as they walked through Golden Gate Park identifying, "fuchsias, rhododendrons, rose geraniums, poppies, and especially nasturtiums with their surprisingly bright yellow and orange blooms and their hidden taste of sweet nectar (we were lucky we knew where to look)."

Research on the childhood experiences that lead to adult conservation values and behaviors has found two recurrent themes – many hours spent outdoors in keenly remembered wild or semi-wild places and an adult who taught respect for nature. The teacher reflections in this collection confirm this research. Moreover, it's wonderful to see teachers creating these same opportunities for the children who will need strong rootedness in nature to deal with the environmental challenges of the twenty-first century.

THE MARRIAGE BETWEEN NATURE-BASED AND REGGIO EMILIA PRACTICES

It's been fascinating to watch the nature-based education movement and the Reggio movement find each other over the past decade. It's a sign of maturation in the nature-based early childhood movement that teachers are committing to diverse ways of documenting their practice and conducting action research to uncover what's actually going on out there when children and banana slugs interact. As Anna Golden, the atelerista at The Sabot School in Richmond, VA notes,

> Documentation, in the sense in which the schools of Reggio Emilia use the word, is a form of "contextual curriculum" or a daily practice of teachers observing the children's activity, documenting through some graphic media, reflecting on the notes and images, and interpreting the children's process and learning.

This kind of Reggio attentiveness to child–nature interactions lends a new depth to teacher insight and allows teachers to communicate more effectively with parents about why it's important to have children outside. Anna's description of different children's experiences with a schoolyard labyrinth is a fascinating example of how teacher inquiry leads to both new understanding, and new curriculum ideas.

THE SURPRISING BENEFITS OF NATURE-BASED APPROACHES

When you start to look at something closely, through the various kinds of inquiry documented in this book, you see things you haven't seen before. This is one of the pleasures of place-based education – the emergence of the unexpected, the counter-intuitive finding. One of the intriguing findings that has cropped up in my evaluation work are examples of the virtue of nature-based work for language development with both language hesitant children and with English Language Learners. Children who never speak inside the classroom speak for the first time out in the woods. Children who arrive at programs with very little English proficiency experience unexpected leaps and bounds in their English competence as a function of farm-based programs. This same finding is nicely illustrated in Isauro M. Escamilla, Sahara Gonzalez-Garcia, and Alicia Alvarez's essay on dual language learners. Their Learning Story about Azel (one of their students) and Tatiana the Turtle is a fine illustration of weaving together an orphaned turtle, storytelling, multiple forms of artistic documentation and family engagement. The authors describe that, "Iterative observations and hands-on investigations over a sustained period of time allows children to play with new words in their home language or English." This approach both enhances language development and deepens children early scientific skills.

Then there are the wonderful essays on infants and toddlers, until now relatively ignored in the nature-based literature. Camille T. Dungy describes taking her babe-in-arms to the California Academy of Sciences where they watch the sea creatures in one of the tanks,

> As we stood quietly, in front of the moon jellies, I felt the baby's heel tap my hip in a rhythm that mimicked the fluttering of the jellies' bells. She was attending to the way these creatures floated through their world, and she was bringing this knowledge into her body.

It's wonderfully surprising to realize that this child is observing, and internalizing the movement pattern of the moon jellies through responsive leg movements. This is the kind of surprising insight that gets captured by the conscientious journaling of these authors.

CHILDREN'S VOICES RING THROUGH

This same kind of conscientious journaling gives us access to children's emergent language and sense-making. As a young father, I committed myself to capturing my own children's language and descriptions and also to capturing our conversations. When I went back and looked at them after a few years, I was both reminded of things I'd completely forgot, and I saw patterns in their interests and thinking that I'd never noticed. The contributing authors to this collection are masters at noticing the good conversation and getting it down before it evaporates from the teacher's memory. Therefore we're treated to fascinating conversations about "bad" black birds, banana slug's antennae, snake stuff, forest fairies, and lemonade trees. On an early forest foray, Marty Gravett and her students come upon a huge tree that had been uprooted and fallen across a small stream. She captures the childrens' attempts to understand what they were seeing:

Hannah: I found a bridge. No I didn't. It's a tree fallen down.
Hunter: It's a tree bridge.
Hannah: No, it's a tree fallen down.
Eric: It's like a bridge.

It's a great example of how spontaneous natural phenomena provoke descriptive language and metaphor-making. These snippets of conversation show up in most of the essays and they bring us right down into the world space and minds of children.

And so, I highly recommend this book to you. It will give you courage to head out into the vacant lot, the city park, the rocky shore, the ratty thicket with your students. These essays will encourage you to keep a sharpened pencil and an accessible journal in your daypack. And the accounts of children discovering the world will tune your ears to the unexpected languages of childhood. Thanks to Daniel R. Meier and Stephanie Sisk-Hilton for corralling all these attentive voices into one place.

ACKNOWLEDGMENTS

We first thank all of the contributors to this second volume on nature and science education in early childhood who provided such wonderful chapters. They are all devoted nature and science educators and believers in the power of the natural world for transforming children's lives. We also thank the children portrayed in this book for leading us along the right nature path, and also their families for giving their permission to have their children included in these chapters. Thanks, too, to the graduate students and other teachers who gave their permission to have their nature teaching portrayed in this book. We also give a big thank you to Misha Kydd, our editor, for supporting this book, and Olivia Powers, for her quick and helpful advice.

I (Daniel) would like thank my coeditor Stephanie Sisk-Hilton for being such a pleasure to work with – always patient, with a good sense of humor, and a real knack for knowing how to connect science, nature, and inquiry. Thank you! I also thank all of the contributors to this book who took the time and energy to support this book and make public their important work in nature education and inquiry.

I (Stephanie) would like to thank coeditor Daniel R. Meier for inviting me to be part of this project, for being so easy to collaborate with, and for keeping alive a focus on the wisdom and intellect of teachers through all of his work. I would also like to thank the amazing early childhood teachers through whom I have learned so much about learning in nature, particularly the teachers of the former Willow Street Schoolhouse – Diana Bickham, Helen Kim, and Ian Kahl. Finally, my greatest thanks to Philip, Max, and Juliet for cheering on and often participating in the research and writing of this book.

INTRODUCTION

> Go into the woods and look carefully. There, growing about six inches from the ground, is princess pine. Her present size gives no indication of her past glories. But admire her ability to adapt; her ability to accept less has ensured her survival.
>
> Marcia Bowden (1989, p. 97)

Marcia's book on nature was published 30 years ago, before the more recent spate of books on and attention to the need for children to get outdoors, unplug their electronics, dig and plant in school gardens, and in general appreciate and understand nature and the outdoors to save our planet and our world.

Like the pithy and yet insightful wonderings and wanderings of the consummate early childhood educator and storyteller Vivian Paley, Marcia encourages and invites us into nature and the world of wonderment and inquiry in small, interconnected ways:

> Go into the woods and look carefully. (p. 97)

> Late fall is a good time to explore stone walls. (p. 55)

> Most children find insects fascinating. Winter is an ideal season to develop that fascination. For then there are not any bees, hornets, mosquitoes, or black flies with which to contend. Before you take the children exploring, they should have an understanding of what they are looking for. (p. 106)

> On a day when children have excess energy, take them outside to dig up a Queen Anne's lace plant. The long taproot goes deep into

> the earth, searching for nutrients. It will take a lot of effort to dig it out! (p. 223)
>
> Sometimes, before I show frog eggs to children, I hand them a hard-boiled egg. They can feel the hard shell and even peel it off. Then we compare the chicken's egg to the frog eggs. This creates great wonderment that *both* are eggs! (p. 155)

These kinds of experiences pull children into what really matters in nature and place-based education – calling on children's powers of attention and focus, of wonderment and joy, analysis and reflection, individual exploration and collaborative discovery, and sifting and sorting of information, data, and concepts over time. This kind of nature learning comes about simply and yet with elegance and sophistication – "going into the woods and looking carefully," looking for "a princess pine" just "six inches from the ground," and learning that "her present size gives no indication of her past glories" for "her ability to accept less has ensured her survival" (Bowden, 1989, p. 97).

Bowden's book is a direct descendent of the great nature writer Henry David Thoreau, who more than 100 years earlier had heralded the wonders of nature, and the power of looking closely and sensitively at the environment to preserve it. Thoreau drew inspiration from observing nature: "How encouraging to perceive again that faint tinge of green, spreading amid the russet on earth's cheeks! I revive with Nature; her victory is mine. This is my jewelry" (April 3, 1856) (Rorer, 2010, p. 33). He attuned his observational faculties and called on his human senses to note and discern animal life: "I stand by the bubbling frogs (dreamers at a distance). They are sometimes intermittent, with a quavering. I hear betweenwhiles a little bird-like conversation between them. It is evidently their wooing" (May 5, 1852) (p. 59). Thoreau sharpened his power of language to record and interpret what he saw and heard and felt:

> I see in a ditch a painted turtle nibbling the edge of a frost-bitten yellow lily pad (in the water), which has turned white. Other pads have evidently been nibbled by him, having many scallops or notches in their edges, just the form of his jaws. (May 24, 1860, p. 74)

Thoreau's observations, his careful documentation, and his elegant prose reveal an inquiring mind and the elevation of the senses to look and see and feel, discern patterns, note anomalies, create metaphors, and chart the cycles and seasons of the natural environment.

NATURE AND INQUIRY

We can continue the line of inquiry from Thoreau to Bowden and others with a focus on nature and inquiry that promotes children's understanding and awareness of core practices in high-quality, developmentally appropriate science education for young children. It is a focus on innovative curricular integration that heightens children's powers of observation, problem-solving, and reflection. It also deepens young children's powers of the mind and intellect as children classify phenomena and artifacts (such as rocks and sticks), look at and understand natural transformations (decomposition), play with time and development (the rate of plant growth), ascertain sequences and stages (the life cycle of the frog), recognize shades of color and shape (leaves across the seasons), watch for patterns and common traits (animal tracks and bird calls), problem-solve (how animals and plants are adapted to diverse environments), stumble upon new discoveries (uncovering the hidden growth of a plant), and hypothesize about historical change in the animal and plant worlds (what did happen to the dinosaurs?).

This new, second edition of *Nature Education in Early Childhood Education: Integrating Inquiry and Practice* is a unified collection of current, cutting-edge ideas, and strategies for linking inquisitive and mindful nature education with the process of teacher inquiry, documentation, and reflection. The book proposes that powerful nature education is conceptualized and carried out by curious, thoughtful educators who are knowledgeable and passionate about observing, documenting, and reflecting on children's nature learning as well as their own teaching practices.

The book is designed for teachers of young children, garden teachers, nature and outdoor learning educators, and others interested in integrating nature education and learning with aspects of inquiry-based learning and teaching across the curriculum. The book will interest early childhood teacher educators who teach courses on nature study, early childhood science, observation and documentation, early childhood curriculum, and inquiry and reflective practice.

The book emphasizes appropriate curriculum design, planning, and relevant pedagogical approaches for linking nature and inquiry in early childhood education. The book links this curricular focus through effective techniques for observation, documentation, and reflection. The linkage of curriculum and inquiry/documentation builds a rich picture of teachers and children learning together through reflective practice.

Nature, as envisioned in this book, encompasses the active learning and discovery of properties, objects, phenomena, and processes in the natural world. Nature is found in rural areas, in forests and streams and mountains and woods, and also indoors, in terraria and books and under a microscope. Nature is also found in suburban and urban areas – under an elevated train track, in an exposed city creek, under rocks and logs in a city park, and in the trees and shrubs in city parks and wild urban areas. Nature can also be found in gardens and other environments designed and built by teachers and other adults – a school site or a communal, public place designed for children and their outdoor explorations and play. Nature is found, too, in those covert and hidden spaces, where children build forts, castles, secret places, meeting places, and quiet corners.

We also think of nature as connected with place-based education (Sobel, 2005), which "teaches about both the nature and built environments" (p. 5). This perspective includes the "history, folk culture, social problems, economics, and aesthetics of the community and its environment" (p. 5). In a related way, we are also connecting with permaculture and diversity, and the idea that we can think about whole systems and design principles through experiencing and understanding patterns and histories in nature. This perspective is also connected with both the nurturing and taking away of one's cultural and social connections to the land and nature as articulated by the permaculture expert Maya Blow:

> [In learning about permaculture] we talk about water, social agriculture, but also who in our lineage grew food and why they left the ancestral land. For a lot of people of color, there is trauma: Did our ancestors leave because they were torn away from that culture? (Fancher, 2019, p. A7)

Maya Blow's views on addressing permaculture through a historical lens and emphasizing cultural loss also has connections with other current ideas linking nature, health, and healing (Akom, 2011; Ginwright, 2016).

Our understanding of the power of nature education in the broad and deep perspective that we take in this book is strengthened by its integration with teacher inquiry, documentation, and reflection. The term *inquiry* has two different but connected meanings in this book. First, it refers to meaningful and high-quality learning for young children. Inquiry-based learning for children engages them in exploring "big ideas," the questions that they have about the world and the core questions that guide scientists', naturalists', and philosophers' understandings of the world around us. Approaching learning as inquiry requires engaging and relevant curricula, environments, and strategies that teach to where young children are developmentally, and are aligned with children's linguistic, cultural, and community traditions and talents. Inquiry-based learning also comes from children's interests – what is intriguing, enticing, puzzling – and the particular, often idiosyncratic, developmental paths of individual children and groups of children. No inquiry-based learning process or set of activities or project is like any other, and the best and the most longlasting of this kind of learning comes from and is tailored to the children at hand. And yet, effective inquiry learning, as idiosyncratic as it may seem in its emergence, remains focused on the questions that are at the heart of all learning: how does the world work? How do I fit into the world? How are things connected? What causes change, and what are its effects?

The book's second meaning of *inquiry* refers to how and why we as teachers observe, document, and reflect on children's nature learning and our own teaching. As shown by Thoreau and Bowden and others, powerful observation involves the thoughtful and sensitive interplay of listening, watching, feeling, and thinking. These are the processes we rely on when we observe children's talk, behaviors, and interactions as evidence to indicate what they are learning. Documentation is an essential part of teacher inquiry, as it encompasses how we use language (our written notes), visuals (such as photography), children's products (the collection of children's work and play samples), and found artifacts (rocks, leaves, animal tracks) to record and document critical moments, elements, and ideas in children's nature learning and development.

Integrating nature study and inquiry is necessarily interdisciplinary, taking in the full range of children's language and literacy learning, artistic development, sociocultural and emotional learning, and cognitive and intellectual powers. As children develop questions and a need to know, they also develop the need for ways to record, compare, and communicate ideas. As the examples in this book show, when children are involved in exploring important and meaningful ideas, opportunities arise for them to go well beyond what we often think infants, toddlers, pre-schoolers, and kindergartners are "ready" to think about, devise, or do. So too, their teachers are challenged to rethink beliefs about children's capabilities and to constantly negotiate lines between free play, context-based skill development, and teacher guided activity.

The ideas taken up in this book do not arise from a single theoretical perspective, and yet the cases and reflections bring to life many of the core ideas that drive our understanding of how young children learn best – Lev Vygotsky's ideas on connecting children's thought, language, and interaction; Jean Piaget's views on children's developmental capabilities to think logically and with precision; modern cognitive science's discoveries regarding how neural pathways develop through the building of explicit connections between experiences, ideas, and memories; ideas about the power and importance of play and stories as learning, championed by educators such as Vivian Paley; and recognition by pioneers such as Lisa Delpit that learning is a fundamentally cultural activity, resulting in advocacy for all children, and especially children of color, to have access to powerful, relevant learning experiences connected to their current and future lives.

The book also echoes important ideas and recommendations from the new National Association for the Education of Young Children's position statements on developmentally appropriate practices, advancing equity in early childhood education, and professional standards and competencies for early childhood educators. The ideas put forth and the practices recommended in this book illustrate the important foundation of conceptualizing and implementing a nature curriculum that recognizes and supports the full range of children's developmental talents and abilities. The book also recognizes that current access to high-quality, meaningful nature education is not equitable across all early childhood sites and that there is unfair, differential access to meaningful nature learning for far too many teachers, children, and families. In this book, then, we argue and show that advancing equity in nature and place-based education is founded upon a sensitive, thoughtful linking of nature education with teacher inquiry, documentation, and reflection. We strongly believe that it is this integration that provides a continual professional growth process for assessing and changing how well we meet the linguistic, cultural, social, and educational talents and needs of all children and all families. We also argue that combining nature education and inquiry provides another avenue to accomplish a number of professional standards and competencies, increasing educators' knowledge of nature education and deepening the tools for observation, documentation, and assessment.

Sixty years ago the biologist and writer Rachel Carson (1962) published her monumental *Silent spring.* Carson's groundbreaking book marked the beginning of our modern attention to the environment, as Carson warned us of the impending dangers to the environment and world of our inattention and damage to nature through our wanton disregard for the earth. She writes, "The most alarming of all man's assaults upon the environment is the contamination of air, earth, rivers, and sea with dangerous and even lethal materials" (p. 6). Sixty years later, we still need to heed Carson's call for protection of the environment as ensuring the protection of humanity and of all peoples. Carson's statement, "There is still very limited awareness of the nature of the threat" (p. 13) to the earth remains mostly true today. And so starting out with our youngest children in early childhood education is our best hope for raising their "awareness" of why and how they can preserve and protect the earth and the future of humanity. This is the ultimate goal of any worthwhile nature and science curriculum and course of study.

We welcome you to our unified collection of stories, ideas, experiences, and strategies for integrating nature education, science, and inquiry in early childhood classrooms contexts. We believe that the book will be both a guide and an inspiration for your work with nature and inquiry, and that you and your children will benefit from its wisdom for many years to come.

THE BOOK'S ORGANIZATION

This new second edition is now organized into four major themes. Part I focuses on the theme of science, nature, and inquiry-based learning in early childhood. In Chapter 1, Stephanie Sisk-Hilton provides a foundational chapter on central ideas and principles of young children's successful science and nature learning and development. In Chapter 2, Daniel R. Meier describes the process of inquiry, documentation, and reflection and also discusses important tools for data collection, analysis, and representation.

Part II addresses the theme of place as teacher. In Chapter 3, Camille T. Dungy chronicles the science and nature learning of her child as an infant, and critically examines the role of adults in nurturing the nature learning of very young children. In Chapter 4, Gita Jayewardene discusses a nature project with her preschoolers in an urban school, and how her nature teaching is founded upon her children experiences in nature in Sri Lanka. In Chapter 5, Darcy Campbell, Kelsey Henning, and Shawna Thompson present a series of stories about toddlers and preschoolers at their independent school in San Francisco's Presidio National Park explore and care for nature. In Chapter 6, Patricia Sullivan presents a story about how one child's comment about a crow started a nature-based inquiry project with connections to race, racism, and colorism.

Part III examines the theme of nature as support for documentation and representation. In Chapter 7, Anna Golden uses varied storytelling methods to tell the story of how her preschool children explored the forest and wild space next to her independent, suburban Virginia school. In Chapter 8, Marty Gravett, who is the early childhood director at Anna Golden's school, describes the power of mapmaking in children's inquiry-based nature learning. In Chapter 9, Jean A. Mendoza and Lilian G. Katz present their perspective on the project approach and its links to inquiry and documentation. In Chapter 10, co-teachers Isauro M. Escamilla, Sahara Gonzalez-Garcia, and Alicia Alvarez examine the role of Learning Stories for understanding the nature exploration of preschool-aged dual language learners in their San Francisco public school.

Part IV looks at the theme of child agency in nature education. In Chapter 11, Mabel Young documents her toddlers' nature learning at her public preschool located in San Francisco's Presidio National Park. In Chapter 12, Heather B. Taylor tells the story of how the inquiry process deepened her understanding of children's nature learning at her forest school. In Chapter 13, Jana Walsh describes how an inquiry approach helped her integrate literacy and nature education for her kindergarten-age children.

Chapters 3 through 13 all feature an opening set of several aspects of "Key Science and Nature Elements" and several "Key Inquiry Elements." We encourage you as read these two call-out boxes in these chapters to note those elements that you find particular valuable, and to keep those in mind as you read each chapter. We wish you all the best in the journey of reading this book and considering how it can strengthen and extend your efforts to link nature education and inquiry.

REFERENCES

Akom, A. (2011). Eco-Apartheid: Linking environmental health to educational outcomes. *Teachers College Record Volume 113*(4), 831–859.

Bowden, M. (1989). *Nature for the very young: A handbook of indoor and outdoor activities*. New York: John Wiley & Sons.

Carson, R. (1962). *Silent spring*. New York: Houghton Mifflin.

Fancher, L. (2019, July 26). Farm at the intersection of permaculture, diversity. *The Berkeley Voice*, p. A7.

Ginwright, S. (2016). *Hope and healing in urban education: How urban activists and teachers are reclaiming matters of the heart*. New York: Routledge.

Rorer, A. (2010). *Of woodland pools, spring-holes, & ditches: Excerpts from the journal of Henry David Thoreau*. Berkeley, CA: Counterpoint.

Sobel, D. (2005). *Place-based education: Connecting classrooms & communities*. Great Barrington, MA: The Orion Society.

Part I

Science, Nature, and Inquiry: Theoretical and Practical Foundations

1

SCIENCE, NATURE, AND INQUIRY-BASED LEARNING IN EARLY CHILDHOOD

Stephanie Sisk-Hilton

Over the past decade, there has been a flurry of writing around the need for children to "return" to unstructured time in nature. While some of this advocacy reveals a nostalgia for a past that never really existed, it also serves as a counternarrative to current efforts to standardize and formalize early childhood learning experiences. In this chapter, I will explore a number of questions regarding the place of nature education in early childhood learning. What do children gain from engaging in nature? What is lost when these opportunities are constrained? In the race to "prepare" children for their academic futures, why slow down and spend time attending to the large, messy, uncontrolled out of doors? To understand what happens when children have relatively unstructured time in nature we must attend to the complex relationship between environment and human interaction. Consider the scene below:

> *Twelve children, ages 18 months to five years, pile out of a van. They walk right past a brightly colored play structure. What has caught their attention enough to make the built playground unappealing? A few of the older children begin to point past the structure, and the younger ones follow their lead. It is geese, pecking at the ground and wandering through the patch of grass next to the structure. The children giggle as some begin to walk like geese, and Diana, their teacher, points out their long, graceful necks. "So they*

can reach down and get their food," says four-year-old Stephen (names of children have been changed). Two children bend their heads down, as though looking for the food. No one chases the animals. The group continues on, picking up the pace as they sense that water is near. They begin running as the small stretch of beach comes into view. The beach looks out over both a sailboat marina and the remnants of an industrial shipyard. This is urban nature. Sand, bay, crabs, birds, and also pavement, cranes, and oil storage tanks in the distance. And yet the children are as focused on the natural world as if they were 100 miles away from the nearest road.

There is an ebb and flow of energy from group interactions to individual explorations and back to the group. One child finds tiny crabs in the water, and soon a small crowd gathers. Joshua, age five, grabs a large shovel and uses it to gently scoop the water, trying to catch a crab. Soon five children are testing different methods, including two-year-old Stella, who cups her hands together, scooping water and saying "crab," but staying well out of reach of the actual animals.

Teacher Diana spots a dead stingray that has washed ashore, and the energy shifts to a teacher-mediated discussion of dead creatures. The children ask where it lived when it was alive, and if it can still sting. The teacher wonders with them. But Jacob, age four, has persisted with the crab hunt, and he arrives at the stingray group announcing, "I got a crab!" He repeats this twice, and suddenly the group energy shifts back to the crabs, first gathered around Jacob's bucket, admiring, and then back to the water as each child grabs a pail and imitates his technique. As children begin to collect the crabs successfully, many of them break from the group and focus only on the tiny living creatures in their buckets.

Juliet, my own four year old, seems to notice me for the first time since arriving, and she shows me the crab in her bucket and explains, "Mama, I'm testing to see if it's alive or dead. I tried putting a stick down there and it didn't pinch, so I'm thinking dead." Her friend Ariana comes over with her own crab in a bucket, and they begin to play a version of house with the crabs. "We need to take care of them so they won't be dead," says Ariana. "They need a blanket." She begins to cover her crab with sand. "No no, they're for real living, Ariana," Juliet responds, looking worried. "They need healthy food," says Ariana, and an argument is averted as they begin looking together for something to feed the crab "babies."

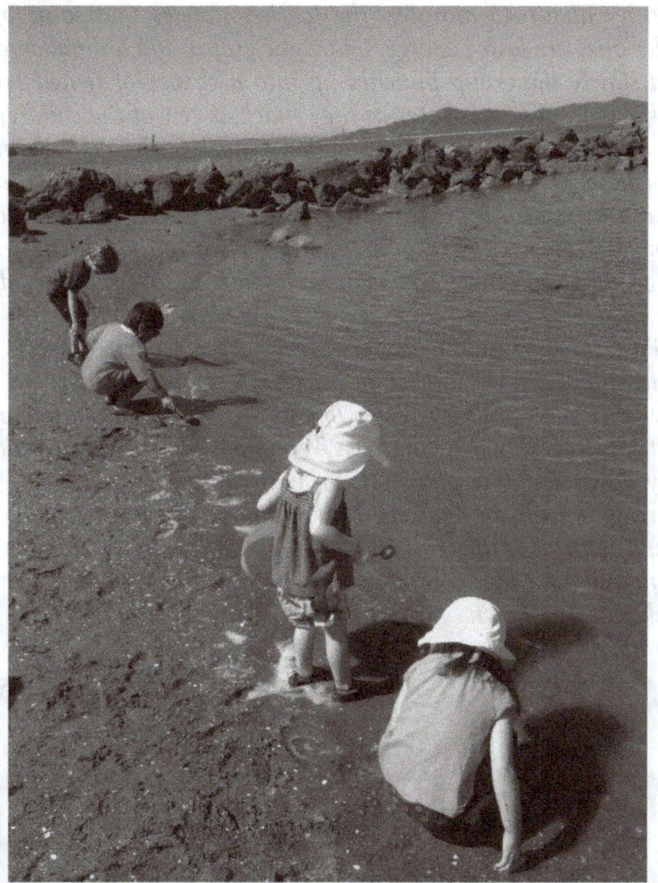

Figure 1.1 Children experiment with tools and methods for catching crabs.
Photo by Helen Kim

Eighteen-month-old Aiden has settled himself in the sand, at first totally focused on scooping and feeling the texture. After a few minutes, he refocuses on observing the older children from his safe perch. He watches them wade in and out of the water for a few minutes, and then holds up a hand for a teacher to take. He toddles his way toward the edge of the water, grasping Teacher Helen's hand. As he begins splashing with his open palm, laughing at the sound and sensation, Helen talks with him quietly.

Four-year-old Lana notices that two-year-old Stella is up to her knees in the water. She reaches out a hand and brings her closer to shore, saying, "not too deep, Stella."

After about 45 minutes, the teacher notices that some of the littler ones are losing energy. Out come grapes and animal crackers, and slowly the group bunches up into a cluster of seated bodies, looking out over the water as they snack. A few of the children are too involved in their work to stop for a snack. Joshua is building an enormous castle and moat system with Teacher Ian. Jacob is alternating between sand castle construction and sea creature collection. And Stella is so enamored with the water that she only stays long enough for one grape before returning to splash at the edge of the bay.

Post snack, children disperse to find their next projects. Suddenly, there is a cry of excitement from the sand castle crew. They have created a path for water to travel from the top of one of the castle turrets down to the bay. Watching the water meander its way down the long path is transfixing even for the adults. Then there is a rush for buckets, and toddlers and preschoolers have found something they can all do, fill a bucket with water, wait their turn, and pour the water down the path, watching in wonder as it makes its way down.

Figure 1.2 A lost bucket provides an opportunity for risk taking and learning about motion in water.

Photo by Helen Kim

In all the excitement, a bucket is lost in the water. Ian, dressed in jeans, gamely wades out to rescue it, and soon he is up to his waist in water. He laughs, and soon he has a group of the four oldest children, "The pre-k kids" wading behind him like ducks, soaked and screaming and delighting in the fact that they are swimming in their clothes. In a couple of minutes they are back, and the ducklings disperse.

Stella, too little to follow the pre-k kids, desperately wants to go deeper into the water. She figures out that she can squat down and create the feeling of being deeper. She squats and begins walking through the water, splashing and smiling ear to ear. Then she falls and begins to cry. Teacher Helen holds out a hand and she comes to shore. The crying stops immediately, and she stands at the shore for a moment, holding Helen's hand and recentering.

I OBSERVED THIS SCENE MANY YEARS AGO NOW, when I tagged along on a field trip with my daughter's preschool, and it has remained one of my favorite examples of the power of the natural environment, combined with skilled adult facilitation, in young children's learning. We live in a small city within a large, urban area. Willow Street Schoolhouse was a home-based daycare facility located in a small house adjacent to a public transit station. The elevated train tracks and commuter parking lot were more noticeable than anything one might call "nature." And yet the toddlers and preschoolers who attended this preschool were deeply connected with the natural world, as was clear in the peaceful, fully engaged 3 hours the children spent at the urban beach.

Diana Bickham, the school's founder, spent years finding ways to connect children's lives to the natural world in this urban setting. In part, she accomplished this by being wholly unafraid of field trips. Nearly every week, all 12 children traveled two blocks by foot, tricycle, and six-child stroller to a local farmers market, where they talked with farmers, danced to local music, and tried foods that some of them, including my own, would be unlikely to try at home. Also on an almost weekly basis, they piled into a van to explore local parks, beaches, and other natural settings. But even on days when they did not leave Willow Street, daily activities were infused with exploration of the natural world. All manner of plants, edible and ornamental, surrounded the yard, many of them planted, tended, and harvested by the children. The area under the train tracks had "forests" of ivy and bamboo to explore, and trees just the right size for preschoolers to develop their climbing skills. Inside Diana's house were animals of all sorts, some permanent residents and some visitors. Each year the children watched silkworms hatch from eggs, fed the caterpillars mulberry leaves from a tree in the backyard, and watched the miraculous spinning of the silk cocoons and emergence of the completely domesticated, flightless moths. Parents often arrived at pick up time to find their child giving a lizard a shoulder ride, assisting in walking one of Diana's dogs, or feeding dandelions to the rabbit. There was an overwhelming sense in this small house that things were cared for: children, animals, plants, and the larger world.

What learning happens in a place like this? What does this focus on exploration of the natural world accomplish in terms of children's learning and development? My answers are grounded in my work as a researcher in science education and child development. And yet in the framework I lay out below I also try to understand what it is like to be a child in a learning environment in which these ideas are brought to life. And so I will interpret my discussion of what we, as a field, know about how children learn and develop scientific ideas with examples from the world of Willow Street Schoolhouse.

A CAVEAT: THE DANGERS OF A FALL/RECOVERY NARRATIVE

In considering what the role of nature education in early childhood might be, it is important to also consider ways in which our understanding of "nature" can both support and constrain our goals. Educators and researchers who consider issues of whose story is being told in our assumptions about goals and structures of education have pointed out that much of the discourse around nature education is premised on an imagined "golden age" of connection with nature that does not reflect the experiences of most people. Advocates for more and better nature-based education accurately cite evidence that most humans are alienated from nature and that increased time and experience in nature can be emotionally and physically beneficial (Louv, 2008; Sampson, 2015). However, these ideas are often intermingled with the invented notion that there was a time in the not-distant past in which humans, and in particular American children, interacted with nature in a non-problematic way. Dickinson (2013) identifies a "fall recovery narrative" in the work of prominent nature education advocates, harkening to a time in their childhood, before increased technology and millennial cultural norms, in which (some) children were free to roam and were assumed to be deeply connected with the natural world.

Kahn uses the term "environmental generational amnesia" to describe the phenomenon of people seeing as "normal" whatever they have experienced, whether pristine, old growth forest or rivers that, while beautiful, are too polluted to drink or fish in. This concept can help explain how adults develop idealized notions that childhood in previous generations was more innocent and better connected to the natural world. In fact, the history of environmental degradation in the Americas stretches back at least as far as the arrival of the first European colonizers, who sought to "tame" the unfamiliar environment and people that they encountered. Kahn's critique points out that each generation's tendency to treat their own childhood as "normal" and desirable ignores or downplays the environmental injustices that were present in that earlier time.

Just as troubling is the norming of the white, middle class, male, heterosexual, able-bodied experience of freedom in the earlier decades of the twentieth century, at a time when laws and cultural norms dictated where people of color, as well as women and girls, were/are allowed to be and were/are allowed to behave. The published memories of a wild, unstructured childhood belong mostly to those who grew up with the privilege of not having to worry about basic safety or economic security. Framing nature education discourse around this one-sided nostalgia can result in approaches that ignore truths about who has access to natural spaces, how decisions are made about preservation, and how to make meaning of human/nature activities such as farming, hunting, and fishing (Flessas & Zimmerman, 2017). These may sound like heavy topics in thinking about very young children's nature experiences. And yet, children begin building their sense of belonging and place from birth, and so for those who design and enable young children's experiences, considering how their perspectives may include or exclude the children in their care is critical.

There are alternate narratives that broaden recorded experiences of our interactions with nature, including Camille T. Dungy's anthology *Black nature: Four centuries of African American nature poetry* (Dungy, 2009), and such stories help reconceptualize human/nature connections. As we consider how we might best support young children to experience and grow in the natural world, it is imperative that as adults we move away from nostalgia, toward a more complex understanding of the troubled but also healing and transformative relationships with nature that humans have had throughout most of our history.

A key component of effective early childhood education is building and strengthening *connections*: to other humans, to content knowledge, and to the broader world surrounding young children. At a cognitive level, strong connections increase the effectiveness of memory and allow for more complex and abstract levels of understanding and problem-solving. From a social emotional stance, connection is how people build feelings of stability and safety that support emotional resiliency and the ability to move toward self-regulation. Connection with nature needs to be considered within this broader construct of how young children make meaning of their place in the world. And to do that requires not nostalgia about how things "used to be," but rather deep immersion into the lives of the young children who are beginning their connections with nature right now.

Consider the Willow Street Schoolhouse example from these differing perspectives. Certainly, the ivy and bamboo under the train tracks, or even the small beach hemmed in by houses and an oil refinery, are far from pristine nature. There could understandably be nostalgia for a time when these areas were wilder, more open, more able for (some) children to explore on their own. However, the environmental degradation of Northern California began hundreds of years ago, and to think of the time just before World War II, when the suburb Willow Street resides in was not yet built, as idyllic is not only untrue, it provides little guidance as to what might be done to improve current children's access to nature. In the area around Willow Street, local environmental efforts have included "daylighting" buried streams, building living shorelines, and planting native plants where non-natives have proliferated for generations. These efforts are not with the intent of returning the environment to that of the mid-twentieth century, but rather to developing wiser and more sustainable human/nature interactions in the current time. Likewise, finding and using pockets of nature does not provide the children with a watered-down version of what they might have experienced 100 years ago, but instead allows them to notice, experience, and connect to their world as it is, and perhaps begin building a vision of what a future world might be.

For the rest of this chapter, we will consider three ways in which children may build connections through experience in nature: complex, interconnected sensory experiences; language development and social connection to make meaning of experiences; and the development of an inquiry stance to build connected understanding of the world. This framework centers the way in which children engage with nature in the moment and over time, not harkening back to ideas about how children "should" be in nature, but rather building upon the curiosity, knowledge and experiences children bring to a specific time and place.

BUILDING CONTENT KNOWLEDGE THROUGH CONNECTED EXPERIENCES

What kind of learning happens when children engage with nature? Consider Juliet and Ariana's exchange about crabs in the opening vignette. Both children believe that the crabs in their buckets are "alive" and both act within their ideas about what that means. For Juliet, her knowledge that living crabs sometimes pinch things leads her to test for life by trying to get her crab to pinch a stick. Ariana focuses on her understandings of how human parents care for the small, living things in their charge, and she tries to cover her crab with a sand "blanket." This upsets Juliet because it contradicts her understanding of crabs needing air. They are able to continue their play without conflict by agreeing that the crabs, as living things, need food.

Throughout this exchange, these two preschoolers draw upon their existing ideas about not only crabs, but more abstract concepts like what makes something alive and how to care for living things. Their experiences with the crabs and with each other may solidify some of their ideas and add new ones as well. Perhaps Juliet's experience with a moving, but non-pinching crab is broadening how she determines that the creature is alive. The two children's brief disagreement about proper care of these creatures allows their ideas to bump against each other and may as a result add to their knowledge of what living things need to survive and how this varies and is the same among different organisms.

This interaction illustrates the complex way in which children build knowledge and understanding over time. Every time a learner is exposed to an experience or idea, their brain connects it to other ideas and experiences in the learner's memory. The richer and more memorable the experiences, the stronger the connections between ideas. Researchers in the fields of cognitive science and early childhood development have demonstrated that this is how lasting learning happens, and how learners are able to progressively consider, develop, and retain more complex and abstract ideas.

For decades, conventional wisdom held that young children were not capable of abstract thought, and in fact many of our decisions about early learning are still based on this assumption. However, there is now significant evidence that even very young children can make generalizations, predict future actions, make inferences, and otherwise engage in abstract mental processes (Fay & Klahr, 1996; Gelman, 2003; Metz, 1997). These advanced capacities seem to be more a function of knowledge and experience than age. Of course a typical three year old exhibits no evidence of abstract thinking in most areas, since they have limited knowledge to draw upon. But providing complex, memorable, social, and content rich experiences builds this knowledge base and encourages connections between ideas, thus building toward the ability to engage in abstract thinking in the area of knowledge.

It is important to note that concepts like "critical thinking" and other hallmarks of complex understanding are *domain specific* (Gelman & Brenneman, 2004). That is, a learner may well exhibit evidence of critical thinking in one specific area while in other areas such reasoning may seem beyond their level of development. Just as an adult's ability to predict the outcome of an event (say, the impact of a 450-degree oven on cookie dough or the force needed to propel a rocket into space) is dependent upon domain specific content knowledge (baking or physics), so too are children's capabilities contingent upon their underlying knowledge of and experience with a particular phenomenon. A preschooler who has grown up playing by the seashore can both describe and predict how tidal movements will affect the sand castle she is constructing on the edge between the compacted sand at the high tide mark and the dry, fluffy sand beyond. A same-aged or even much older child without this experience will be mystified when the once far away waves begin eating away at his creation. Likewise, children with divergent cultural experiences show significant diversity in abstract thought, a finding that points not to the superiority of one particular set of experiences but rather back to the idea that how children experience the world, even as infants, forms the framework for future reasoning (Carstensen, Zhang, Heyman, Fu, Lee, & Walker, 2019). Development of abstract thinking and problem-solving is dependent on rich and complex learning experiences, whether for a three year old or for an adult learner.

Building connections between ideas, skills, and context is essential in order for new learning to be useful in constructing complex understanding (Duschl, Schweingruber, & Shouse, 2007; Metz, 2008). Children who are given a set of objects and asked to sort them by color, size, or other property have no reason to connect this to meaningful activity in the broader world. Children who examine the diversity of shells at a beach develop ideas about the kinds of animals that they are a part of, and continually revisit their ideas as they encounter new evidence, thus creating a context in which sorting and classification are meaningful, important, and memorable skills. When children have time to explore and experience natural phenomena, especially in conversation with each other and with knowledgeable adults, they are better able to build their capacity to problem-solve and consider "big ideas" (Metz, Sisk-Hilton, Berson, & Li, 2010; Sanders-Smith, 2015).

The stronger and more salient the connections between ideas and experiences, the more resilient children's understanding becomes, and the more easily they can retrieve and use these ideas. In the case of Juliet and Ariana, it is unlikely that either of them had engaged in crab caretaking before. Their conversation was based on their existing knowledge of what other living things need (for instance, food and blankets). They worked to integrate this new creature into that prior knowledge. When Ariana tries to put a "blanket" on her crab, this is at odds with Juliet's understanding of what live animals need, as opposed to say, baby dolls or even human babies. She says, "No no, they're for real living," indicating that she thinks Ariana is treating them as a toy or something else not "for real" living. In this small moment, the two children are adding to their schemas of living vs. non-living things and the needs of animals (Gelman & Lucariello, 2002).

We see in such small moments the tremendous power of experiences in the natural world to support children's cognitive development. Experiences in nature are not fully controlled or designed. Animals behave in both predictable and unpredictable ways. Tides are predictable events, but individual waves can be surprising, requiring children who are building a sand castle to constantly revise their estimations of the best spot to position their construction. Diana Bickham explains how she feels children learn through returning many times each week to "the sand area," a small play area under the elevated train tracks, surrounded by child-climbable trees, "forests" of ivy and bamboo, and sometimes squirrels:

> I really feel that kids are happy exploring, and the fact that nature doesn't give you cookie cutter designs. It is always different the next day. Always. You've got that built into nature. So if you go the next day, the sun is in a little different place, and the tree is different, and the weather may be different, then you have the children. Their interest may be building on what they've done already [or a new idea]. And you keep conversation with them, so that they're not left to their own devices.... When they realize they've got so much freedom and yet they're being taken care of, it's just beautiful.

As Diana describes, it is both the predictability of repeated experiences and the ever-changing nature of the environment, the children, and the conversations they have that allow them to build their feelings of competence and their understanding of the world around them.

When young children have the opportunity to build significant content knowledge, they are able to engage in reasoning that otherwise seems well beyond their developmental capabilities (Duschl et al., 2007, p. 53). Experiences in the natural world that encourage them to explore and make meaning of the environment around them are ideal for supporting young children's development of scientific understanding and ways of knowing. A key component of these experiences, as referenced by Diana above, is supported use of language. That is the idea we will take up next.

DEVELOPING LANGUAGE TO SUPPORT EMERGING UNDERSTANDINGS

Children's seeming limitations in reasoning are based on limited experience not only with ideas and objects, but also with language. Opportunities to engage in ideas and observe phenomena over time provide a context for developing vocabulary and modes of discourse that deepen understanding and facilitate engagement in inquiry. Gelman and Brenneman (2004) describe a preschool program that explicitly teaches the ideas of "observe, predict, and check" as a way to approach inquiry into the natural and physical world. Children engage in both simple and complex experiences that build upon their existing ideas. Equally importantly, teachers support children's talking about their ideas through providing relevant terminology and opportunities to describe and compare ideas using increasingly rich language. Gelman and Brenneman note "One of the great surprises for us is how readily children take up seemingly difficult new words [in relevant contexts]" (p. 153). Consider the many preschoolers who memorize a seemingly endless list of obscure dinosaur names. Words themselves are not an obstacle for most young children, but they must have relevant experiences and opportunities to use them in order for specialized words to become part of their working vocabulary.

Of course, vocabulary is only one piece of language development. Equally important are opportunities to engage in different forms of discourse. It is not enough to let a group of young children loose in a natural environment and teach them the names of things that they find. Rather, one key role of the preschool teacher is to engage children in different types of conversations based on their experiences. The teachers at Willow Street Schoolhouse are masters of "I wonder" conversations, invitations for both children and teachers to make predictions and compare ideas. During our beach visit, I heard several such conversations, including the following, while walking past the flock of geese at the end of the trip:

Diana [noting the geese's necks bent toward the ground]: I wonder if they are looking for something down there.
Stephen: Bugs. Diana, they are looking for bugs because they eat them.
Connor: Looking for bugs!
Juliet: Or maybe, mama, do geese eat bugs or grass?
Stephanie: I don't know. Can you see if they are eating something?
Juliet: I think they are eating the grass. Stephen, look. They are pulling on the grass.
Stephen: Or maybe it's to get to the bugs. Because they live on the grass.

At that moment, the energy shifted again and the conversation ended. But in just a few seconds, two children had constructed predictions about the function of an observed behavior, and a third, younger child, was participating through listening in and mimicking. In the coming weeks, they are sure to see more geese and are likely to bring up the topic again. Meanwhile, back at school, they will observe silkworm caterpillars eating mulberry leaves, a bearded dragon eating crickets, and perhaps a local squirrel searching for food. In each of these situations, the teachers may initiate "I wonder" conversations. Little by little, the children will build their understanding through words and in conversation with others.

"What would happen if" conversations are invitations to further investigation, a way to build both language and scientific process skills. When the Willow Street children were building their sand castle with Teacher Ian, he initiated this type of discussion, and also supported children initiated "what ifs." For instance, he wondered aloud what would happen if they poured the water more quickly. A couple of children rushed to try the idea, but five-year-old Joshua first discussed his prediction with Ian. Later, a child suggested that two people pour water at once, and Ian remarked, "Oh, that might make it even faster," modeling a prediction based on observation.

The "I wonder" and "what would happen if" conversations are similar to the "observe, predict, and check" framework that Gelman and Brenneman propose for supporting language development and science knowledge building in preschoolers. Children are invited to not only test their ideas, but also to communicate and informally compare their ideas with others. As they do this, the need arises for new words to express their ideas, and teachers play a critical role in providing the vocabulary at the right moment. The teachers at Willow Street do very little "talking at" children. Rather, they engage in real conversation with them as the opportunity arises. This models the "real world" ways in which people communicate with one another. The children become partners in communication and knowledge construction. These context-specific, just-in-time conversations allow children to both hear and participate in increasingly sophisticated ways of reasoning and making meaning of the world.

ENGAGING IN INQUIRY: THE DANCE BETWEEN CHILD AND ADULT-MEDIATED EXPERIENCES

In his classic essay arguing for the primacy of an inquiry orientation to science teaching and learning, Bruce Alberts proposes that teaching through inquiry means, "allowing students to conceptualize a problem that was solved by a scientific discovery, and then forcing them to wrestle with possible answers to the problem before they are told the answer" (Alberts, 2000, p. 4). At first glance, this description seems to apply better to formal science classrooms than to early childhood environments. And yet the activities of the youngest children engaged in the natural world are often wonderful exemplars of learning through inquiry. Young children have not yet learned to wait patiently for an adult to tell them "the answer" to a puzzling phenomenon. In some ways, that may actually make it easier to facilitate inquiry with three year olds than with 16 year olds. Unlike their older counterparts, most preschoolers need very little prompting to generate their own ideas about a puzzling phenomenon.

Let's return for a moment to the building of the sand castle during Willow Street's trip to the beach. It began when Teacher Ian sat down and began making sand "towers" by filling a cup with wet sand and unmolding it onto the beach. Joshua soon joined him, and without prompting he copied Ian's activity, making his own circle of towers. Ian then began connecting the towers with a series of moats, and he and Joshua had a conversation about Joshua's interest in castles and his prior knowledge of moats. Joshua went to get a bucket of water and filled a moat, expressing surprise when the water both broke through the wall of the moat on the downhill side and absorbed into the sand. He and Ian then worked to reinforce the walls. In the next attempt, the walls held, but the water still either absorbed into the sand or settled in a "pond" at the lowest point of the moat. At this point, Joshua cried out in excitement, which signaled a group of children to come observe and join in. Soon several children were fetching water, watching it

Figure 1.3 Sand castle building becomes an inquiry into the movement of water on slopes.
Photo by Helen Kim

travel down different pathways, and repairing and reinforcing walls based on their results. As energy began to wane, Ian stepped in, suggesting that they try to make a channel that went all the way to the bay. The children eagerly set to work on this project, experimenting with gravity, water movement, and even the idea of "sloshing," as they became more and more accurate at filling their buckets only to a level they could carry without spilling. In all, this activity went on for well over an hour. Some children moved in and out, and others remained steadily engaged for the duration.

In the race to acquire "skills" at younger and younger ages, we sometimes forget that there is incredible skill building going on when children have the opportunity to simply mess around with ideas and materials, particularly when an adult or more knowledgeable other provides gentle prodding toward new ideas. The sandcastle building project shows how context-embedded inquiry learning can happen through play in natural rather than built environments. The children had at their disposal sand, moving water, a few buckets and shovels, and most importantly an adult who was willing to provide greater skill when needed but also to let the children's ideas take the lead. At first, a single child engaged in fairly typical sand castle building, copying his teacher, and in so doing began to observe properties of the sand and water. As he worked, his experiences with the materials led to questions, which Ian took up through wondering aloud with the child and occasionally making suggestions. This led to a gradual shift from castle building to observing water movement through gulleys built in different shapes, with different slopes. By the end, children were testing the effect of water volume on speed of flow, gaining context-specific, memorable science knowledge.

The role of the teacher in supporting this type of inquiry is critical. The children might well have explored water flow to some extent without an adult present. However, they likely would have lacked the skill to bring their different ideas to life, and they might not have persisted with "wonderings" that built upon one another in an organized way. Through Ian's involvement as a participant, rather than as simply the initiator or "boss," he allowed the children to experiment in a way that might have otherwise been beyond their capabilities.

Repeated experiences in nature, with different levels of adult mediation, teach children the process of wondering about a phenomenon, developing predictions based on experience and knowledge, and revising ideas based on evidence. As much as literacy and math, these are "basic skills" in a world with a critical need for problem solvers and knowledge builders.

IS IT PLAY OR IS IT SCIENCE?

Observing great nature education for young children is a delightful pastime. For much of time I spent observing children at Willow Street, the children were "just playing." They were running up and down the beach, sometimes stopping to ponder stingrays, sometimes just feeling the difference between wet, hard-packed sand and the softer stuff further up the beach. They were sometimes discussing differences between living and non-living things, sometimes just sitting and gazing out. And yet it is the unhurried time experiencing the world that ultimately allows children to make sense of it. As the chapters that follow illustrate, "play" and "science" are deeply intertwined. Young children move in and out between pretend adventures with fairies and examination of the tree stumps in which they might live. We need not prevent this mixing of imagination and investigation. On the other hand, we need not assume that young children reside only in a world of fantasy and make believe. Children take up big, important ideas through "just playing" (NAEYC, 2009). By situating this play in natural spaces, where the environment provides both constancy and change, and by engaging children in discussion of what they notice and wonder, we can help children ask and begin to answer their own big questions about how the world works.

Early childhood educators have always known the power of play as teacher, and research bears this out. Children who have extensive, relatively unstructured time to play in a supportive social environment tend to have better academic and social outcomes than children who experience more constrained, "formal" learning structures instead of (rather than alongside) play (Sanders-Smith, 2015). This is particularly important to consider when examining equity and access to high-quality early childhood programs. From their earliest school experiences, children have unequal access to the types of rich, multi-faceted learning environments that support long-term knowledge building, and schools inequitably privilege certain types of knowledge and experience that best conform to "school-like" knowledge (Delpit, 2012). A commitment to nature-based education for our youngest children is a fairly simple step toward addressing this persistent gap in opportunities to learn.

Further, play provides ways for children to bring their cultural knowledge and experiences to bear on the learning enterprise. Many of children's activities in nature are global in their practice: physical play, hiking, camping, fishing. But *how* they are enacted is mediated by culture, for instance, in differing ways that cultural groups conceptualize the connection between humans and other animals (Dickinson, 2013). Play in nature allows children to make meaning of the world within their own cultural understanding and to expand their ideas through social interactions. Considering how children learn through time spent playing in nature, then, requires that we expand our understanding of what it means to be in and with nature. Playing in a bamboo stand underneath the train tracks might seem less consequential than time spent in a national park or more bucolic setting. And yet for a young child, noticing the changes to the bamboo and exploring what lives on or near it over the course of a year of outdoor play may well be a more powerful learning experience than gazing in awe at natural wonders that appear less touched by human activity.

Early childhood educators have the opportunity to change the dialogue around what "good education" looks like, based on our emerging knowledge of how children learn to make meaning of the world. Relatively simple steps such as facilitating outings into the community beyond the school help build children's competence interacting with the world around them and lead to opportunities to facilitate inquiry in both planned and "just-in-time" ways. Toddlers and preschoolers do not necessarily need an official curriculum, but they need rich, open-ended environments and teachers who engage with them in making meaning of the world. Diana Bickham sums up this approach in her description of her students' weekly outings to a nearby farmer's market:

> I wish I could say that they were completely invested in learning about produce [laughs] because it's all right there, but [there are so many other things to notice]. Right now, they've been really interested in a little patch of dirt that has a parking lot on three sides of it, a patch of dirt with plants. And they try to collect as many snails as they can within that plant. It's a plant that's doing just fine with all those snails in it. But I think the snails hide in it. So they get so many snails. And the music is going on. And we do get fruit an we usually have something to eat. I think it's the whole trip. It's the walk. There are a lot of favorite places we do along the way.... There's a place where the dirt is very slippery, and all the little acorn looking seeds that come off the tree make it very slippery, so someone's always falling. And yet, we'll say, "now this is very slippery, would you like to sit on your bottom first and then slide down?" And they'll say no, and then they'll fall.... You know it's just so funny to me that they want to challenge themselves with that. So it's not just the destination of the farmer's market. There's a lot of talking, a lot of singing.... It's the same old, and yet not.

It is that cycle of routine and novel, of "the same old, and yet not" that allows children both the safety and the stimulation to build new ideas, attach them to existing ones, and become people who deeply understand and care about the world around them.

REFERENCES

Alberts, B. (2000). Some thoughts of a scientist on inquiry. In Minstrell, J. and van Zee, E. H. (eds.), *Inquiring into inquiry learning and teaching in science* (pp. 3–13). Washington, DC: American Association for the Advancement of Science.

Carstensen, A., Zhang, J., Heyman, G. D., Fu, G., Lee, K., & Walker, C. M. (2019). Context shapes early diversity in abstract thought. *Proceedings of the National Academy of Sciences*, 201818365.

Delpit, L. (2012). *Multiplication is for white people: Raising expectations for other people's children.* New York: The New Press.
Dickinson, E. (2013). The misdiagnosis: Rethinking "nature-deficit disorder." *Environmental Communication: A Journal of Nature and Culture, 7*(3), 315–335.
Dungy, C. T. (Ed.). (2009). *Black nature: Four centuries of African American nature poetry.* Athens, GA: University of Georgia Press.
Duschl, R., Schweingruber, H. A., & Shouse, A. (2007). *Taking science to school: Learning and teaching in grades K-8.* Washington, DC: National Academy Press.
Fay, A. L., & Klahr, D. (1996). Knowing about guessing and guessing about knowing: Preschoolers' understanding in indeterminacy. *Child Development, 67*(2), 689–716.
Flessas, B. M., & Zimmerman, T. D. (2017). Beyond nature talk: Transforming environmental education with critical and queer theories. In Letts, W. & Fifield, S. (eds.), *Stem of Desire: Queer Theories in Science Education.* Leiden: Brill.
Gelman, S. A. (2003). *The essential child.* Oxford: Oxford University Press.
Gelman, R., & Brenneman, K. (2004). Science learning pathways for young children. *Early Childhood Research Quarterly, 19,* 150–158.
Gelman, R., & Lucariello, J. (2002). Learning in cognitive development. In Pashler, H., and Gallistel, C. R. (eds.), *Stevens' handbook of experimental psychology, third edition, vol. 3* (pp. 10, 395–443). New York: Wiley.
Gopnik, A. (2009). *The philosophical baby: What children's minds tell us about truth, love, and the meaning of life.* New York: Farrar, Straus, and Giroux.
Louv, R. (2008). *Last child in the woods: Saving our children from nature-deficit disorder.* New York: Algonquin Books.
Metz, K. E. (1997). On the complex relation between cognitive developmental research and children's science curricula. *Review of Educational Research, 67*(1), 151–163.
Metz, K. E. (2008). Narrowing the gulf between the practices of science and the elementary school science classroom. *The Elementary School Journal, 109*(2), 138–161.
Metz, K., Sisk-Hilton, S., Berson, E., & Li, U. (2010). Scaffolding children's understanding of the fit between organisms and their environment in the context of the practices of science. In Gomez, K., Lyons, L., & Radinsky, J. (eds.), *Learning in the disciplines: Proceedings of the International Conference of the Learning Sciences (ICLS).* Chicago, IL: International Society of the Learning Sciences.
National Association for the Education of Young Children (NAEYC). (2009). *Developmentally appropriate practice in early childhood programs serving children from birth to age 8.* Washington, DC: NAEYC.

Sampson, S. D. (2015). *How to raise a wild child: The art and science of falling in love with nature*. New York: Houghton Mifflin Harcourt.

Sanders-Smith, S. C. (2015). Class and pedagogy: A case study of two Chicago preschools. *International studies in Sociology of Education*, *25*(4), 314–332.

2

NATURE EDUCATION AND THE POWER OF INQUIRY, DOCUMENTATION, AND REFLECTION

Daniel R. Meier

NATURE AND INQUIRY – KEY PRINCIPLES AND STRATEGIES

In this chapter, I discuss several foundational principles for using inquiry for conceptualizing, teaching, and reflecting on nature education for young children. I especially emphasize the role of the inquiry cycle, models for conducting inquiry, inquiry tools and strategies, and Learning Stories. In presenting each inquiry element, I provide examples from early childhood educators working with infants, toddlers, preschoolers, and early primary grade children. I also refer in certain places to aspects of inquiry presented and discussed in the chapters that follow in this book.

BEING MINDFUL AND INTENTIONAL

The effective and meaningful linking of nature education with inquiry and reflection is intimately connected with our awareness of ourselves as active learners, and our attention to the subtle and often hidden moments and instances of nature and place-based education (Sobel, 2015; Stribling, 2017). The ecologist and naturalist J. Drew Lanham (2016) shares his passion for nature:

> What do I live for? I eventually realized that to make a difference I had to step outside, into creation, and refocus on the roots of

> my passion. If an ounce of soil, a sparrow, or an acre of forest is to remain then we must all push things forward.... To help others understand nature is to make it breathe like some giant: a revolving, evolving, celestial being with ecosystems acting as organs and the living things within those places – humans included – as cells vital to its survival. My hope is that somehow I might move others to find themselves magnified in nature, whomever and wherever that might be (p. 6).

Let's now look at the perspectives of a few early childhood nature inquirers, and see how these educators have taken up Lanham's passion. For example, Shenna Rodeo, an infant/toddler teacher, noticed a powerful change in her approach to teaching and relationships to her children through linking nature and inquiry.

> I have come to understand the importance of being mindful of the minor details that occur during learning and teaching moments that I am able to witness or partake in. I cherish my newfound patience, observational skills, and attentiveness to the children's work, play, and interactions. I have also developed an immense respect for the way that nature can directly influence one's life, evoking emotions and as a tool to spark a reflective and artistic mind.

Stefanie Stoddard, a preschool teacher, found instant rewards and insights in her first experiences with nature and inquiry (Stoddard, 2012):

> Nature is something that I never necessarily thought played an intricate role in my practice as a preschool teacher. Having a school in the middle of a busy street, four stories high in the heart of San Francisco, and circled by a chain-link fence, you tend to lose sight of the beauty around you and the way that nature can be a piece of every growing puzzle in teaching. I try to draw on several new strategies in my teaching, such as being more purposeful in planning, being reflective in my practice, slowing down moments and observing what is immediate, chronicling change, and comparing and contrasting my children's and my own feelings and experiences in nature.

For Isauro Michael Escamilla (2012), one of the authors of Chapter 10 in this book, linking nature education and inquiry has deepened his relationships with children:

> I started listening to the children and to what they were saying, and to realize that I had been hearing, but not really listening to my students for years. I realized that I had to dedicate the time to reflect on what it means to actually listen to children, to their voices, thoughts, ideas, and how this ability and openness to listen can support children's growth as learners.

Emily Bugos, an experienced infant/toddler teacher who was relatively new to conducting inquiry in an intentional way, realized that linking nature exploration for her young children with inquiry and reflection needed to start with initiating her own interest in nature. Emily embarked on a series of outdoor hikes and took notes and photographs as a way to document her early nature exploration.

> During this nature visit, I felt calm, nostalgic. I felt connected not only to the place around me, but to my memories. Despite hiking this trail several times, I took in new sights and sensations. I began to think about the nature experiences I was providing for my infant classroom – What were they experiencing each time we stepped outside? What were they learning? How was our outdoor space contributing to their mood? How was it contributing to *my* mood? I wanted them to feel the calm connection that I felt on that hike. I wanted them to make new and exciting discoveries, to help them feel grounded in and curious about the world around them.

INQUIRY CYCLE

The overall goal of inquiry, documentation, and reflection is "to make self-conscious efforts to improve" our teaching and practice (Hatch, 2006, p. 2). Successful and powerful inquiry follows Andrew Stremmel's structured and yet flexible cycle (Figure 2.1) consisting of posing a problem or puzzle, designing an inquiry plan, collecting data, analyzing and reflecting on that data, and reflecting on possible changes in instruction (Hatch, 2006; Henderson, Meier, Perry, & Stremmel, 2012).

While it may not always be possible to complete this inquiry cycle in all nature-based inquiry projects, the essential goal is to become immersed in some aspect of this process, and to tinker with and deepen our inquiry knowledge over time.

A Good Place to Start

There are so many good places to start your nature inquiry, and finding a suitable set of inquiry goals and a comfortable and "doable" inquiry process takes a certain measure of time, planning, experience, and trial

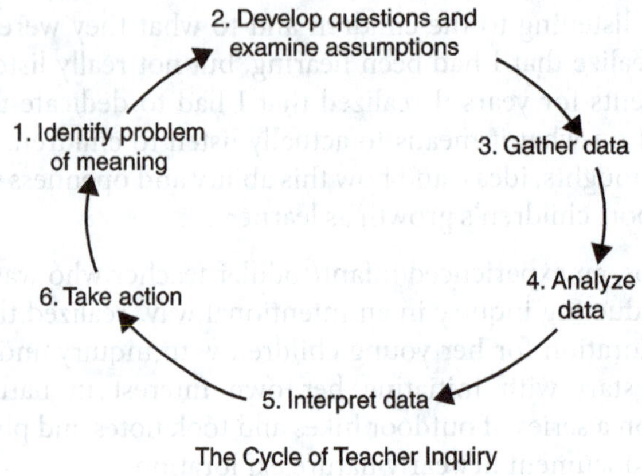

Figure 2.1 The inquiry cycle.

and error. In this section, I describe the varied ways that early childhood nature inquirers have started their nature inquiry.

Starting Small and with Intentionality – Emily Bugos

Emily Bugos, the infant/toddler teacher, initiated a new focus linking nature, inquiry, documentation, and reflection. Emily wanted to put more intentionality behind the outdoor space she was creating for her infants, and so she began to take observational notes in a teaching journal as she watched and interacted with the children outside. Emily began cultivating time to take the infants on morning walks around her site, and recorded these walks via photographs and videos. With the help of her instructional coach, Emily also began to observe a particular child in the classroom to better understand the child's social–emotional needs, recording a daily observation of his drop-off and transitions between indoors and outdoors. Emily wanted to use multiple forms of documentation to document the children's experiences with nature at school, as well as her efforts to make outdoor play a more integrated part of the infant room's daily routine.

> *Emily's Nature Journal*
> After I helped Enzo out of the stroller, he stood on the grass, wobbling slightly on the soft, uneven surface. He walked a few steps before plopping down. He sat and touched the blades of grass, running his palm over them. There were several small pink and white flowers around us. I picked one and held it out to him. "Look, Enzo. A small flower. What do you think?" I asked. Enzo

reached out with his thumb and forefinger and grasped the flower by its petals. He held it up and looked at it. "Ooooh," he said. I leaned forward to smell it, exaggerating the sound I made as I sniffed at the petals. Enzo brought the flower down and rested his hand against his leg as he stared at me briefly. Then he lifted the flower back up and loudly exclaimed, "WHOA." He held the flower up in front of his face. Another teacher was sitting in that direction. She asked, "Are you showing me your flower? It has pink and white petals. How does it feel?" Enzo repeated "WHOA" and continued to examine the flower.

In writing this and her other initial observations, Emily goal was to keep her observations objective and clear without adding her own thoughts as a witness or participant in this event and without adding her own ideas or assumptions about what Enzo was thinking or feeling in that moment.

Spontaneous Inquiry – Patricia Sullivan

Patricia Sullivan, the author of Chapter 6, uses inquiry and documentation to examine important intersections between social justice, equity, and nature education. Pat's nature inquiry with her children started with one child's spontaneous comment about a bird.

Pat's Nature Journal
David likes Steller jays because they have a cool mohawk and blue eyebrows. They watch us from the trees sometimes and mimic the call of hawks to scare the squirrels away from the nuts. When actual hawks appear, the jays dash for the trees, warning everyone of the danger. Suddenly, all at once the jays flew away, and David and I stare through the glass at the branches above the deck rail as a chicken-sized crow lands silently.

"Oh no!" He says, dread and worry spreading across his face. "That's not a good bird!"

He freezes, alarmed but clearly eager to run outside and save the squirrels, who were still seating, oblivious to the danger.

"Why do you think that's a bad bird?" I ask.

"Because it's black," David replies.

David's brief comment became the impetus for an inquiry-based project with the children around colorism in the animal world at large, and its implications for race and bias in human relationships.

Planning a Wider Inquiry Focus – John Nimmo and Beth Hallet

John Nimmo and Beth Hallet (Nimmo & Hallett, 2008) wanted to investigate how their nature curriculum and garden at a university-based early childhood center integrated aspects of "social class, disability, and community support" (p. 36). Nimmo and Hallett wanted to increase outdoor risk-taking for the children, increased negotiation of different relationships with peers and adults in nature and a shift in teachers' apprehension about their personal involvement with nature education. Further, in working with the school's Diversity, Equity, and Bias Task Force, they wanted to deepen the children's understanding of the diverse child and family relationships with nature and gardens. Nimmo, Hallett, and the center's teachers documented critical conversations with the children about social and cultural variation as linked with gardening and nature education. For example, one teacher engaged and documented conversations with children about cultural and environmental variations in housing on a global level. The school also used a survey to ask families about their views on home–school connections around food, gardens, and cultural diversity, as well their ideas for a collaborative garden at school.

QUESTIONS AND STATEMENTS – THE LANGUAGE OF AN INQUIRY FOCUS

How do professional naturalists, ecologists, conservationists, and others approach the use of questions and puzzles in their inquiry and scientific work? Let's return to J. Drew Lanham (2016):

> What is wildness? To be wild is to be colorful, and in the claims of colorfulness there's an embracing and a self-acceptance. We scientists are trained to be comfortable with the multiple questions that each new revelation may elicit. Like sweetgum trees, which find a way to survive in the face of every attempt to exclude them, the questions we ask are persistent resprouts, largely uncontrollable. There really aren't hard-and-fast answers to *most* questions, though. Wildness means living in the unknown (p. 5).

There is no correct way to frame the initial goals or frame for your nature inquiry. You can start your inquiry project with a question or set of questions or statements, or they might appear later once your project unfolds. Sometimes, the questions appear and disappear, replaced by more relevant and pertinent ones.

Emily Bugos, for instance, discovered a set of questions as she hiked in the outdoors and wrote down her reflections:

> I began to think about the nature experiences I was providing for my infant classroom – What were they experiencing each time we stepped outside? What were they learning? How was our outdoor space contributing to their mood? How was it contributing to *my* mood?

Emily's questions came to her spontaneously and organically, spurred on by her hikes away from school.

Beth Hallet and John Nimmo, on the other hand, started their project with a statement rather than a question: "We wanted to explore the important role of the garden in children's learning," and to "share images that frame our adventures in the garden with children and draw from our larger goals for children – about who they are and how the learn about the world" (p. 1).

Both questions and statements are effective; it's a matter of deciding which linguistic form best moves you forward at the start of your nature inquiry, and which gives you the most passion, impetus, and direction.

PROFESSIONAL COLLABORATION AND DIALOGUE

At some point in your nature inquiry work, it is helpful to turn to your colleagues and engage in professional collaboration and dialogue about what you are seeing and discovering, and how it links to your teaching and leadership. Alex Dutton (2012), a veteran director at an emergent curriculum preschool with an inquiry focus, believes that "collaboration is a key part of doing project work well," and to check in with colleagues "who may see the children's work, conversations, and ideas in a different way" (p. 15). Through her inquiry work, Alex has learned that "finding out where a project would lead depends on how well I listen to the children" (p. 10) and her engagement and dialogue with colleagues.

There are a number of ways that we can pursue collaborative nature inquiry. In a *co-inquiry* model, educators work together on their inquiry work within a systematic forum for sharing one's inquiry discoveries and challenges. Effective co-inquiry groups often use an established meeting protocol for group members to present and to respond to their ongoing observations, discoveries, problems, and issues (Abramson, 2008). The co-inquiry model does require dedicated time and space to meet and share, and an ongoing commitment from teachers and administrators to attend group meetings and maintain a high level of trust and risk-taking.

A number of authors in this book collaborate on a regular basis with their colleagues to deepen their nature inquiry work. For instance, the authors of Chapter 10 share how their nature inquiry work is embedded in their long-standing teacher inquiry group, and the authors of Chapter 5 discuss how their school's nature inquiry is founded upon the school's foundational principles of learning and dialogue.

OBSERVATION AND DOCUMENTATION

In this section, I describe several tools for strengthening our observational and documentation skills and knowledge. As you read this material, please think about which tools appear most promising, and how you might adapt and use the tools in your nature inquiry.

CAPTURING CONVERSATIONS – AUDIOTAPING

Children learn about nature through interaction and conversation, drawing upon their personal experiences, cultural assets, and languages. For example, Marisa Nunez audiotaped and captured her preschool children's conversation about the spiderlings (Nunez, 2012).

Alex: Look, we found spiderlings, baby spiders.
Daniel: Yeah, baby spiders.
Alex: Look, they are yellow and black. There are so many. Cool!
Daniel: I think they are sleeping.
Alex: No, they must be cold. The sun is not out.
Daniel: No, they miss their mommy. She left.
Alex: Maybe she went to get food.
Daniel: Oh, like rolly pollies.
Alex: And worms.
(Megan, another child, comes to join Alex, Daniel, and Marissa.)
Megan: Teacher, what are you doing?
Marissa: Alex and Daniel found spiderlings.
Megan: Spiderlings?
Alex: Remember, they are baby spiders. Look, they are so small.
Daniel: Be careful, gentle.
Megan: They are scary.
Alex: They won't bite, they are babies.
Daniel: The mom will bite. She went to find food.
Megan: And the daddy? He went to find food.
Daniel: I do not see him, maybe.

Marisa captures this age-appropriate conversation with an audiotape recorder, and this snippet of conversation shows young children's talent for spontaneously discussing and trying to explain natural phenomena, and provides documentation Marisa and the children can revisit and reflect on later.

PHOTOGRAPHS

Photographs are a powerful tool for capturing a small moment or series of moments in children's nature exploration and learning. While educators and other adults are often the primary photographers, even young toddlers can use inexpensive cameras to capture aspects of nature exploration that they find intriguing. In Chapter 7, for example, Anna Golden describes how her young children photographed and drew about one special place in the forest adjacent to their school.

Alex Dutton (2012), the preschool director, has found that using photographs in nature inquiry helps to:

- step out of the immediate teaching moment as we focus on taking a photo of a child;
- capture a single action or physical movement in children's nature play and discovery;
- tell a story that records and indicates children's developmental growth in nature learning over time;
- provide a visual reference for studying nature objects and artifacts that can't be transported back to a classroom;
- revisit photographs to remember nature exploration and learning;
- revisit photographs for new insights, discoveries, and reflections;
- complement and add to documentation of children's conversations and our written stories of children's nature learning.

Let's now look at a few examples of nature inquirers taking photographs as part of their nature inquiry. When Marisa Nunez, the preschool teacher, first observed her children's fascination with the spiderlings in the school's grassy area, she took photographs to document the children's discovery (Figures 2.2 and 2.3).

Photographs, in addition to audiotaping, allowed Marisa to step back and not guide the children's learning as she normally did: "I just stood back, letting the children explore. I listened to their explanation of why the mother was gone, or what type of food the spiderlings eat."

Adrianna Ochoa, a preschool teacher, documented her children's interest in birds and butterflies in her school's garden. One day one of

Figure 2.2 Spiderlings.

Figure 2.3 Spiderlings.

her children was particularly interested in a hummingbird's nest that he found in the garden (Figure 2.4).

Since Adrianna and the children wanted the nest to remain outside for the absent birds, the photograph provided a visual record of an intriguing artifact that they could revisit again and again.

The children then became interested in butterflies, which were growing inside the classroom. When it came time to let their butterflies go outside, Adrianna noticed that one butterfly's wing did not look right, and she gently fixed its wing, and as it prepared itself for take off, Adrianna let one of her children hold the butterfly (Figure 2.5).

Adrianna's photograph captures this magical moment for the child, and her written documentation adds another level of documentation and reflection.

> How amazing it must be for a child to hold a butterfly. I remember as a child looking for rolly pollies with my friends at school and ladybugs in my grandmother's garden, but never in a million years would I have ever imagined holding a butterfly. It was definitely a great experience for me and hopefully a meaningful experience for the little boy who was the only one who got to hold the butterfly before its official flight.

Figure 2.4 Hummingbird's nest.

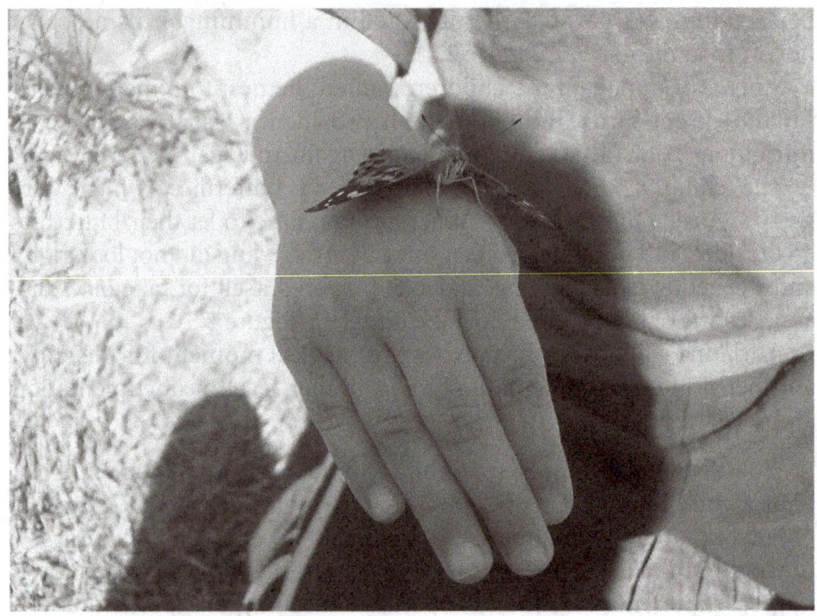

Figure 2.5 Butterfly before taking flight.

DRAWINGS AND PAINTINGS

When we encourage children to draw and paint in nature, we promote an effective symbolic and representational mode of observation, documentation, and analysis. Drawings can include children's maps, designs for structures in natural spaces (Galizio, Stoll, & Hutchins, 2009), and renderings of trees and animals and artifacts. Children can record their drawings in nature or in the classroom via a nature journal or simple clipboard with paper. They also benefit in their drawing from small handheld or table microscopes and also light tables and overhead projectors that illuminate certain aspects of artifacts and observational scenes. As Marcia Baghban (2007) observes, "Children draw pictures and write to organize ideas and construct meaning from their experiences" (p. 21).

Art and writing, then, add levels of symbolic representation to their nature inquiry as children create works of art (painting, drawing, dictating, labeling, writing, making marks) that represent natural elements (the branches of a tree or dried flowers or a bird's nest), characteristics (colors of a butterfly), processes (decomposition), and cycles (tadpoles to frogs) in nature education. The authors of Chapter 10 and Chapter 11 in this book feature children's drawings and Chapter 8 depict children's maps.

Artifacts

The observation of natural artifacts is another powerful form of documentation, reflection, and learning for children, for us, and for families. In nature inquiry, artifacts are most often left in their natural setting once children have observed and recorded aspects of an animal, plant, rock, water, or other nature element. On occasion it is appropriate to bring back an artefact or animal (fallen bird's nest, part of a bee's honeycomb, dried flowers, rock, branch, leaves, banana slug) to the classroom or school for temporary observation and documentation. The integration of artifacts and animals in nature inquiry is particularly powerful for very young children, infants and toddlers, who do not yet have the oral language to use for description and analysis. See for instance, Camille T. Dungy's observations in Chapter 3 on the objects that captivate her infant daughter. As Dungy and other nature inquirers have shown, infants and toddlers rely on their physical senses and benefit from revisiting concrete and sensory-based artifacts.

JOURNALS

Journals are a low-tech, highly effective tool for using written notes and photographs for observation, documentation, and reflection. The nature scientist Bernd Heinrich (2011) describes the value of written field notes:

> As I have searched for answers to biological questions that popped into my mind as I was watching birds or insects, I have meticulously documented my observations, and this documentation has made the difference between simply being a witness to nature and being one who identifies themes and questions (p. 38).

The use of a journal also lends itself to observing, documenting, and reflecting on the beauty of nature with a sense of aesthetics and beauty. Here is Henry David Thoreau writing about a moment in nature in a journal entry dated March 31, 1857, which is excerpted in *Of Woodland Pools* (Thoreau & Rorer, 2010):

> As I rise the east side of the Hill, I hear the distant faint peep of Hylodes and the tut tut of croaking frogs (wood frog) from the west of the hill. How gradually and imperceptibly the peep of the Hylodes mingles with and swells the volume of sound which makes the voice of awakening nature! If you do not listen carefully for its first note, you will probably not hear it, and, not having heard that, your ears become used to the sound, so that you will hardly notice

> it at last, however loud and universal. I hear it now faintly from through and over the bare gray twigs and sheeny needles of an oak and pine wood and from over the russet fields beyond, and it is so inseparable from it....

Thoreau's journal entries are attentive to sensory experiences in nature ("I hear the distant faint peep of Hylodes"), to listening in nature ("If you do not listen carefully for its first note, you will probably not hear it"), to the power of description ("over the bare gray twigs and sheeny needles of an oak and pine wood and from over the russet fields beyond"), and to identifying patterns and relationships in nature ("and it so inseparable from it").

Let's now look at the nature journals of a few early childhood nature inquirers. BreAnn Stewart, a toddler teacher, and her colleague took their young children outside in two large strollers, which seat four children each, alongside the waterfront in San Francisco.

> *BreAnn's Nature Journal*
> The farmers' market happens on Tuesdays during our stroller ride. My co-teacher and I noticed the large grapefruit and offered some for the children to try. One child held the whole grapefruit to her nose and smelled the citrus scent. After trying the grapefruits and pomelos many of the children asked for more. As we continued our stroller ride we found a tower of bananas inside the Ferry Building. Some of the children pointed to the tower and said, "Bananas over there." The children became frustrated as we discussed that we could not try the bananas. Thinking back, maybe the children were confused as to why we were able to try the grapefruit but not the bananas.

The journal entry allowed BreAnn to document the children's collective interest in the sensory experience of smelling the fruit, as well as their children's developmentally appropriate confusion that they couldn't smell all the fruit.

Like the scientist Bernd Heinrich's use of journals just discussed, BreAnn also used her journal to document patterns as well as anomalies in their walks along the wharf.

> *BreAnn's Nature Journal*
> For several weeks, we have walked along the dock searching for a boat. We had not been able to find one until today. We paused in front of the boarding gates and watched the boat take off. As we stopped I realized that one of the children continued to look

down. I followed her gaze and noticed that the suds appear in the water from the boat taking off. Very softly she said, "Bah-bul" as the suds looked very similar to soapy water bubbles, which we had recently played with in our classroom. I was amazed at how long the suds held her attention. The entire time that we were watching the boat she was watching the suds. It makes me think how often as teachers we intend for a project or activity to yield a specific outcome that we miss the children creating their own learning experience.

BreAnn uses the journal entry to document the sudden appearance of a boat, observe one child's spontaneous fascination with the suds in the water, and to reflect on easy it is for us to miss children's real science and nature discoveries and connections.

Marie Bourdier, a parent and preschool teacher, kept a nature journal that documented her nature experiences both with her own children and the children in her preschool classroom.

Marie's Nature Journal

As we started on the trail I couldn't help notice again how dry and spiky everything was, but what an elegant landscape that created; something to be said about the shades of beige and gray. I marveled at the thistles: Why did nature make them so? What are they meant to defend against? Not a millimeter of them was left spike-less, even with a third of those spikes no animals would dare to eat them! I wondered what Michael Pollan (2007) would say about them, he explained in *The Botany of Desire* that apple seeds are bitter to ensure the survival of the species, what about thistles? I noticed that green was coming in, through the dry and grey, maybe from the previous week of rain, maybe spring is around the corner. That's what I need to do, I thought, talk with my colleague about transforming our kitchen/dramatic play area at school into a science/garden area; prepare for spring. I realized I felt refreshed, ideas were springing about work and I am excited about going back to school.

Marie's journal entry allows her to integrate several inquiry elements, which range from straightforward observations ("I couldn't help but notice how dry and spiky everything was"), reflections based on nature literature ("I wondered what Michael Pollan would say about them …"), and new ideas for her teaching ("talk with my colleague about transforming our kitchen/dramatic play area into a science/garden area …").

Adrianna Ochoa, the preschool teacher, added to her photography documentation through the use of a nature journal:

> *Adrianna's Nature Journal*
> I noticed a hummingbird this morning. I got the children to follow it with me. Little did we know that hummingbird had built a nest in one of our trees. I stared at it for so long. I was amazed. The only other nest I had ever seen was the nest I had taken down from our tree a couple weeks back. The nest was pretty big, and the hummingbird nest is so tiny compared to it. I was fixated. I kept trying to find ways to get the children interested in going back. Luckily, the children were as enchanted as I was with the idea of having a hummingbird nest in our yard.

Writing in her journal enabled Adrianna to document the surprise appearance of a hummingbird nest, and to link this discovery with the feeling of enchantment that she and the children shared in this event.

POETRY

The linking of nature and poetry often conjures up powerful images and metaphors for re-seeing and re-experiencing human senses in nature. For example, in the professional poet Nikki Giovanni's "Winter Poem," the author uses "simple" language to describe a "simple" phenomenon in nature, a falling snowflake, but does so with a simple narrative beginning ("once a snowflake fell on my brow"), sensory experience ("a web of snow engulfed me"), feeling ("i reached to love them all"), and a change in identity ("i stood perfectly still and was a flower"). Reading and listening to her poem, we will never see or touch or taste a snowflake in the same way again; or if we've never seen an actual snowflake, we now can envision its potential magic.

Poems are an excellent way, then, to "freeze" and hold images, feelings, insights, and sightings in nature. In her journal entry about the hummingbird, Adrianna Ochoa added a haiku poem.

> *A Tree's Delight*
> A hummingbird sits
> pondering the day's beauty
> waiting for new life.

The addition of poetry, which can easily be shared and understood by young children, are pocket-size additions to journal writing that resonate with our emotional, personal, and cultural connections to nature as adult learners and inquirers.

STORIES AND ANECDOTES

Stories and anecdotes provide another effective way to observe and document children's nature experiences and learning, and to record our own reflections on children's inquiry-based discoveries. The anthropologist Karen Kramer (2011) reflects on the value of story as an elevated form of observation and insight:

> While repetitive observations are the sustenance of science, they can obscure connections and pigeonhole imagination. Understanding the scientific data we collect also requires being alert to clues about inter-relationships that are often outside the initial research problem. Narrative by nature is relational … and somewhere in there is a story, a really good story that you will repeat time and time again (p. 127).

Stories allow us to document the varied directions of children's nature learning, the process of our teaching, and the involvement of families (Dutton, 2012; Gallas, 1995; Meier & Henderson, 1997; Meier & Stremmel, 2010; Paley, 1981).

Returning once again to Adrianna Ochoa's nature inquiry, Adrianna also wrote a short story about Richard, one of her students, and his interest in the bird's nest that Adrianna had found earlier. Here is an excerpt from that story:

> Spring has finally arrived. The children all join us at the small picnic table; a surprise awaits. A bird's nest has been found and the children are cautiously observing it. Richard walks cautiously across the yard. Finally reaching the table he takes a peak over Sean's shoulder. "A bird's nest!" he shouts. The table clears up and Richard waits for his moment He grabs the bird's nest with both hands and turns it over. "What are you doing?" I ask. "I am taking the leaves out of the bird's nest," he says. "Why are you taking the leaves out?" "Because the bird's will be sad," he says. I assume he means the birds don't like a dirty nest, just like most of us do not like a dirty home. I wonder if I should stop him or let him continue. As I begin to let him know the bird nest is an old one and that those birds have flown away, he turns to me and says, "Put it back on the tree."

Adrianna put the nest back and Richard went to join the other children in their animal play outside in the yard. Adrianna's story has important elements of a small, well-told story – engaging characters (Adrianna, Richard, the absent birds), intriguing objects (bird's nest), a problem or predicament (dirty bird's nest which is not in the tree for the birds), a mystery (where the birds are), external spoken dialogue (Adrianna and Richard converse), internal thought (Adrianna's assumption that Richard does not want the birds to have a dirty nest), and a measure of narrative resolution (Richard tells Adrianna to put the bird's nest back on the tree for the birds when they return).

WRITING AND REFLECTION

Toward the end of a nature inquiry project or journey, whether it has lasted days or weeks or months, it's often helpful to sum up for ourselves where we started, where we went, and our next steps for teaching and inquiry. Elissa Calvin, an outdoor education preschool teacher, documented and examined how she could strengthen her role and teaching at her preschool:

> When I began this inquiry, I already had a sense, from experience and the relevant literature on nature and young children, that time in nature greatly benefits young children. As recess time continues to diminish across the country and some preschools feel the pressure to introduce more and more academic type learning, this time in nature becomes even more essential and harder to come by. I do not take for granted that my school places a high value on this concept and that most classes take a weekly walk to the Presidio [the national park in San Francisco] with the children. It is now ingrained in our school culture. Teachers who were once hesitant to leave our school grounds now mentor new teachers on how to get started in nature exploration.

At the close of her project, Elissa also reflected on her inquiry journey:

> This project opened my eyes to specific ways that natural settings can help children have greater success in social competence for themselves and for each other. The Presidio, our backyard National Park, provided me with a perfect setting with so many varied environments that provide different materials and experiences for the children. Our walks took us to Andy Goldsworthy's sinuous Woodline sculpture, an overlook by the Lyon Street Steps where you could see Alcatraz, a space with a dense canopy overhead and hundreds of owl pellets at our feet, and a large sandy expanse of land with lots of downed trees and sticks. Each of these areas offered specific gifts, such as bone hunting, tree climbing, stick play, and others such as insect identification and fort building. I hope my program will continue to take advantage of the

nearby Presidio and all it offers; there may be wild places that we have yet to discover that could unlock new curriculum or strategies for helping children reach new enzotones in social competence.

IN CLOSING

In this chapter, I have presented a number of ideas and strategies for observing, documenting, reflecting, and acting upon the interconnectedness of our social, educational, and political lives in natural world and built environments. There is great pedagogical and professional power in this interconnectedness, and when we use the tools of inquiry, documentation, and reflection as discussed in this chapter, we can remake our relationships with children, families, colleagues, and the environments in which we all learn and grow.

Much of our success in integrating inquiry and nature and place-based education also depends on who we are as individuals, as members of multiple communities, and on our jointly constructed nature experiences and knowledge with children and adults. Through the process of inquiry, documentation, and reflection, we learn to recognize and register our wanderings and wonderings in nature in increasingly sophisticated ways. We learn to create and use an expanding toolbox of data collection and analysis tools for finding patterns, connections, anomalies, dead-ends, and U-turns in our pedagogy and relationships in and around nature and place. I hope that you found this chapter helpful in reflecting on your own goals for connecting inquiry and nature and place-based education, and that you now have new ideas and strategies for achieving your nature inquiry goals. As you read the remaining chapters in this book that tell specific nature inquiry stories from varied early childhood settings, keep in mind this chapter's toolbox of inquiry ideas and tools.

REFERENCES

Abramson, S. (2008). Co-inquiry: Documentation, communication, action. *Voices of Practitioners, 3*(2), 1–10.

Baghban, M. (2007). Scribbles, labels, and stories: The role of drawing in the development of writing. *Young Children, 62*(1), 20–26.

Dutton, A. S. (2012). Discovering my role in an emergent curriculum preschool. *Voices of Practitioners, 7*(1), 3–17.

Escamilla, I. M. (2012). Understanding nature learning in the city. San Francisco State University. Unpublished paper.

Galizio, C., Stoll, J., & Hutchins, P. (2009). We need a way to get to the other side!: Exploring the possibilities for learning in natural spaces. *Young Children, 64*(4), 40–48.

Gallas, K. (1995). *Talking their way into science: Hearing children's questions and theories, responding with curricula.* New York: Teachers College Press.

Hatch, A. (2006). Teacher research: Questions for teacher educators. *Voices of Practitioners, 2*(1), 1–5.

Heinrich, B. (2011). Untangling the bank. In Canfield, M. R. (ed.), *Field notes on science & nature* (pp. 33–48). Cambridge, MA: Harvard University Press.

Henderson, B., Meier, D., Perry, G., & Stremmel, A. (2012). The nature of teacher research. *Voices of Practitioners*, 1–7.

Kramer, K. (2011). The spoken and the unseen. In Canfield, M. R. (ed.), *Field notes on science & nature* (pp. 109–127). Cambridge, MA: Harvard University Press.

Lanham Drew, J. (2017). *The home place: Memoirs of a colored man's affair with nature.* Minneapolis, MN: Milkweeds Editions.

Meier, D., & Henderson, B. (2007). *Learning from young children in the classroom: The art and science of teacher research.* New York: Teachers College Press.

Meier, D. R., & Stremmel, A. (2010). Reflection through narrative: The power of narrative inquiry in early childhood teacher education. *Journal of Early Childhood Teacher Education, 31*(3), 249–257.

Nimmo, J., & Hallett, B. (2008). Childhood in the garden: A place to encounter natural and social diversity. *Young Children, 63*(1), 32–38.

Nunez, M. (2012). Learning to explore and document in nature. San Francisco State University. Unpublished paper.

Paley, V. (1981). *Wally's stories.* Cambridge, MA: Harvard University Press.

Pollan, M. (2007). *The botany of desire: A plant's-eye view of the world.* New York: Random House.

Sobel, D. (2005). *Place-based education: Connecting classrooms & communities.* Great Barrington, MA: The Orion Society.

Stoddard, S. (2012). Nature exploration. San Francisco State University. Unpublished paper.

Stribling, S. M. (2017). The transformative power of action research. In Baily, S. F., Shahrokhi, F., & Carsillo, T. (eds.), *Agency, advocacy and leadership: The power of teacher action research in schools* (pp. 27–38). Boston, MA: Sense Publishers.

Thoreau, D. & Rorer, A. (2010). *Of woodland pools, spring-holes, & ditches.* Berkeley, CA: Counterpoint.

Part II

Setting as Teacher

3

BABIES AND NATURE

The Act of Noticing in Infancy

Camille T. Dungy

Box 3.1 Key Science and Nature Elements

- The connection of a novel experience, visiting moon jellies at an aquarium, with the knowledge of more everyday nature experiences such as walks through the neighborhood
- The importance of providing complex, adult language juxtaposed with opportunities for the infant to make her own meaning in non-linguistic ways
- The "dance" between adult-mediated experiences and child-led wondering and observation
- The difference between what adults find fascinating in the natural world and what fascinates and holds the attention of a young child

Box 3.2 Key Inquiry Elements

- Knowing when not to intervene and simply observing infants and toddlers in nature
- Letting young children follow their own interests, at their own pace and time
- Using oral language to explain natural phenomena with and for infants and toddlers
- Reading and Interpreting scientific printed matter and information
- Engaging infants in multi-sensory experiences

Infancy is the land of change. It is the land of giants and surprises, miracles and marvels. In infancy the whole world is ancient and there are timeless laws that rule you and everyone around you. In infancy the whole world is new and anything might happen anytime. Watching the world shift, discovering its wonders, can be deeply engaging for a baby. As a parent, I am learning to see the world anew through my baby's awestruck eyes. I am learning the ways that we as adults can bring nature to our youngest children and help infants notice and engage in nature from their earliest experiences. Through basic activities like walking with our babies, talking to them, encouraging play and exploration, we help infants learn about nature. With proper attention, parents and caregivers can support productive early nature experiences.

One of the most important steps in helping a new human being interact with the world around her is learning when to get out of her way. I am constantly teaching myself not to let my adult focus and adult fears direct my infant daughter's access to the world. Though I am necessarily vigilant about my daughter's safety and comfort, I am also vigilant about learning to let her follow her whims. Frequently, I find that even as small as she is, she manages to divine aspects of the

Figure 3.1 Watching the world shift, discovering its wonders, can be deeply engaging for a baby.

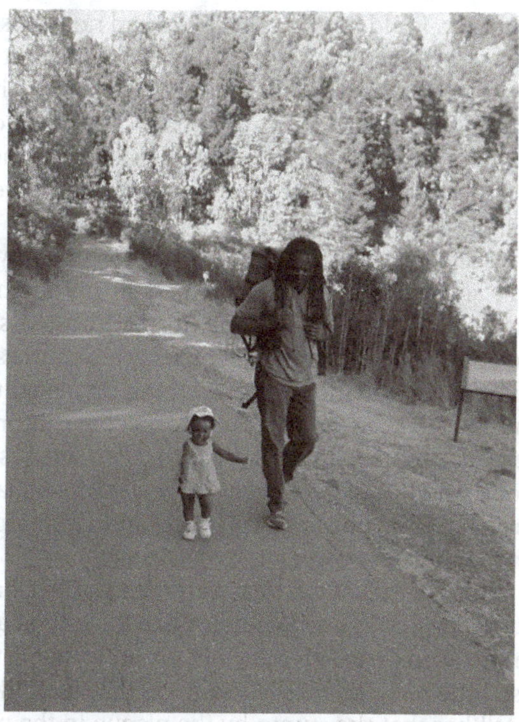

Figure 3.2 Finding the right path and then letting the infant child lead, that is a wonderful way for babies and adults to learn about the world.

world's beauty I would have overlooked. Finding the right path and then letting the infant child lead, that is a wonderful way for babies and adults to learn about the world.

Consider the day my daughter and I visited the moon jellies in the California Academy of Sciences. It was one of the afternoons when the Academy opens its doors to the public free of charge, so the corridors were packed with parents and children. I was focused on moving through the crowd as we proceeded toward our destination. My daughter was safely on my back in the Ergo, so what she was able to see was largely directed by me. I assumed we were looking at the same things, and I assumed I was showing her the most interesting animals in the room.

The moon jellies floated toward us and away, directed by a current our human eyes could not perceive. The lighting in the tank augmented their bioluminescence and made the jellies look improbably delicate. I was mesmerized, and I assumed the baby was too. I explained what we were seeing, how the jellies were moving, what and how they would eat. I told her that the jellies had no bones, or heart, or brains, and in these ways they were inherently different from her. I told her they were also quite similar. Jellies, like babies, live in a cycle driven by eating and evacuation. The baby I carried on my back learned that jellies, like babies, have not developed a means for self propulsion, so they are at the mercy of forces that carry them wherever the forces will.

I read the placard on the wall to the baby, informing myself as much as her. I don't always have to be the expert in my infant daughter's company. I'm willing to ask questions, to read posted signs, and to refer to guide books. I am responsible for securing sources of information that will be the foundation for everything my daughter will learn hereafter, and so I take it as my duty to become informed and to convey to her what I know and what I learn. Perhaps it seems silly to talk to someone who doesn't yet have the power of language, but soon enough she *will* have the power of language, and I am largely responsible for strengthening her power.

Because I want her to have a clear command of her native tongue, when I'm out walking with my daughter I like to point at a tree and say something more than "tree." I want her to understand that a maple tree has those little seedpods, called samara, that look like hovercraft propellers. I tell her that the stump by the plaque in the park near our house is from one of the oldest oaks in a city named for such trees. I want her to know that the redwoods in that same park were planted to commemorate ancient ancestors of the second and third growth coast redwoods now found in the hills surrounding us, that the trees lining our sidewalk are plums and will bear a hard bitter fruit in late spring. When I can, I tell her what facts and history I know about the nature we find around us. I name what I can name, the flowers, the squirrels, the birds and the honeybees, and I try to learn what I don't know right alongside her. I will have to take the time to look up the name of the twinned beauties leafed out on the bluff across the street. I want my daughter to have a broad knowledge of the language she was born into and the world that has received her. Her treatment of both will be informed by what I have passed on, and so I feel it is my responsibility to speak to her, as fluently as possible, about the world in which she lives. It is my responsibility to instill in her, even before she has the power to speak, a dedication to caring about what she discovers in the world.

Words are important. Silence is important too. I have to teach my baby the value of being quiet in the world, the value of letting her senses engage completely with the environment around her.

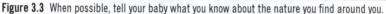

Figure 3.3 When possible, tell your baby what you know about the nature you find around you.

Eventually, I stopped talking and I let the silence of the jellies' world surround us. Accustomed to noise pollution as we are, the sonic resonances of the natural world can be quite startling. At first everything might seem quiet, without the wall of sound we humans so frequently create, but soon new noises become apparent, and these noises have as much to teach us as any human words. As important as it was for me to tell my daughter what I could about the wonders of the jellies, I knew there was an aspect of experience that required me to shut up and let her take what she could from her encounter without my intervention.

Language imposes a mode of understanding the world that is, in many ways, foreign to a baby's most developed modes of understanding. Babies are alert to the new sensations they experience around them daily: the breeze blowing through leaves and onto their little arms, the moist smell of wet leaves on a creek bed, the sound of skittering leaves on the gravel. This is true for the youngest babies, who regularly move in and out of sleep, as well babies nearing their toddler days, who spend quiet moments watching and feeling. The world without words holds plenty of learning opportunities for infants. Engage as many senses as you can.

My daughter needed to encounter the jellies visually, because babies register so much knowledge through sight. There is a reason so many child-focused zoos and aquariums have touch pools and petting stations. Being able to encounter the world tactilely is a foundation for greater comprehension and connection. When possible, get your babies outside so they can encounter nature first hand, literally. Where touch is safe for the baby and the plant, animal, or mineral the baby is observing, let him use his hands to learn. If touch is inappropriate, remember there are other physically involved ways that a baby can experience the world. As we stood quietly, in front of the moon jellies, I felt the baby's heel tap my hip in a rhythm that mimicked the fluttering of the jellies' bells. She was attending to the way these creatures floated through their world, and she was bringing this knowledge into her body.

When I had gotten my fill of the jellies, I moved on. I walked at a speedy clip, cutting through the crowd like the rays we'd seen in a busy tank. I was searching for the next thing that I thought would engage my baby. But the baby had a mind of her own. *Whoa-oh!* she said. At first I thought she was responding to the general ambiance of the place. In the aquarium things are darker than they would be outside. The light is blue and shimmery, vibrant and magical, and I thought she was reacting to that. Or maybe her verbal reaction to the jellies I so admired was delayed, I reasoned. With these assumptions, I was underestimating her capacity to take in new material. I was misinterpreting her cues. Not for the first time, I was to learn from my daughter that there is more to the world than meets *my* eye. Teaching an infant about the world can be a learning process for adult caregivers who are open to learning new things. As I kept moving, my daughter craned in the opposite direction, and soon her body's resistance made her will evident even to me. For the first time that afternoon I followed the baby's lead. Something I ought to have done from the beginning.

What the baby had seen was unmistakably wonderful, a giant sea bass, weighing close to 165 pounds, maybe four feet long and three feet tall, apparently defying the laws of gravity her infant games of drop-the-object suggested ruled everything in the land. Whereas I found the moon jellies beautiful, their small bodies fluttering through the blue might have been relatively unremarkable to a new human being who'd already seen balloons and butterflies, plastic bags and hummingbirds move similarly through space. Researchers who study infant cognition report that babies register incongruities by focusing their gaze longer on objects or actions that seem improbable or surprising. The giant sea bass created a new set of possibilities for my daughter. This might have been the largest animal she had ever seen. It was huge considering all she had seen thus far were plate-sized fish or smaller. Huge as it was, it wasn't sinking. It wasn't swimming. It wasn't even floating with the current like the jellies. That giant sea bass was stationary in the water, unmoving and unmoved. The baby wanted to take a longer, careful look at this miraculous creature, hovering over the rocks and sea vegetation, fluttering the little wing-like apparatus her mother would soon tell her were called fins. Though there was much that was familiar about this manifestation of the world's possibilities, there were as many things about it that were absolutely new. Whoa-oh indeed!

What could my daughter take from this lesson were she older? New knowledge about buoyancy and swim bladders, about the relative density of water to air and how this effects the laws of gravity, about the endangered state of sea bass along the Pacific coasts, and about the fact that the largest animals on Earth live in the water. Watching the bass with her, I told the baby all of these things, but who knows what she took from the encounter. Likely something about the elasticity of her assumptions about scale, possibly something about potential modifications to the rules she was learning about gravity, maybe something about the range of beautiful creatures she's liable to see in the world. I won't ever know. I have to be okay with simply providing the groundwork for the exposure.

When introducing infants to the wonders of the natural world it is crucial to remember that what is awe inspiring to you might appear ho-hum to a baby and vice versa. Therefore, it behooves the caregiver, and the baby, if the caregiver takes time to attend to where the baby directs her attention. If researchers know that infants register their attention to new objects or incongruencies by focusing their gaze longer in the direction of those changes, and we know that gaining a greater understanding of how things change and under what circumstances is a building block for knowledge, one thing we can do as caregivers of infants is to heed where our babies' gazes land.

I took my baby girl to a redwood grove and set her beside a 315-foot tree. The adults all looked up at the tree, amazed, and we expected the baby to be equally transported by its enormity and grandeur. This was not to be. The little one just played with the gravel she found below her. Closer to her birth length of 21 inches than to this tree's diameter of 21 feet, nearly everything the baby had ever encountered was taller and older than she. What made this tree so special? *These things I'm*

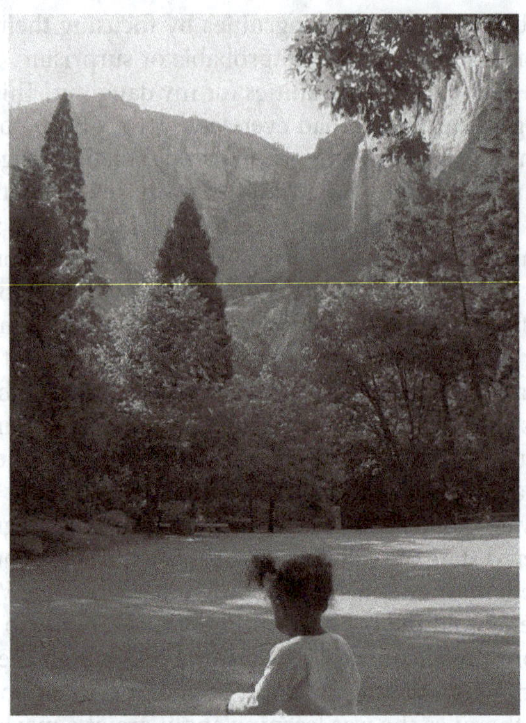

Figure 3.4 Remember, nearly everything will seem taller and older than your baby.

playing with now though, she seemed to be telling us, *these are amazing. Look how this one glitters like nothing I've ever seen before, and this one is black as the hair I curl around my little hand when I'm nursing. These are wonderful, these little hard things I'm holding. What do you call these?* She seemed to want to know. Even the gravel under our feet can be miraculous to the inquisitive baby.

My daughter's interest in rocks has not waned as she's developed. The house next door has a gravel walk, and two out of three times she is allowed to walk by herself somewhere near it she will toddle over to the gravel path and run her tiny fingers over the small pebbles. She will pick them up and sift them through her hand. I have to explain to her that the rocks aren't good for the neighbors' roses and so she should not pour the rocks into the roses. I have to tell her not to throw the rocks. Often in a hurry, I have to pick her up and physically remove her from these objects of her affection. But whenever I can let her just play with these rocks or others, I let her. I let her pile them and measure their varying sizes. I let her note the dirt revealed beneath the gravel. I let her attend to what insects, spiders, and small plants travel across or make their homes amid the gravel. Who knows that my little girl won't one day become a geologist or petrologist. This baby is focused on rocks, so I will teach her how rocks have shaped our world. Pushed in front of glaciers to scour our valleys and mesas, tectonically shifted to form our mountains and faults, broken down by lichen, by water, by wind, by the force of man, the pebbles in the neighbor's driveway are a part of the continuity of the firmament our whole existence depends on. The giant redwoods are amazing, certainly, but so are the little rocks.

Developing an appreciation for the natural world means understanding that things are often driven by forces that are beyond your power to control. This is a reasonable knowledge set to bring along when introducing infants to the natural world. Though we are used to being the ones responsible for directing the infant's life and actions, in cases where we are working to develop their relationship with nature it is often helpful to step back and let nature run its course. Set the baby on the grass to see what her little legs discover. First prickles, then softness, then a space for delight. Let this discovery unfold in its own time. Don't rush it. Don't work too hard to choreograph the child's encounter. Give it time. What will she do? What will she feel? How

Figure 3.5 Set the baby on the grass to see what her little legs discover.

will you talk to her to help her understand what she's feeling? When will you keep quiet and leave her at peace to take it all in? Notice what your baby notices and move her in the direction of her discoveries. Move slowly, allowing time for the new sensations to seep in. If she looks toward an orange flower, call it what it is, *California poppy*. Bring her body closer to the flower and linger awhile so she can come to know it in her own way.

I am aware that I am describing a parenting experience in an environment with a world-class aquarium, ready access to a redwood grove, friendly neighbors with gravel walkways and roses in their front yards, and time to linger. Perhaps this is not your experience. Much of the hesitation to introduce infants to the natural world stems from a perceived absence of access to nature. This is particularly true for urban dwellers, but is also true in suburbia where nature is so well-managed as to be nearly imperceptible. In such communities, where we have retreated indoors into climate-controlled homes or we have relegated "nature" to the city park or the zoo, daily encounters with the natural world might appear more difficult for the parent or caregiver of an infant. These encounters should not be impossible, however.

Much of the introduction of an infant to the natural world simply means moving through the world with increased intentionality. When a column of ants navigates the cracks in a sidewalk, stop and let the baby watch their progress. Baby's little eyes register difference and scale very early on, so you can point out all the ants then show your baby the ones who are carrying objects. Even if you don't have time to linger long, you can take a brief moment to comment on what you see as you and your child move through the world. When you have a little time to spare, seek out opportunities at local animal and plant facilities like zoos and botanical gardens. If you don't have something like that around, you can take the baby to the local garden supply store and wander through the potted plants. One of the most useful ways to develop an appreciation of the natural world in a baby is to make that world part of what she understands as normal. Is there a way to plant a butterfly bush somewhere on a porch or in the yard where the baby will encounter it regularly? That bush will grow, and the caterpillars and butterflies that make it their home will provide a life science lesson. Baby's vocabularies expand through exposure, and as parents and caregivers we can use innumerable opportunities to expose our infants to the many ways we speak about the world.

When my daughter was about nine months old, and again when she was roughly 14 months old, we were joined on our regular nature walk by a four-year-old boy and a six-year-old girl. As we entered the mouth of the nature trail, a managed path lined with wild blackberry bramble on one side and creekside shrubbery on the other, the children looked around in obvious trepidation. They wanted to know if there would be snakes, if there would be mountain lions or bears. I had to tell them that bears had long since been exterminated in the area where we were walking, that the likelihood of seeing a mountain lion in the middle of the day in a densely populated area was quite slim, and that this wasn't the terrain for rattlesnakes, the only snake they really had to be cautious about in California. Then I told them what they should do in the unlikely event that they did encounter one of these creatures, what to look for and how to protect themselves from harm. Once the children knew what was in store, and how to keep themselves safe, they calmed down considerably. They were able to enjoy the trail, to ask more questions, to identify some of the plants they encountered. The second time they came on the walk they weren't looking for what would hurt them. Instead, they wanted to see how the plants they'd encountered on their first foray had grown. Spending time with children who had not been raised to wander in nature, it occurred to me that this sort of walk will be second nature to my daughter (pun intended). Being outside will be her normal. She will develop a sense of comfort in natural spaces.

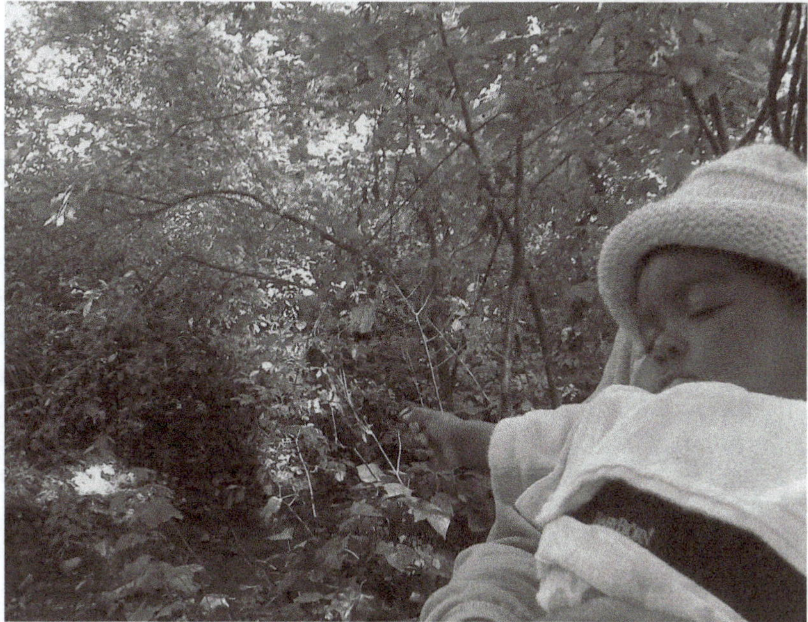

Figure 3.6 Even sleeping babies benefit from getting out into nature.

From the time she was a week old, I've taken my baby on walks through the neighborhood, hikes in regional and national parks, and strolls through nature centers. I've shared the world with her, identifying what plants and creatures I could, telling her how to safely navigate trails, warning her against doing things that invite unnecessary risk. At first she was as likely to be sleeping as watching, but she was there with me, carried in a pack close to my body or pushed ahead of me in her stroller. My voice, calling its catalog, registered as one of her life's constants. When she began to use language, I was able to reap the fruits of my labors. As she approached her second birthday, barreling out of the land of infancy and into the land of the toddler, she grew much more likely to engage with the world on my terms, using words.

Walking through the neighborhood either she or I would call out the words that identified the world around us: squirrel, bluejay, live oak, redwood, lenten rose. *Dat?* She would ask, as we walked by something we'd yet to identify. Her question was developmentally appropriate, *What is this thing?* she wanted to know. It also pointed to the fact that I had instilled in her a desire to assimilate her environment into her own lived experience, an important step in coming to care for

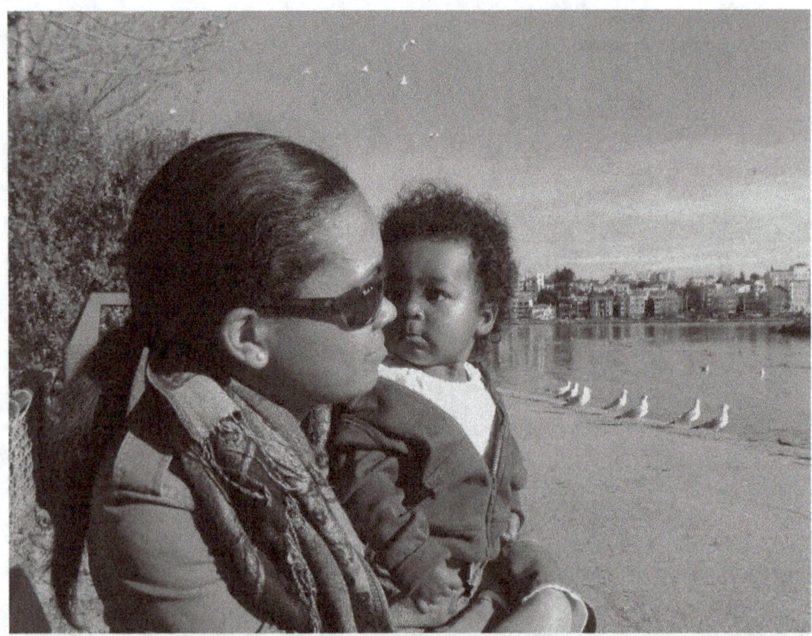

Figure 3.7 The process of looking and seeing and naming, discovering and turning back to look at what we've discovered again, all these are the lessons of infancy.

and about the world. On a walk with friends, when she was just over 22 months old, my daughter stopped at a stand of orange flowers and said, "Poppy," recognizing by name for the first time the state flower of her native home. How proud a moment this was for me, because I knew that my lessons had not been in vain.

I am just as proud to know that she is comfortable sitting quietly in the world. I have watched her admit the sounds of the birds and the rushes without the need for comment. The morning she stopped at the stand of poppies she moved closer for a better look, and I slowed with her. If I have taught her some things, she has taught me too. She has taught me to slow down when something amazing is in front of me, to take a closer look in order to broaden my understanding.

As she moved through infancy, I took my daughter places I thought she should go in order that she might see things I thought she should see. I came to realize that if I followed her attention I could discover amazing wonders and I could help her learn even more about the world. It didn't always take fancy aquariums or carefully weeded gardens to show my daughter the world's beauty. The butterfly bush in her daycare was enough some days. The bunch of basil I bought at the farmer's market and put in a vase on the kitchen counter where we could watch it grow a new set of roots. The key was to engage as many of her senses as possible. I found things she could see as well as smell, could touch and hear, and even taste. Sticks and stones and leaves and dirt and beetles could sometimes offer up more opportunities for genuine connections with the wonders nature than elephants and eagles and 3000-year-old trees.

I try as much as possible to slow down and notice what she notices, where her gaze rests, how her body reacts when placed in proximity to something new. What we overlook we can see again through infants' eyes. What we see all the time, we can see anew. The process of looking and seeing and naming, discovering and turning back to look at what we've discovered again, all these are the lessons of infancy. They are the fundamental ways we help infants notice and engage with nature. They are the fundamental ways we help infants experience the world.

4

OVERCOMING OUR FEARS

Embarking on a Nature Journey

Gita Jayewardene

Box 4.1 Key Science and Nature Elements

- Repeated exploration of similar creatures in their habitats and in a "laboratory" setting (with magnifiers and paper)
- The connection between learning to care for and respect small creatures and learning about how these animals are adapted to survive where they live
- The symbiotic relationship between children's efforts to understand and to represent (through drawing and language) their understandings
- The importance of following the interests of children while providing structures, skills, and knowledge to expand their understanding

Box 4.2 Key Inquiry Elements

- Observe children's nature exploration in the different contexts of the school yard and neighborhood garden
- Ask open-ended questions and "wonder aloud" about children's questions and problems

- Record children's behaviors via written notes and children's conversations via audiotaping
- Examine the effect of mixed-aged groupings on children's level of cooperation and problem-solving
- Collect and analyze photographs of the children's nature explorations as visual evidence of their learning over time

A PASSION AND INTEREST IN NATURE AND INQUIRY

I GREW UP IN CEYLON, now called "Sri Lanka," a small island in South Asia surrounded by oceans and rain forests, where most backyards teemed with wildlife. Most of my childhood was spent in small cities on the island and also in a city not far from the capital of the country. In the tropics small creatures manage to creep into people's homes upsetting many residents, but they did not bother me. I have a very pleasant childhood memory of looking for gecko's eggs behind my father's bookshelves (their favorite place to lay eggs) and placing them in empty match-boxes lined with cotton wool. Then I waited impatiently until the baby geckos hatched. When they finally came out, I tried to keep them as pets, but to my dismay they always ran away.

So is it any wonder that the young children I teach associate me with animals and plants? Very often I hear them calling me, singling me out from all the other teachers, when they see a worm, a bee or any other creature that they want to take a closer look at, but are a little hesitant or cautious to do so. They quickly take my hand and take me over to their findings, knowing that I am not scared or squeamish of these creatures of the earth. My students also love to listen to stories of my childhood, how I caught dragonflies, grasshoppers, worms, frogs, and other creatures and about my pet fox, peacocks, squirrels, and porcupine among others. They listen to my stories and want to hear more. One of their favorite stories is how I raised two small fox cubs who did not have their mommy to raise them. They love to hear how I fed them milk with baby bottles. I have always wondered how this innate curiosity of nature, in young children, that seems to be so strong, can be destroyed so easily, and turn these children into people who are afraid and far removed from nature. Durrell (1988) says that we are born with an interest in the world around us. Watch a human baby or other young animal, he says, crawling about, investigating and learning with all of their senses, discovering what life is all about.

Once, at a staff meeting about teaching science to young children, I mentioned that teachers should try not to exhibit their fears of animals in front of young children, and one of my coworkers said, "Gita, you grew up in the jungle, that is why you are not scared of animals, and we are city girls!" But I don't believe that just because someone lives where there is an abundance of wildlife or nature that he or she learns to love or be loathsome of nature. Sure, most children living in natural environments will learn to tolerate encounters with creatures just for survival, but I believe that children need someone who can be a role model to show the importance of respecting and taking care of nature. As Durrell (1988) points out, no creature is horrible or loathsome; they are just a part of nature same as we are. I learned to respect nature from my father who was a naturalist by hobby. He had an abundance of knowledge about trees, plants and other aspects of nature. I grew up understanding that the earth does not belong only to the human animal but also to all other living and non-living things of nature. As teachers of young children, it is our responsibility to sustain children's natural curiosity without instilling unnecessary fear of the natural world.

I agree that "there is an innate need for children all over the world to be close to their elders, and this closeness and the involvement of the elders with the children, helps them to learn about the activities of the elder who is followed" (Hay, 1980, as cited in Rogoff, 2003, p. 239). Because I am passionate about nature, I wondered if I could be the elder whom my young students would follow around, helping them maintain and foster curiosity about nature. I believe that young children need to experience nature first hand by seeing, touching, smelling and hearing to establish a bond with nature. I agree that "curiosity alone is not enough for children to develop skills and promote their understanding" and that "adult guidance is essential" for "children to develop the skills of scientific inquiry" (Worth & Grollman, 2003, p. 27).

INQUIRY AND NATURE – STARTING OUR JOURNEY

I set out to explore and find answers as to how I could fulfill this responsibility of giving my young students hands-on experiences with nature at my university childcare center. I followed Cochran-Smith and Lytle's (1993) advice that teacher inquirers find answers to puzzling questions by listening to ourselves and to our students. I also followed Hubbard and Power's (2003) three important elements for successful inquiry. First, be humble and recognize that you have much to learn from your students and their communities. Second, approach your students and their needs to guide your teaching. Finally, have a willingness to share your story (p. xvi).

I decided that my students should have hands-on experiences with nature to explore, investigate, ask questions, and make sense of what they observed and experienced. I also wanted my students to learn collaboratively with same-age peers as well as older children. I focused on five of my children who were three years of age and five children were five years of age. In this way the younger children would benefit from the older students' language, mathematical, social, and problem-solving abilities, and the older children could become teachers and practice their more advanced nature knowledge.

In terms of my own inquiry work in this process, I was an active partner in their learning and a co-constructor of knowledge. I asked open-ended questions and wondered aloud about a question or a problem, and in so doing I tried to spark their interest and advance the children's thinking. I was mindful of the Reggio Emilia approach (Edwards, Gandini, & Forman, 1998) where "the teacher's role centers on provoking occasions of discovery through a kind of alert, inspired listening and stimulation of children's dialogue, co-action, and co-construction of knowledge" (p. 10). While we often consider "thinking" as something we do solely by ourselves without any connection to the outside world, Rogoff (2003) reminds us that thinking also involves interpersonal and community processes working together with individual processes. My children worked together to solve their problems, asking and answering questions, arguing with each other, and in the process broadening their nature knowledge.

We explored first our school's yard located in urban San Francisco, and then expanded our nascent nature curriculum beyond our school environment. Taking a team approach to nature inquiry, I discussed my research with Laura, my assistant teacher, who agreed to help me take pictures and observe the children. Unfortunately, she was not fond of the natural world and did not like small creatures like slugs and snails. I assured her that she did not need to touch any of these creatures. To my relief, she agreed to our inquiry project. Then I wondered what I could find in our urban play yard covered only with woodchips and cement, two trees, a few planters and some trees around the school. I explored the possibility of bringing nature into the classroom to add to what little aspects of nature I could find in our own yard. I also explored the neighborhood to find possibilities to take the children on nature walks. I was glad to find a small but beautiful garden called the Garden for the Environment (http://gardenfortheenvironment.org/pages/garden.html) tended by some neighbors.

STARTING WITH OUR IMMEDIATE SURROUNDINGS

In Sri Lanka, I used to walk to school and walk back home. My school was about a mile away. On either side of the road were different trees, bushes, and plants where many kinds of birds and other species lived. My father used to say that when he was a child walking the same road to school it was different because there were more trees and animals. During his childhood my father said that this same road was not tarred but was just earth and gravel and people traveled by foot or rode in bullock carts. When I was a child, there was less wildlife for me to enjoy along the way to school. Still, myna birds, parrots, big black crows and rufus babblers, and small hawks were a common sight on my way to school. My father also told me that he saw monkeys jumping from branch to branch chattering happily eating wild mangoes and other fruits such as ripe jackfruit, breadfruit, different kinds of leaves, flowers, and insects.

I was not very hopeful that I would find enough specimens for my students to observe solely from our school play yard. But we do have many bushes with purple flowers that bloom from spring through the end of fall that attract many honeybees to the annoyance and fear of most teachers and the curiosity of the children. We also have many large trees surrounding our center but are out of reach of our children. These trees are home to many kinds of birds such as hummingbirds, blue birds, and woodpeckers and also to squirrels. I never had the chance to explore these trees and bushes around our school during the ten years I have worked at the center. As spring was near, we started hearing different bird calls from the birds in the area, and my students and I also talked about making a bird sanctuary. Then I started collecting information on how to build one. I was certain that there were also many other creatures that were making these trees and the bushes under the trees their home. I decided to get some advice on different methods of looking for different kinds of creatures from Durrell's (1988) *A Practical Guide for the Amateur Naturalist*. But until then my students and I explored under our planter boxes to see if we could find any creatures to observe. When we removed our long planter, the children were surprised to see a colony of woodlice and a slug living under it. Our nature journey had begun.

Be Gentle With the Wood Lice – Respecting Small Creatures

On our first day of our nature inquiry (February 6), the children and I placed the wood lice that we found under our planter in containers with magnifier lids and placed them on a table. I also placed some of the wood lice on a white sheet of paper on the same table. I took out our magnifier to give children a closer look at the bugs.

Lee: Yukky! Squish it!

Gita: No one hurts the bugs that we pick! Why do you want to squish it Lee?

Lee: Bugs bite!

Gita: All bugs don't bite. These wood lice don't bite.

Lee: Mmm. But, but … my mommy say they bite!

Lena: He is moving! He is upside down!

Moses: Wow! Lot of legs!

Karn: Can I hold it?

Gita: Yes, you can. You have to be very gentle when picking them up.

Karn: Why?

Gita: Because they are very tiny and they can get squished if we are not careful. (I gently scoop the bug with a small paintbrush and my finger and place it on Karn's palm. Karn looks at me with a questioning look, as if to get reassurance that the bug won't bite him.)

Karn: The roly-poly is ticklish. (giggling) (See Figure 4.1)

Moses: Where's the little one?

Lee: The big one ate it! I think he needs food.

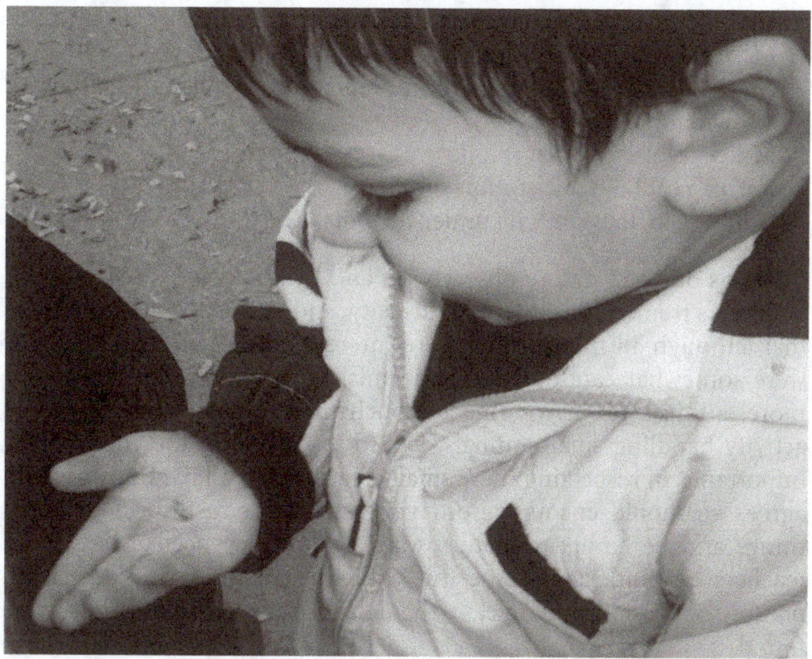

Figure 4.1 "He feels ticklish."

Next I asked the children if they wanted me to provide paper and markers to draw the woodlice; I wanted to see if they would represent any aspect of their learning through drawing. These three year olds had not done any representational drawings, although a few had started drawing human figures with a head with eyes, legs, and arms coming out of the head. Karn asked for my pen and started to draw lines to represent the many legs of the bug and drew a wavy horizontal line over the vertical lines.

Representation and reflection are critical ways in which children make meaning and develop their own theories from their work (Chalufour & Worth, 2003). The point of encouraging children to represent what they have learned through a cultural tool such as drawing is not to force children along but to show them the possibility of making a connection or finding a relationship between their drawings and their own experiences (Cadwell, 1997).

After everyone got a turn to observe these creatures, we decided that they needed to return to their home under the planters. We placed them under the same planter where we found them to show respect for the lives of these tiny creatures.

Moses: Where are the roly-polies?
Gita: Remember we put them back under the pots?
Moses: Why Gita?
Gita: Because that is their home and they are happy in their own home!
Moses: Oh!
Karn: Yeah! No one stomps on them?
Gita: Yeah, they are safe under the pots.

This was our first nature observation and I noticed the three-year-old children's tremendous interest, curiosity, and attention. I also observed that although all the children were interested in these creatures, they were somewhat cautious and squeamish at first and only later were more enthusiastic in wanting to touch them. As this was their first activity handling small animals, I tried to convey to the children the importance of respecting these small creatures. As all naturalists would agree, we should encourage our young students to respect all living things and be compassionate toward them. They need to see us as teachers as gentle and respectful with the creatures we select from nature to observe and release them later back to where they were found.

Moses' Slippery, Cold Slug – Encouraging Children to Take the Initiative

The very next day (February 7), three year olds Karn and Moses were digging in the sandbox. Suddenly Moses went near the wall of the sandbox and moved his face closer to what looked like a dried leaf that was wet and sticky after the rain. Moses turned toward Karn and said, "I found a bug!" Karn called me in an excited voice, "Gita, come here, we found something!" It was a small slug slowly crawling toward the bushes. I gently picked up the slug and took it to the picnic table. Sujee, a four year old, also joined us. Teacher Laura brought the magnifying glass and a sheet of white paper for the table.

Karn: What is it?
Moses: A bug.
Ollie: No it is not!
Lee: It snail.
Gita: Yes, it is like a snail, without a shell.
Karn: Who break it?
Lena: Not me!
Gita: Slugs don't have shells

Moses slowly extended his forefinger to touch the slug. He touched it and quickly withdrew his hand, wiped his finger on his jacket sleeve, and looked at me and said, "Touch is cold, it is slippery, cold."

Sujee: I want to touch it! (She picks up the leaf with the slug on it and examines it intently.) (See Figure 4.2.)
Ollie: (Then Ollie picked up the slug.) Look he is doing poo-poo! He is going poo-poo. I don't like this one, poop come in my hand. (Shows his finger to me smiling.)
Gita: Now let's put the slug on the paper and see what happens. Don't touch it. Look at his head. What is happening to his head?
Sujee: Something is coming out!
Moses: Yeah! What is it?
Sujee: I think they are his ears.
Lee: Eyes, little eyes.

Ollie gently touched the antennae and they went in again.

Ollie: They gone!
Lee: His shell broken?
Gita: Slugs don't have shells.
Lee: I have lots of shells at home.
Karn: In Mexico I picked shells.

Ollie: Shells are dead! My mommy said.
Karn: I have a sand dollar. It broke!

We carefully put the snail away where we found him. Karn wanted to draw the slugs. After he finished drawing he said, "Gita, write this is a mommy slug, this is a baby slug, this is a family."

The children initiated this activity, found the specimen all by themselves, and wanted to look at it with me. I was glad that they did not try to squish it with their shovels like they used to do sometimes before we started our nature observations. Nature activities initiated by children themselves, such as what took place during the "slug observation." give children a sense of accomplishment and pride. The children always have a choice to participate or not to participate, especially in the yard where there are so many outdoor activities to choose from. Therefore, the children who found the specimen and participated in the observation were self-motivated to learn about the slug.

I agree with Lowry (1998) that children acquire new scientific knowledge only if we give children unhurried experiences and the motivation to participate. I have also noticed that children who are highly distracted while taking part in teacher-directed activities, usually become highly interested and motivated when participating in nature

Figure 4.2 "I want to touch it."

activities such as the "slug activity." After only a few days, my students had developed a habit of asking for paper and markers to represent what they have seen and learned. They also ask me to write down what they say on their nature drawings.

SHELLS – BUILDING ON NATURE EXPERIENCES

The next day (February 8) I chose a book on snails and slugs and also a book on seashells and took them outside into the yard. I had recognized from our previous nature observations and conversations that the children were also interested in snails and shells. We looked in the book at different kinds of snails, slugs and also other creatures with shells. Laura also brought our collection of shells to the table for us to examine.

Gita: What do you think these are? (Pointing to the shells.)
Karn: Shells!
Gita: Do you think they are animals?
Alex: They are dead! They don't have legs.
Gita: What do you think? Do you think they have legs?
Karn: Mmmm they slide.
Alex: No they don't! They crawl.
Karn: Yeah, they do! I saw a movie, they slide.
Moses: I think some shells have legs. Octopus have legs.
Alex: My daddy said octopus drop their legs!
Gita: Yes, if another animal tries to catch an octopus by its leg, he can drop that leg and run off! Their legs are called tentacles.
Rick: Yeah! Examining a sand dollar, and mumbling to himself, "flower."
Karn: Why?
Alex: He run away! I saw a movie.
Gita: If he drops one tentacle, how many legs do you think he will have?
Karn: Mmmm five legs!
Gita: Let's show eight fingers. One drops, and counts to seven. Seven. But you know, he can grow another leg!
Karn: Wow!
Rick: Hole! (Looking inside the hole of a sea urchin and shaking it.)

In this activity, four year olds Rick and Alex joined three year olds Karn and Moses, and all the children touched the shells, shook the sand dollars, examined the soft and smooth shells, and the rough and bumpy ones. They also looked inside a broken sand dollar. Rick asked me for the tabletop magnifying glass, which he called the "telescope," to get a closer look at the shells (see Figure 4.3). Since the tabletop magnifying glass had its own stand, Rick did not need to hold it and could use both of his hands to move the shell as he observed it under the magnifying glass.

During the drawing activity Rick drew accurate sketches of a sea urchin and a sand dollar (see Figures 4.4 and 4.5).

Alex watched the other children drawing shells and said he was going to draw the ocean because the shells live in the ocean.

This mixed-aged activity enhanced the learning of all the children. They observed the shells, asked questions, disagreed with each other, provided answers and hypothesized, and in general were motivated to draw and discuss the shells. I also recognized their enhanced observational skills through their detailed drawings of the shells as the children tried to learn and make sense of their natural world (Colker, 2002).

Our First Nature Walk – Exploring a Neighborhod Garden

Five days later (February 13), the three year olds were excited to go on their first nature walk to the Garden for the Environment a few blocks away from school.

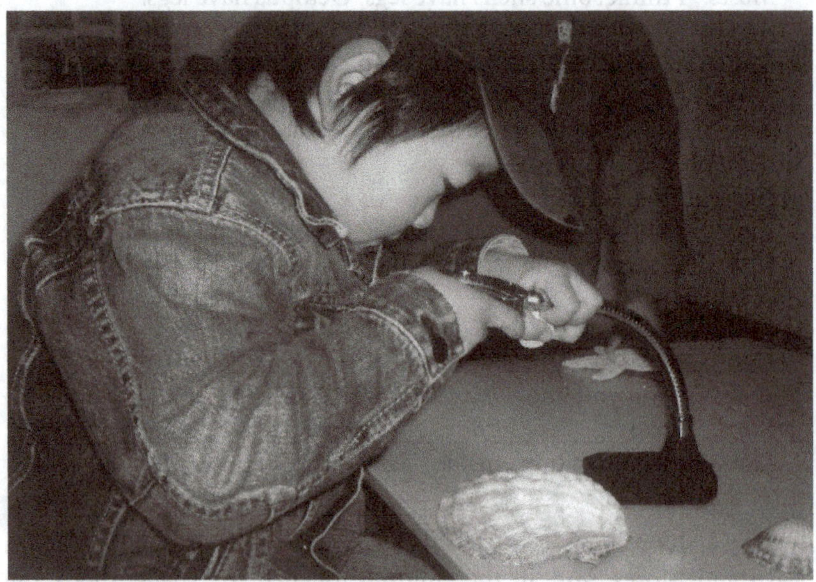

Figure 4.3 Rick observing slug family.

Figure 4.4 Rick drawing.

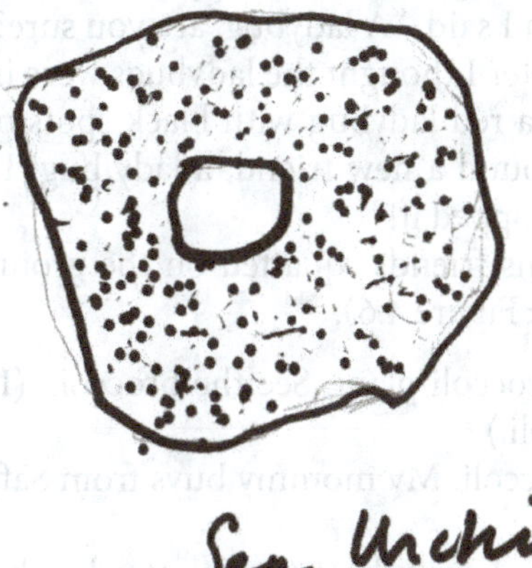

Figure 4.5 Rick's sea urchin.

Lena: Gita where are we going?
Gita: We are going to a garden. What do you think we would see?
"Flowers," "trees," "birds," a "lion," were some of the replies. I asked what else we would find on the flowers and plants.
Karn: Bugs!
Moses: Worms!
Laura, the children and I set out on our first nature walk. A few blocks down the street, we passed some Douglas fir trees, and Moses stopped and pointed to a tree.
Moses: That tree has a lot of hands!
Laura: Oh yes that tree does have a lot of branches.
Karn: I hear birds, but I don't see them.
Lena: They are hiding. (Lena walks up to the tree and touches the bark.)
Gita: What does it feel like Lena?
Lena: Feel like snake.

Every week we took walks up and down the street and then back to school. So, this walk to the garden was a real treat and a big adventure for the children. I heard the excitement in the children's voices and the curiosity in their observations of this new experience. As soon as we entered the garden gate, Moses stopped and pointed to the ground, "Look a bee, a bee, I see a bee!" he said. The children gathered round the bee. I asked the children what they thought the bee was doing on the dirt. Moses said, "I think he is looking for food. Oooh, he is gone. I see him again!" We observed the bee for a while and started walking along the path into the garden. Suddenly, Karn shouted, "Gita, Gita, I see a ladybug!" Then I said, "A ladybug, are you sure?"

As it was still winter I thought the ladybugs were in hibernation. But sure enough it was a red ladybug with black spots on a large broccoli leaf. Karn said, "I found a new friend, a lady bug! I want to take him home, oooh no, I dropped it!"

Then Karn and his friends squatted on the ground and looked for the lost ladybug (see Figure 4.6).

Gita: This is a broccoli plant. See the broccoli. (I pointed to the head of broccoli.)
Moses: I like broccoli. My mommy buys from Safeway! I go with mommy.
Elena: Look Gita, I see a bee! (Looks at a bee hovering around some flowers.)
Moses: Bee bite!

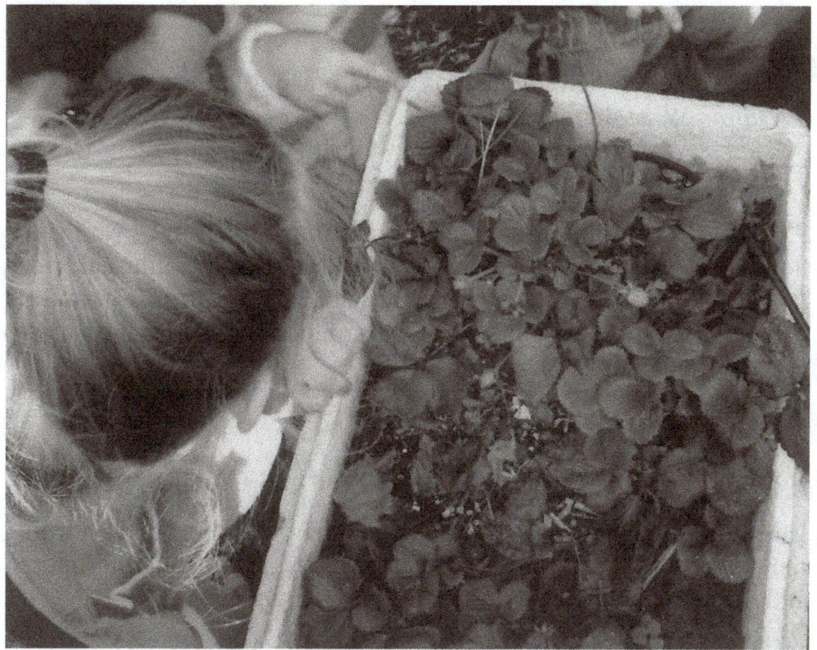

Figure 4.6 "Where's our ladybug?"

Gita: Yes, they do sting, if they are scared or angry, but they usually don't sting if you don't bother them.

Moses: It is NOT OK to hit, right Gita?

Gita: Yes. What do you think the bee is trying to do?

Elena: He is trying to eat the flower.

Gita: Yes, you are right he is looking for food. He has something like a straw in his mouth to suck the sweet water "nectar" out of the flower.

Moses: I like to blow bubbles with my straw! Where's the bee?

Gita: There, he is flying away. Where do you think he is going with the nectar?

Lena: Home, to eat honey.

We kept moving as it was almost lunchtime, but the children were so absorbed by their surroundings that they did not complain. On our way out the gate, we stopped near a large lemon tree. Laura squished a leaf, smelled it and said, "I love this smell!" Then all the children wanted a turn to smell the lemon leaf.

Karn: That's my lemon. My mommy likes lemons! (Touching a lemon.)

Laura: What color are the lemons?
Lena: Lello.
Moses: Yellow! (Everyone took turns touching the lemons.)
Laura: What do they feel like?
Moses: Water. (The lemons were wet with dew.)
Karn: Soft.

At the bottom of the lemon tree I saw a clump of helleborus with green flowers. I brought the children's attention to these unusual green flowers. Lee looked at the flowers and said, "wow!" Then Karn noticed a sweet pea pod, hanging down from a fence and he reached out to touch it (see Figure 4.7).

Laura: What does it feel like Karn?
Karn: Soft. Can I take it home?
Gita: Touching the peapod. Yes, it is soft and smooth.

Later, after nap time, I was curious to find out what the children would remember from their experience at the garden. I gathered the children and asked them what they saw at the garden that day.

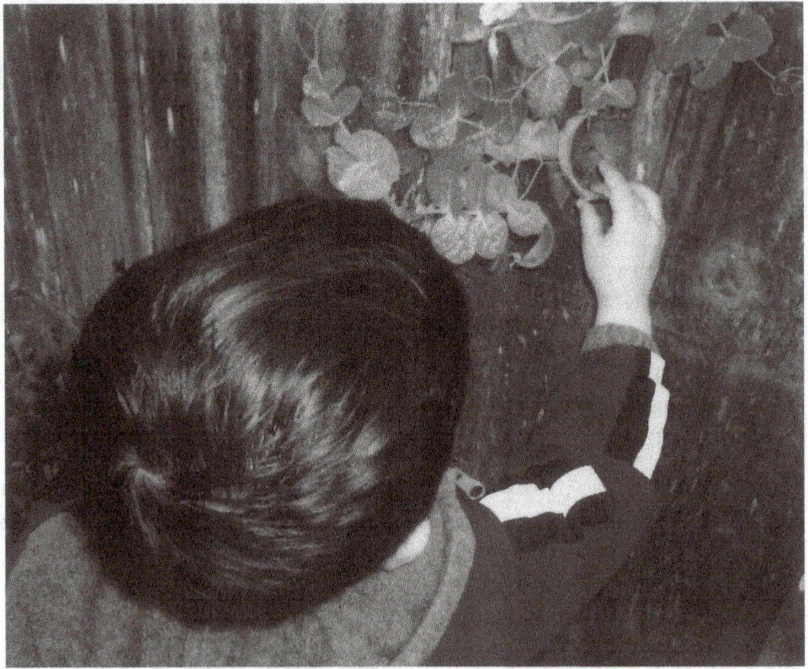

Figure 4.7 Karn touching the pea pod.

Karn: My friend ladybug. It flewed away. I want to take it home.
Katy: I saw green flowers and apples in the apple tree. (The apple tree with apples was from her imagination as we did not see any apple trees with apples.)
Lena: I saw a bee and a lemonade tree!
Moses: Bees, but no birds. They were hiding.
Olly: I see a spider!
Gita: What else did you see?
Olly: I want to see a apple tree. Only sticks in the apple tree. We couldn't find the apple tree. (As it was winter all the leaves had fallen off the apple tree) I saw a black thing with dirt. (I think what he was referring to was the compost bin.)
Elena: The lady bug crawling on a leaf. (She crawls on all fours to show me.)
Karn: Strawberries, and mmmm a broccoli!
Gita: Do you think we should walk to the garden again? (They all said yes.)

These young children, some of whom had just turned three years, were curious and inquisitive about what they were discovering and it helped that there were no time restrictions. The openendedness of our garden exploration allowed the children to "appreciate beauty, express creativity, and perceive patterns and variety in sensory dimensions of their worlds and themselves" (Torquati & Barber, 2005, p. 40). I was pleasantly surprised that Lee remembered the "green flowers" because I never imagined that any child would be interested enough as to remember the "green" flowers. Often Lena brings lemonade with her lunch and so calling the lemon tree the "lemonade tree" was her personal and quite developmentally appropriate connection. Of course Karn remembered "his friend the lady bug" and Moses his "bee." Olly seemed to be disappointed that he did not see the apple tree but only sticks on the tree. Overall, the children's level of interest and curiosity during our nature walk helped them remember what they saw, smelled, touched, heard, and discussed.

When I analyzed the children's conversations I could see that the children constituted their own theories of the world through their own interests and observations. For example, Lena probably realized that her drink at lunch was made of a fruit that grows on trees, and it does not just come from the grocery store shelf. The children who were interested in the strawberries and the broccoli plant may have also learned that these fruits and vegetables are grown somewhere before coming to a store. Lee may have realized that flowers come in different colors including green. Karn and Moses may have learned that ladybugs and bees need plants for their food and that ladybugs live on plants and that bees take the nectar and fly away to their home. I realized that the children's visit to the garden, seeing new plants and small creatures and listening to bird songs, helped them become more aware of their physical and sensory surroundings.

OVERCOMING OUR FEARS AND STARTING OUR NATURE CURRICULUM

Our first nature activities and discoveries occurred over the short span of several days. I was delighted that the children, Laura, and I had such deep engagement with nature - small creatures, plants, flowers, the outdoors - and we had forgotten our early fears and hesitation about exploring nature. We were then ready to continue our nature journey. Over the next several weeks, we explored flowers and plants; creatures such as spiders and scorpions (in plastic cases), squirrels, ladybugs, newts, worms, woodlice, tadpoles, and frogs (we had a firebelly toad) and birds (we had two parakeets); build a bird sanctuary; acted out animal actions and behaviors in our tumbling area; shared and discussed nature books; sang nature and animal songs.

The children also continued to make increasingly detailed and accurate representational drawings of plants and flowers and small creatures from their observations. Their representational drawings showed their evolving scientific capabilities as well as their aesthetic development. I continued to analyze their drawings, reflect on my photographs of the children's nature learning, and to record and reflect on their nature conversations.

In my own inquiry learning, I also became more alert to the children's questions, answers, and their conversations with each other and I learned what they know, their theories about the physical and natural world, and their interests in nature. We both had a renewed sense of alertness to the activities and conversations that unfolded and were meaningful to the children in learning about the natural and scientific world.

When I first started working with young children in San Francisco, one of the first observations I made was the fear and alienation the children and teachers had about nature. Then I realized that San Francisco was a city and this alienation from nature was just a fact of life for contemporary children in a modern society. I knew that young children's biological attraction to nature diminishes very quickly if significant people in children's lives do not nurture it. Now I realize even more the urgency of having curriculum and "nature elders" to encourage nature education in early childhood.

REFERENCES

Cadwell, L. B. (1997). *Bringing Reggio Emilia home. An innovative approach to early childhood education.* New York: Teachers College Press.

Chalufour, I., & Worth, K. (2003). *Discovering nature with young children.* St. Paul, MN: Redleaf Press.

Cochran-Smith, M., & Lytle, S. L. (1993). *Inside/outside: Teacher research and knowledge.* New York: Teachers College Press.

Colker, L. J. (2002). Teaching and learning about science. *Young Children, 57*(5), 10–11.

Durrell, G. (1988). *A practical guide for the amateur naturalist.* New York: Knopf.

Edwards, C., Gandini, L., & Forman, G. (eds.) (1998). *The hundred languages of children: Advanced reflections on Reggio Emilia approach to early childhood education.* Greenwich, CT: Ablex.

Hay, D. F. (1980). Multiple functions of proximity seeking in infancy. *Child Development, 51*, 636–644.

Hubbard, R. S., & Power, B. M. (2003). *The art of classroom inquiry: A handbook for teacher-researchers.* Revised ed. Portsmouth, NH: Heinemann.

Lowry, L. F. (1998). *NSTA pathways to the science standards: Guidelines for moving the vision into practice.* Elementary school ed. Washington, DC: National Science Teacher Association.

Rogoff, B. (2003). *The cultural nature of human development.* New York: Oxford University Press.

Torquati, J., & Barber, J. (2005). Dancing with trees: Infants and toddlers in the garden. *Young Children 60*(3), 40–47.

Worth, K., & Grollman, S. (2003). *Worms, shadows, and whirlpools.* Newton, MA: Education Development Center, Inc.

5

NATURALLY SPEAKING

Children and Teachers in Dialogue with Nature

Darcy Campbell, Kelsey Henning, and Shawna Thompson

Box 5.1 Key Science and Nature Elements

- Children's open-ended exploration of natural habitats
- Observation of cyclical change and growth in natural spaces
- Science knowledge stemming from long-term, repeated engagement with flora and fauna
- Use of scientific terminology and vocabulary in small-group and whole-group discussion of scientific and nature artifacts and processes
- Regular observation of animal habitats and patterns of use and change

Box 5.2 Key Inquiry Elements

- Audiotaping children's conversations
- Photographing children's spontaneous discoveries and social interaction in nature
- Recording teacher observations and insights via written notes and journal entries

- Documentation of children's nature explorations and learning inside and outside of the classroom
- Documenting children's nature learning and engagement in repeated visits to familiar places in the national park surrounding the schools

Most people have had some experience in nature, they have walked in the woods, held a frog gently near the water's edge, tended a garden, marveled at the diligence of ants at a picnic, been moved by an Ansel Adams photograph, but to step beyond an "experience" with nature and come to care for nature means that one is moved, inspired, and in awe of its beauty and power. This doesn't usually happen in just one visit to a national forest, or one encounter with a sweet-smelling flower, or one's first visit to the zoo, but develops over time, deepens as we come to observe, connect, label, discuss, and imagine this beauty and power over and over again. To care for nature is to come into a relationship with nature, to feel one's connection to it, to *not* see it as separate, but as part of who we are, and *how* we are in the world. In this chapter, we explain the context of Cow Hollow School (CHS) and our cycle of inquiry, and then provide two brief narrative accounts of how put our inquiry and nature play and work into action with children and families.

OUR SCHOOL

CHS began its life, like many preschools, in the base of a church building with many space limitations. Although it was not larger than a small house garage, we were fortunate to have access to a tiny brick courtyard. Well-tended flowers and our neighbors' apple tree often provided us with valuable learning gifts of rotten apples, robins, and snails. We collected and noticed the attributes of leaves, and the children learned to be very gentle with the plants and living things. Living creatures and natural materials collected right outside our door became conduits for researching and strengthening the children's empathy, awareness of patterns, and sense of belonging in an ecosystem.

Three years later we moved to the Presidio, a national park on the northwestern edge of San Francisco, where we remain nestled between the woods and the water, surrounded by eucalyptus and cypress trees (Figure 5.1).

Figure 5.1 Adjacent to the Cow Hollow School and its fenced play yard, three year olds roam in "The Forest."

Our school is surrounded by wildness, and we acknowledge that it is a part of our learning environment – it is a teacher too. Through an inquiry-based curriculum with the children, and our school's emphasis on documentation and reflection, we have learned what it means to feel a sense of ownership and to take care of our natural surroundings. A core set of principles guide our rich inquiry and play-based curriculum:

- every child is capable and competent;
- children learn through play, inquiry, investigation, and exploration;
- children and adults learn and play in reciprocal relationships with peers, family members and teachers;
- adults recognize the many ways in which children approach learning and relationships, express themselves, and represent what they are coming to know;
- process is valued, acknowledged, supported, nurtured, and studied;
- documentation of the learning processes acts as memory, assessment, and advocacy;

- the indoor and outdoor environments and natural spaces transform, inform, and provoke thinking and learning;
- school is a place grounded in the pursuit of social justice, social responsibility, human dignity, and respect for all.

Our theoretical framework, inspiration, and pedagogical choices are firmly rooted in social-constructivism. We find inspiration in the research of Jean Piaget, who viewed the acquisition of knowledge as a continually developing process, and the mind as an aggregation of cognitive structures that are changed and connected to one another. We also look to the work of Lev Vygotsky, whose research focused much on the adults' role in a child's construction of knowledge and meaning. The term "scaffolding" is used to describe the process by which a more knowledgeable learner guides a young learner through certain steps with warmth and responsiveness, joint problem-solving, and guided participation. Last, the educators from the schools of Reggio Emilia, Italy, provide us with a context for asking questions, and pedagogy of listening to reflect on our images of nature education.

OUR CYCLE OF INQUIRY IN NATURE

To facilitate the children's meaning-making and deepening awareness of their place in the natural world, we guide the children through the cycle of inquiry from the children's discoveries, questions, and problems in their outdoor learning environments. Our inquiry-based learning model is founded upon the following elements:

- children see themselves as thinkers;
- everyday acts of teaching and learning lead to thinking;
- process is valued, acknowledged, nurtured, and studied;
- dialogue is essential to learning;
- collaboration is valued;
- strategies for listening are developed;
- children grow up without sacrificing their present identity and stage in childhood.

These points of inquiry and investigation create a framework for long term, in-depth examination and representation in our project work. The children's projects, linked to their discoveries in the outdoor environment, represent beauty, intelligence, creativity, and respect for the world. Our project work offers opportunities to:

- make connections and expand awareness;
- represent experiences and provide a context for ideas;

- extend language;
- build relationships, reveal commonalities, and make note of diversity;
- engage minds and encourage wonder;
- evoke process, not product;
- analyze dialogue and experiences;
- make meaning with and for the children;
- establish identity of the classroom community.

The inquiry-based project work supports the children's caring for our immediate natural world, and our three nature-based dimensions are:

1. Sense of Place, learning to know the Presidio and its creatures and plants.
2. Sense of Ownership, learning to take care of their surroundings.
3. Sense of Stewardship, learning to advocate for their surroundings.

To more clearly illustrate how these three dimensions guide our nature inquiry work with young children, we now present two brief stories illustrating linking inquiry and nature education. Shawna first describes her experiences over the course of two years with a group of 16 three-to-five-year-old children, and then Kelsey tells the story of promoting a sense of place in nature with her 17 three-to-five-year-old children.

The Story of the Troll Bridge – Learning about the Presidio and Stewardship

Developing a sense of belonging within the classroom community and in the outer surrounds was our primary goal our morning group of 3.5 year olds, half of whom were new to our program. Along with my co-teacher, Trevor Valentino, I (Shawna) took walking trips of four children twice a week, so that each child experienced a walking trip twice a month, to one location, the beloved "Troll Bridge," an area named for its old brick bridge over a small creek, with lush vegetation and a climbing tree nearby (Figure 5.2).

Many of our cherished walking destinations around the Presidio have been named by our children and/or teachers. The process of labeling a place is to establish a relationship with our surroundings. By taking recurring visits to the same place each week, over a long period of time, our hope was that children came to feel more comfortable with each other and more familiar with their environment, and a

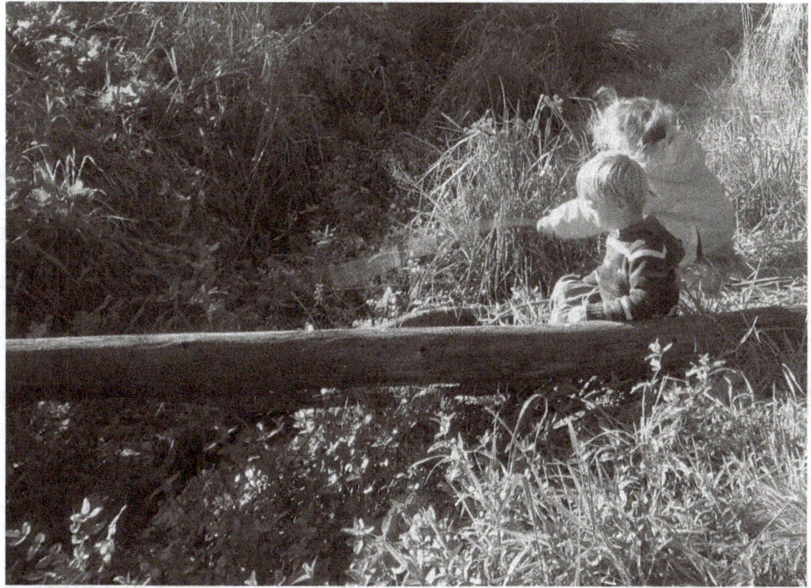

Figure 5.2 Children play at the stream, a place they lovingly know as the "Troll Bridge" and enjoy pretend fishing.

nearby place offered time to nestle in. As Nabhan and Trimble (1994) attest, "A few intimate places mean more to my children, and to others, than all the glorious panoramas I could ever show them. Because I sense their comfort there, their tiny hand-shaped shelter has come to epitomize true intimacy for me."

To create an air of reverence and to set our intentions as observers and visitors to our special spot, we silently tiptoed down the trail, not uttering even a whisper. A quiet, magical approach invited the children to hear the birds announcing their arrival, to keep their eyes open for any changes since their last visit. A favorite activity was "fishing" in the stream with sticks and peeking inside the bridge for any signs of the troll, inevitably leading to a debate on his existence.

At the end of October, the entire class, along with several teaching parents, visited the Troll Bridge together. The parents contributed a Day of the Dead celebration for the children in lieu of a Halloween celebration, as we had chosen as a school not to provide a Halloween celebration. Teachers and parents chose to have a "parade" (walk) to our favorite spot to honor all creatures living and dead, fitting in well with both our nature studies and the spirit of the Day of the Dead. On that day, the group ventured a little farther and played near an old large tree stump. To their surprise, they discovered something new: an animal's den. While Trevor and I posed questions to the children to prompt their theories and questions about the den ("What do you notice? Who lives here? Are there any clues?"), parents were quick to jump in with answers ("deer don't live in the Presidio, but coyotes and skunks do"). We gently stopped them and redirected them to instead listen to the children's ideas; it was too soon to give facts – the spirit of surprise and wonder need not be quelled by adult logic.

The discovery of the den launched a new cycle of inquiry. In the data collection phase of our inquiry, we took repeated visits with clipboards and pencils for children to record the shape of the den and any new features they noticed (it just rained; will it still be there? Will it have changed at all?) (Figure 5.3).

Some of these investigative walks were led by teaching parents who took notes and reported back to the whole group what was discovered, with a focus on the children's thoughts and actions. A first step in all of our project work is to find commonality within the children's ideas and to root them in co-constructing theories. To begin this process, Trevor, my co-teacher, and I guided the children in listing all animals

Figure 5.3 A small team of researchers pause at the site of the animal den to make observational recordings.

that they believed lived in dens. Rather than focus on solving the mystery of to whom the den belonged, we extended the learning by pondering dens. What are the features of dens, how are they built? Where are they built? What do they provide to the inhabitant? As a result, the children became rich storytellers about forest animals, revealing the three to four year olds' values of safety and family. Their subsequent play involved building dens of sticks in our forest, becoming a family of hawks (or bears or raccoons) with babies to nurture. We made note of how quickly the children's elaborate stories brought them together, adding depth to their connections, and ability to negotiate.

Our den research then led us on many adventurous walks through the Presidio, with children looking for possible animal homes, classifying them based on identifiable features. After several trips into the forest, the children became expert stick builders, leading to an extended study of weaving in the following spring semester. The children experienced an increased awareness of animals that inhabit the Presidio and became attuned to looking out for them. With the children and their families, we had successfully developed a rich sense of place within our social and natural community.

The following year, Trevor and I were quite fortunate to stay with this same group of children. In the fall, we continued our walks through the Presidio, venturing ever farther up the Ecology Trail, a hiking trail behind our school. As with every new school year, we offered new prompts and provocations as well as revisiting stories from the previous year to find again our common threads to establish our learning community. Our fall project work involved revisiting the children's expertise in weaving and stick homes and coming to know our new classroom pet gecko. Later in the fall, the children made a new discovery along the Ecology Trail: a beautiful space inside the forest that had a large, mysterious stick structure erected, closely resembling a dinosaur skeleton. At a reporting meeting in which the children who were on the walk reported on what they found, we wondered about how it had gotten there. I said to the children, "Was it the forest fairies? Andy Goldworthy? A group of students from the Bay School?" After a long quiet pause, a child said, "Must have been the forest fairies."

Soon after this initial conversation, the children named their special spot in the woods, Fairy Land. Using logs and natural materials collected on the Ecology Trail, the children built their own Fairy Land in the classroom, complete with little fairies made from clothespins and fabric. Their stories and representations demonstrated the sense of ownership they developed in co-constructing the concept of Fairy

Land and what it meant to them. The children returned to Fairy Land on several occasions with their journals, collecting, recording, and telling stories about the fairies. On one of these visits, something terrible was found: a bag of dog waste was left on the fairies' special dinosaur skeleton. The children were extremely offended and concerned; they felt it their duty to help protect the beauty and safety of Fairy Land, on behalf of the fairies.

Upon returning from winter break, we asked the children what they wanted to do or study next at Fairy Land, and a lively conversation ensued around three main ideas: construct something scary like a puppet to protect Fairy Land from "bad" litterers, post a sign telling all visitors not to leave their trash, and more closely investigate fairy homes. Three committees were formed to investigate these goals. Each committee visited Fairy Land several times as researchers within their specific focus. The puppeteers took detailed notes of the trees from which they planned to hang their puppets. They debated with each other on which materials were best and most durable to use for the outdoor location, and they discussed scary features, such as fireballs and spikes. They researched papier machè and connected to their previous work in wire weaving, deciding to make wire frames for the puppets.

The trash committee looked for more signs of trash along the Ecology Trail and interviewed the many dog walkers along the trail, asking them what they do with their dog bags. In doing so, they found out that some dog walkers leave the bag along the trail and pick it up on their way back to their car. In preparing to construct their sign, the trash committee decided to test out many different types of glue on wood samples to find the most effective. The third committee, the fairy home investigators, took photographs of the many entrances to fairy homes that they found in Fairy Land. While revisiting their photos and making fairy drawings, the children decided to construct a fairy elevator for the fairies, so that they could help the fairies more easily reach the entrances that were higher up on the tree. The children decided to construct a pulley system for moving the elevator up the tree, traveling to the hardware store to gather the necessary parts (Figure 5.4).

Throughout the spring the children stayed committed to their projects, and since their gifts to the fairies were meant for an audience, the children and teachers planned a special "Revealing Day" at Fairy Land and invited their families. The class also decided to organize a trash pick-up day, which happened to coincide with Earth Day. To include the family perspective in this plan, teachers notified families in advance, who, through the weekly online journals, were well aware of

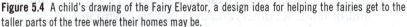

Figure 5.4 A child's drawing of the Fairy Elevator, a design idea for helping the fairies get to the taller parts of the tree where their homes may be.

the children's investigations in the forest. All of the families were supportive of the trash pick-up plan, and one accompanied us on the walk. While we rarely prompt the children to engage in this kind of environmental responsibility, these particular children were not only ready for the activism, they sought it out due to the sense of stewardship they felt for the special places in the Presidio that they had come to love and care for.

THE STORY OF THE HURT TREE: DEVELOPING SENSE OF PLACE THROUGH NATURE INQUIRY

Our year in the classroom began with my co-teacher, Jenna Betterly and I (Kelsey) finding ways to bring our lively group of 17 three-to-four-year-old children, otherwise known as the Little Bay class, together. As a social constructivist school, it is always our goal and our responsibility to create a collaborative classroom community and a place in which we co-construct our knowledge about the world. We spent the first few months of the school year prompting them with various entry points such as storytelling and revisiting "the troll bridge," just described by Shawna in the previous story, to begin looking for the "spark" of inquiry.

Despite our efforts to bind this group together and create a sense of belonging, we saw that the children were still thinking more as individuals rather than as a community. During one of our weekly meetings, Jenna and I decided to reframe our thinking and our approach to inquiry with this particular group of children. In our meeting, we came to the conclusion that this group of children felt a deep connection to the troll bridge and we collectively decided that we would use the troll bridge as a third teacher and our way to try to bind the children together. Keeping in mind one of our guiding principles at Cow Hollow School that "every child is capable and competent," we began by asking ourselves three questions to guide our collaborative inquiry:

- How do children develop a sense of competence in tool use, a way for children to represent what they are coming to know and their theory-making as an important aspect of critical thinking?
- How do children feel a sense of power and influence in their social and nature community?
- How do children come to understand how their actions impact and/or influence others and their natural environment?

Through our exploration in nature and with natural materials, we used these questions to frame our work with the Little Bay children going forward. Once we had reflected on our own perspectives, we more clearly saw what would potentially guide the children to begin thinking as a collective community. Toward the end of our first semester, a "spark" happened.

THE SPARK

The "spark" happened on one of our weekly walks to the troll bridge, which our group of children had consistently visited over the year. Many of the children felt as though this place in the Presidio was special to them. They felt a sense of belonging as individuals, but were still struggling to have a collective mindset and connection to this special place. On this particular walk, the children noticed a tree that had been chopped down. When they approached it, one child saw that there was sap on the tree. Seeing this as a possible opportunity for a spark, Jenna and I rushed over to the tree and said, "Oh no, the tree is bleeding!" Our intention was to attempt to engage the children in something potentially important for us as a community. As Carolyn Edwards and colleagues in the *Hundred languages of children* (2012) states, "The teacher needs to enter into a kind of intellectual dialogue with the group of children and join in their excitement and curiosity" (p. 151). By doing this right away, the children showed concern over the tree and began discussing among each other what had happened to the tree and what they could do to help. The children seemed to enthusiastically and collectively agree that this tree needed the Little Bay's attention.

DOCUMENTING

We started out by guiding the children in documenting the details they noticed and wondered about the hurt tree. Each time we revisited this space, we asked the children to take a moment to look more closely and prompted them to ask questions. The children took their field journals, which they had used before, with them on our walks to the troll bridge as a tool to record their theories (Figure 5.5 and Figure 5.6).

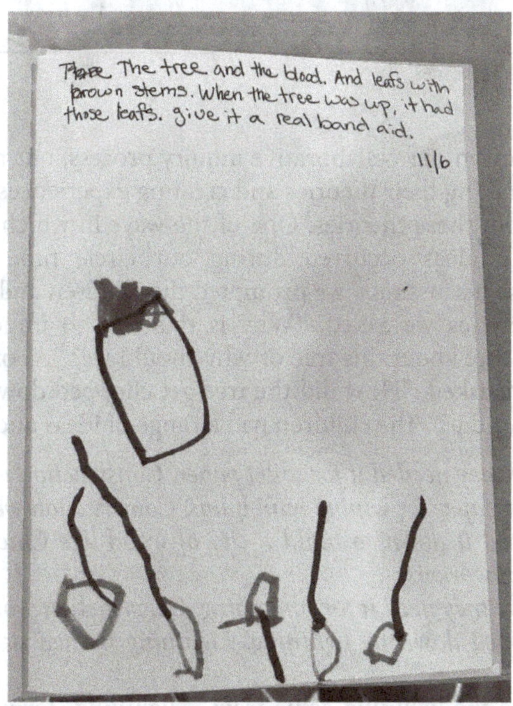

Figure 5.5 Recording theories.

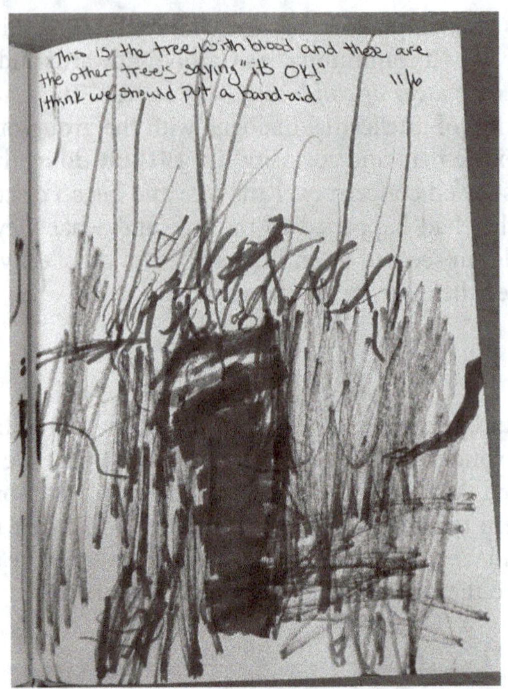

Figure 5.6 Recording theories.

At this point in our collaborative inquiry process, our role as teachers involved taking their theories and creating experiences for the children to test out these theories. One of the ways in which we revisited the children's ideas occurred during our circle time discussions. Through these discussions, we prompted the children and ourselves to think critically, as we asked, "Why is this tree so important?" and "Why do we care about this tree or why should we?" At one particular circle time we asked, "How did the tree get chopped down? And who do you think did it?" The children had a range of ideas and theories:

JS: Maybe they needed it for toilet paper. Construction workers.
AN: Toilet paper for wiping bum bums. Construction workers.
JC: Chopped it down to build a city of wood like Chicago. Construction workers.
GT: Maybe they need it for something. Construction workers.
AN: Chopped down by lightning. Lightning needed it to build a bridge.
LB: Maybe the lightning came from a lightning storm in winter time.

EL: A thief chopped it down because he needed to kill it.
EN: The construction workers needed it to build a bridge.
LB: Someone who is really mean to the tree. Maybe a river.
MCE: A beast used his horns and chopped it down in the night.
LL: A crocodile maybe.
GT: A pirate chopped it down with a sword.

Through this conversation, we saw that the children had big ideas about the power of others, as well as their own sense of agency.

REVISITING AND TESTING THEORY

As a way to honor the children's ideas, maintain their engagement, and as a way to revisit and tell stories about the "hurt tree" while inside our school building, the children used their developed tool skills to make a tree forest out of cardboard and tape, sticks, wire, paint, and natural materials (Figure 5.7).

Once we had set our scene, we had the backdrop to think critically about why and how we were telling the story of the "hurt tree." At this point in our inquiry, Jenna and I wanted to support the children by creating dialogue, sharing materials and ideas, listening to differences

Figure 5.7 Recreating the forest.

of opinion, and offering time and space for each of the children to express their ideas. We hoped that these factors would help the children to work together and develop empathy toward something in their natural environment. And they did! The children used their cardboard tree forest to test and play out their theories about how the tree became hurt. The children took on the roles and characters of construction workers and animals and used different materials to experiment with their ideas and construct new theories.

AN: (talking to a construction worker) Cut down a different tree not the bleeding tree.
LB: That tree will be able to grow back. Oh no! They are trying to get into our territory (to the construction workers).
AN: We're protecting you from bad bugs!
MCE: All the chopped down trees are bleeding. The people chopped down this one because it was too small.
AN: Another storm is coming!
MCE: Get out of the storm.
LB: Oh no! I'll get my fairy friend.
MCE: Oh boy, let's get out of here. Kelsey, there's a storm. We need to hide (the construction workers).
AN: Oh no, I heard a boom of lightning. The storm killed one of my praying mantises. This guy is sad. Wait he's still alive he actually had protection from the storm. The storm brought the fire and it's bad for bugs.
MCE: The fire keeps the blood of the tree warm.
AN: the fire is hurting the bugs and other trees though.

Their ideas around how the tree became hurt and how they could now help the tree showed us that they desired having power and influence to care for their environment. So we came back to the fundamental question, how do we help? We knew we couldn't fix the tree, but we could do something to help it feel better. Many of the children initially had the idea that the tree needed a band aid, so that is where we began. We studied photographs of the hurt tree and then worked together to decide what the band aid should be made out of and what it should look like. When it was finished, a group of children went to the Troll Bridge to attach the band aid (Figure 5.8).

This, once again, gave action to their idea of how they could help.

Through coming to know and care for the hurt tree, and knowing how they think they can influence each other, others, and the tree positively and collectively, the Little Bay class gained a collective identity of being the protector of trees. The "Hurt Tree Project" helped to set the

Figure 5.8 Helping the hurt tree.

foundation for being a citizen, not just of their classroom but of the entire school community and its local environment. The Little Bay children came to care about something beyond themselves. Through the process of collaborative inquiry, this group of children began to think more critically and collectively about the environment and developed a sense of responsibility to protect nature – particularly trees.

OUR NEXT STEPS FOR INQUIRY AND CARING FOR THE ENVIRONMENT

In this chapter, we have presented two brief stories that show our how collaborative inquiry with young children can promote our school's guiding principles of place, ownership, and stewardship. At our school, adults and children collaborate in co-constructing our relationships with the immediate, natural world. Adults introduce and lead children on their initial discoveries of natural spaces. Adults model the attitude toward nature that children emulate. A critical piece of this modeling involves inquiry, documentation, and reflection. Developing a lasting, impactful relationship takes time. We must not rush into the mindset of exposing young children to the harm we've done to our environment and our generation's responsibility to fix past generations' negligence. If we want our children to be true stewards and protectors of nature, who continue a lifelong relationship with the outdoors, we must first respect children's rights to have meaningful, joyful contact with wild elements.

REFERENCES

Edwards, C., Gandini, L., & Forman, G. (eds.). *The hundred languages of children: The Reggio Emilia experience in transformation*, 3rd ed. Santa Barbara, CA: Prager Press.

Nabhan, G. P., & Trimble, S. (1994). *The geography of childhood: Why children need wild places*. Boston, MA: Beacon Press.

6

DISCOVERING THE BRILLIANCE AND BEAUTY IN BLACK

Patricia Sullivan

Box 6.1 Key Science and Nature Elements

- Children's open-ended exploration of natural habitats
- Knowledge of animal (birds) movement and feeding preferences and patterns
- Knowledge of local birds stemming from long-term observation and discussion
- Use of scientific terminology and vocabulary in small-group and whole-group discussion
- Linking of scientific knowledge to children's developmental sense of social justice and equity

Box 6.2 Key Inquiry Elements

- Engaging children in conversations about nature and animal life
- Photographing children's spontaneous discoveries and social interaction in nature
- Recording teacher observations and insights via written notes and journal entries

- Reflection on key connections between nature exploration and observation with critical race reflection
- Use of artifacts and reference books to stimulate discussion and reflection with young children

"Let's go feed the squirrels," I say, just after seven in the morning, as I lead David to the back door and the shelves where we keep the wild animal food. David doesn't like to be the first to arrive at school. He anxiously watches the door, waits for his friends to arrive if I don't find an activity to distract him, so every morning we feed the feral cats, the birds, and the squirrels.

This is a complicated process. The wild cats, who were born in my neighbor's yard, have been coming to our back door for five years and are always right outside when I open it. The youngest always runs inside for me to pet his fluffy white fur before he joins his more cautious friend. I have two containers filled with food and hand the third to David to carry up the stairs to the deck rail, where the squirrels are already waiting. We pour the cat food in the dishes first, so they aren't hungry when the birds arrive. David pours the cracked sunflower seeds on the rail and I add the shelled peanuts because they always roll. Then we quietly walk back inside to watch from the window, which looks out on our backyard and the adjacent park.

"Squirrels are crazy!" David chuckles, as we watch them jump and leap about trying to eat, keeping other squirrels from eating at the same time. With one eye on the food, they watch as less dominant associates try to grab a bit of breakfast. When the older squirrels chase one to the left, another comes from the right in this crazy squirrel food dance. We have seen as many as 15 leaping and flying from the nuts to the rail to the tree branches just above. Sometimes when we are laying down the nuts, they don't even hop away. They just sit on the rail and wait for us to step back. A few times when we ran out of nuts, the squirrels perched themselves in the trees and shrieked what could only be described as demands for someone to get to the store and get those nuts. We've tried other things, like crackers, grapes, raisins, even blueberries, but squirrels are finicky. They don't even like almonds.

The Steller jays arrive last. They wait for the squirrel frenzy to die down. They're not afraid of the squirrels and often will eat right next to them. David thinks they just don't like all the moving about. Unlike the squirrels that only come in the morning and just before sunset, the Steller jays have memorized our meal times. They come in the morning with the squirrels, but in the spring and summer when we eat snack and lunch outside on picnic tables, they come again several times a day and call to us to put out more nuts. If we don't act quickly enough and the back door is open, they will fly into the house and get the nuts themselves because they know exactly where we keep them. Steller jays are not as particular as squirrels about their diet. They also like pasta and tater tots.

David likes Steller jays because they have a cool mohawk and blue eye brows. They watch us from the trees sometimes and mimic the call of hawks to scare the squirrels away from the nuts. When actual hawks appear, the jays dash for the trees, warning everyone of the danger. Suddenly, all at once the jays fly away, and David and I stare through the glass at the branches above the deck rail as a chicken-sized crow lands silently.

"Oh no!" David says, dread and worry spreading across his face. "That's not a good bird!" He freezes, alarmed but clearly eager to run outside and save the squirrels, who still were eating, oblivious to the danger.

"Why do you think that's a bad bird?" I ask.

"Because it's black," David replies.

As a Black woman living in America I am hyper-vigilant about color, and Black in particular. I know that David is a three year old, but he already has made some decisions about color and meaning that may possibly shape his feelings about himself, other people, and the world for the rest of his life. David is Samoan and within his family there are many shades of brown. His older brother Tino is a warm caramel, while he and his little brother Andrew are a light tan. In her article for *TIME*, Tharps (2016) warns that "the pervasiveness of a color hierarchy in the outside world seeps into the household and becomes part of the implicit and explicit teachings of parenting."

> In this country, because of deeply entrenched racism, we already know that dark skin is demonized and light skin wins the prize. And that occurs precisely because this country was built on principles of racism … The privileging of light skin over dark is at the root of an ill known as colorism. (Tharps, 2016)

By ignoring the issue of color and the values our children attribute to color we may be inadvertently contributing to color bias.

We all have favorite colors. Mine is orange. It reminds me of a warm autumn day, when the leaves have just begun to fall and occasional cool gusts of wind remind us that winter is coming. David says his favorite color is red because Spiderman is red. As the other children arrive, we ask about their favorite colors. Leo likes blue, Sue and Adele pick pink and purple, and Liam surprises us all with yellow. He says it's the color of happiness.

It felt a bit heavy-handed asking the children to list the colors they felt were good and bad. Discourse like this often perpetuates the thinking you are trying to avoid. Instead my co-teachers simply cut out a bunch of color shapes and put them on the table, with glue sticks and a background color of their choice. The children are between the ages of two and four – three boys and two girls. Each child picks a background color. All the children pick white except Sue who picks blue. Circles, squares, triangles and rectangles are all cut in red, blue, green, pink, purple, gray, white, brown, and black. As the children pick colors and make pictures with their shapes a pattern emerges. Nobody picks black. Sue and Adele create a landscape. They use shapes to create flowers, houses and trees, with a big yellow sun circle in the sky. The boys are more abstract, stacking pieces on top of pieces like a construction project. Even in their zeal to use the glue sticks, they don't choose the black shapes. We present this activity again a week later, using only the color black. Again, each child picks a background color, this time the children pick their favorite colors as background. They use the black shapes to make faces. The color black becomes the absence of color, rather than a color all its own.

A few years ago there was a huge clearance sale at a very popular chain of toy stores just before they went out of business. I waited until the sale was just about over before I decided to pick over the remains. On the shelves of realistic stuffed animals there were very few left and all of them were black. There was a black panther, a black dog, a black gorilla, and four black bats. I bought them all. I got rid of all the stuffed animals in our collection that were unrealistically colored. No pink bunnies. I watched the children play with the animals and without exception they used the black stuffed animals as monsters and villains, terrorizing the others. Was I witnessing the development of color bias?

The first question to ask: How do we use colors in our school and are we contributing to color bias? Looking over all the art projects, I realize that we only use the color black on Halloween. In our crayon box we have dozens of colors to choose from, but the colors used most often are red, blue, and green. The children even try to use white on white paper. Black is reserved for eyes, the inside of holes, caves, and the occasional witch or monster. These color activities lead us to begin to think about color associations. What do we like and what color is it?

The children are eager to play this game. We start with their favorite colors. Red is very popular. Besides Spiderman, they also like apples, flowers, fire trucks, cars, and popsicles. Blue likes included sky, water, and cotton candy. As we continue, we notice that many of their likes are associated with concrete things within their experience. Pink is associated with dolls and orange with jack-o-lanterns. Even brown was favored for trees, mud, and sand. But black has no favorite until finally one of the boys shouts, "Batman!"

This project could have easily veered into the universe of superheroes, but my co-teachers and I want to keep the focus on color and the perception of good and bad colors, so we make the conscious decision to recognize we have at least one thing that the children like that is black and that we need to help them add to that list. Based on our understanding that the children's associations with color are directly related to their personal experiences, we need to find things within their world that we can add to the list of things they like that are the color black.

As nature is our focus, we looked to the natural world for examples and we were surprised to see that many species present in a variety of colors. Penguins, orca, and bats are consistently at least partially black, but animals that they are much more likely to encounter at the zoo or at home, like cats, dogs, pigs, goats, sheep and horses, come in many colors. On trips to the zoo we find that the children like the black goats, not noticing the color because the color was insignificant: some were brown, some were black, and some were multi-colored. This was also true of the sheep and horses. The question then becomes: What animal are these children mostly likely to encounter in nature that is almost exclusively black? We find the answer in birds.

San Francisco has a diverse wild bird population. There are sparrows, finches, mourning doves, pigeons, seagulls, hawks, robins, wood peckers, jays, parrots and three types of black birds: cow birds, starlings, and crows. We return to David's original idea: crows are bad birds because they are black. Rather than focus on the color of the birds, we focus our inquiry on the birds themselves.

The one thing we know about crows is that they like peanuts. They don't care if they were shelled or unshelled, roasted or raw. If we put out peanuts early enough in the morning, eventually a crow will come. We watch from the window as the crow eats with the other birds and squirrels. Seldom aggressive, a single crow will often take turns going after a pile of nuts, walking away to eat and coming back for more. After eating for only a few minutes the bird takes off only to return minutes later with a few friends.

"He brought his family!" David says excitedly. There are five or six crows now eating our nuts. We watch as they rotate to the nuts. One always sitting on the branches as a sentry to keep the others safe. There is a lot of squawking and screeching as they communicate with each other and I worry that the neighbors might complain about our project. After they leave, we notice that they didn't eat all the nuts, leaving a few for the grateful jays. We talk about what just happened and the children are happy about the crow that left to get his family. It was nice of the crow to bring the others to enjoy the nuts, rather than keep them all to himself. Are crows really bad birds? The children are still unsure. Finally, I ask "Would we like crows better if they were white?"

I've asked undergraduate early childhood education students that same question, and the answer is the same – yes, crows would be more favorable if they were white. This perception of crows as evil isn't only about colorism. Crows have been used as a symbol of evil and bad omens in literature for centuries. From Apollo to Aesop, crows in ancient literature were depicted as magical creatures that could flock to a battle, foresee the victors, and feast on the bodies of the defeated. During the middle ages and the plague that engulfed Europe, crows were symbols of death, seen circling in the sky over villages littered with corpses. Doctors wore masks made in the image of crows that they used to keep themselves safe from the plague (Savage, 2005). Grimm's fairy tales perpetuated and engrained the crow's evil persona by associating them with villains such as the evil queen in Sleeping Beauty and the cabalistic witch from Hansel and Gretel. In the Wizard of Oz, the crows are recurrent reminders of malevolence, first on Dorothy's farm stealing corn and later terrorizing the scarecrow as servants of the wicked witch of the west. We could only find one well-known reference to crows in children's literature that didn't fit the stereotype, however, the crows created by Disney for his children's classic Dumbo were unabashedly racist. Disney studios even named the lead crow *Jim Crow* after a character invented by a white comedian from the early 1830s who sang in blackface, perpetuating the mockery of Blacks in America by showcasing the minstrel show genre which became so pervasive that when segregation laws were established, they became known as Jim Crow Laws (blackpast.org). Anthropomorphizing crows with evil intensions and racist stereotypes provide the context for which crows are feared, hated and routinely killed by humans.

Abandoning the history, we decide to focus instead on scientific investigation of crows, and there we find some impressive facts about crows to share. We collect some reference books about crows for children; *Crows! Strange and wonderful* (Pringle, 2002), and an age-appropriate picture book, *As the crow flies* (Keenan & Duggan, 2012), giving us some insight on the daily life of crows. We also add a few reference books to our nature book library; *Crows – Encounters with the wise guys of the avian world* (Savage, 2005;) and a beautiful photographic journal, *Bird brains* (Savage, 1995) allowing the children to see close photographs of crows and jays. The children love the story *Thank you, crow* by Michael Minkovitz and Jose Medina (2018) that tells of a special friendship between a boy and a crow that brings him trinkets. Through an internet search on crows we found the film made for PBS, *A murder of crows: Birds with an attitude* (Fleming, 2010). Surprisingly, the children are fascinated by the documentary. The girls, Sue and Adele, are particularly interested in the fact that crows can recognize faces and warn their babies about people that might harm them. After just a little research, the teachers and children create a list of things we learned about crows:

- crows stay with their parents until they are five years old;
- crows can live in the wild until they are 20 years old;
- crows mate for life;
- crows are the smartest birds;
- crows have a language and dialects;
- crows watch and learn from people;
- crows are the only birds that not only use tools, but make tools;
- crows can perform a series of tasks to get to the food they want;
- crows mourn the death of one of the flock;
- crows collect things;
- crows play.

In observations on our nature walks we discover that the crows in our neighborhood do not nest or live in the eucalyptus trees, which are the trees that line the edge of the park outside our gate (Figure 6.1).

It is in this large expanse of the park where the children play in nature, and make their nature discoveries on their own (Figure 6.2), with a partner (Figure 6.3), or in small groups (Figure 6.4).

We travel farther through the park to places where large pine trees grow and find more crows in the branches. This is where we begin to leave more peanuts. Concern that the crows might not find the peanuts left scattered on the ground inspires the children to place them carefully under the trees, and a few on the benches. They sit to wait for the crows to come, but quickly begin running and playing under the trees. The teacher notices that the crows are watching, and probably waiting for the children to leave, so she takes the group to the playground next to the trees and watches from a distance. Sure enough, the crows come and take all the nuts, even those scattered in the grass.

Figure 6.1 The eucalyptus trees.

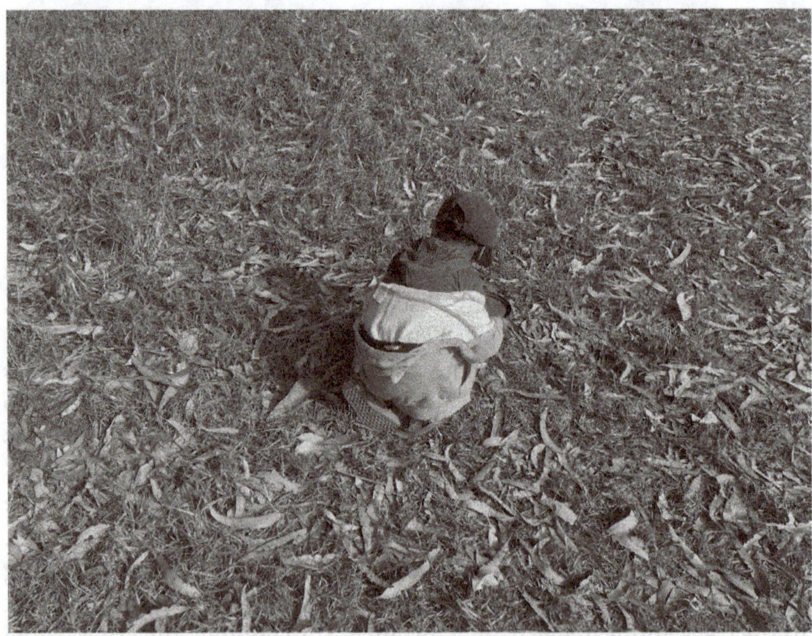

Figure 6.2 Nature exploration and discoveries by a solo child.

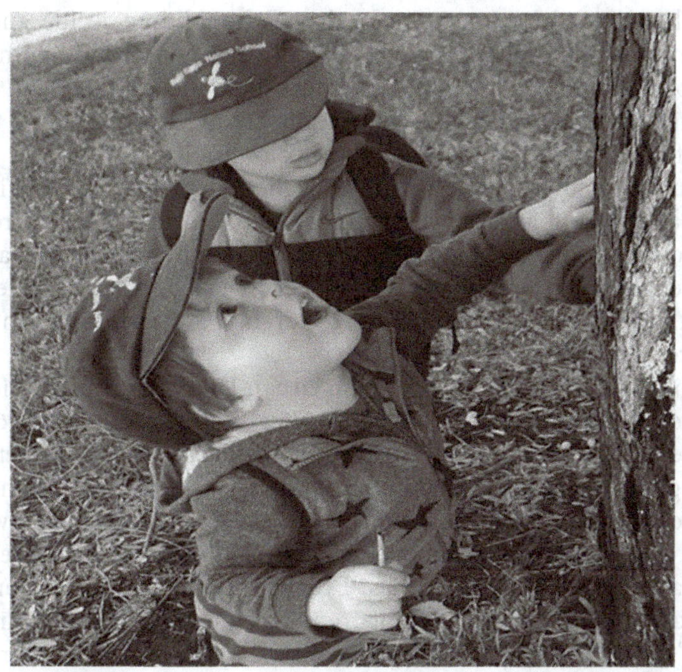

Figure 6.3 Nature exploration and discoveries with a partner.

Figure 6.4 Nature exploration and discoveries in a small group.

"They knew those nuts were for them," the children decide, and they all promise the crows always to return to the playground with nuts. Happily, we find something in nature that the children can easily identify, associate a positive connection, and we can add crows to our list of things we like that comes in the color black.

Our last activity (although none of these discovery projects is ever over and we will always bring nuts to the playground), is the creation of crow costumes for the children. Nothing is more fun than adding feathers to an art project but when it becomes wearable art, the excitement becomes an activity that the children and the teachers can enjoy and revisit.

Colorism is a word found in the Urban Dictionary (urbandictionary.com). Although it's credited to Alice Walker (Tharps, 2016), the concept of color hierarchy exists in nearly every culture. Preferences for light skin are evidenced in paper bag tests, bleaching creams, and Photoshopped images of famous faces. Celebrities courting a worldwide audience lighten their skin, hair, and eyes to increase their appeal, perpetuating color bias. Even as filmmakers, television networks, and publishers attempt to add color diversity to their children's catalogs, they often lighten dark skin to make the characters more attractive. We have come a long way from stereotypical portrayals of ugly bad guys in black and attractive heroes in white, however, recent replications of the Clark Doll Experiments indicate that a statistical majority of Black, White, Asian, and Latino children still maintain a white bias, even after America's first Black president served two consecutive terms in office (Cooper, 2012). Although I would be the first to say that people, even as young as the children in my classroom, can't easily make the multi-cultural leap from black animals to Black people, breaking the colorism barrier through an exploration of color may be an easy starting point, especially in schools and classrooms that are not diverse.

It may not be enough for teachers and parents to help children recognize that there are no bad colors, just like there are no bad skin colors, an especially important lesson for non-Black children. It may not be enough for teachers and parents to highlight notable figures like Barack Obama and Martin Luther King because these exceptions can't outweigh all the other negative images and stereotypes about Black people insidiously woven within the fabric of American culture. Teachers and parents of young children are understandably reluctant to talk about race and color, but maybe they can begin with something more basic, like simply appreciating and connecting with some of the wonderful things in this world that come in the color Black.

REFERENCES

Cooper, A. (Producer). (2012). *CNN special report: race and children* [Aired on CNN March 5, 2012]. Retrieved from https://youtu.be/wYkUMqxr_o8 on January 20, 2019.

Flemming, S. (Producer). (2010). *A murder of crows birds with an attitude* [Motion picture on DVD]. Canada: WNET. PBS Television Broadcast for NATURE.

Keenan, S., & Duggan, K. (2012). *As the crow flies.* New York: Fiewel & Friends and imprint of MacMillan.

Minkovitz, M., & Medina, J. (2018). *Thank you, crow.* Oklahoma City, OK: Penny Candy Books.

Pringle, L. (2002). *Crows! Strange and wonderful.* Honesdale, PA: Mills Press.

Savage, C. (1995). *Bird brains: The intelligence of crows, ravens, magpies, and jays.* San Francisco, CA: Sierra Club Books.

Savage, C. (2005). *Crows: Encounters with the wise guys of the avian world.* Vancouver, Canada: Graystone Books.

Tharps, L. (2016). The difference between racism and colorism. *TIME,* October 6, 2016.

Part III

Nature as Support for Representation and Aesthetics

7

CHILDREN EXPLORE THE FOREST

The Power of Wild Spaces in Childhood

Anna Golden

Box 7.1 Key Science and Nature Elements

- Engaging in multiple forms of representation (drawing, writing, photographing, clay) as a way to make meaning of experiences in the natural world
- Recording in the moment (by drawing on clipboards) and retrospectively, the latter leading to synthesis of ideas
- Creating a plan, and to some extent anticipating results, prior to engaging in investigations and projects
- Negotiating meaning with other children by comparing and co-constructing representations of the natural world

Box 7.2 Key Inquiry Elements

- Using story to collect, reflect on, and represent inquiry data
- Using observational notes to capture children's nature explorations and teacher insights
- Using audio and videotaping to document children's oral language, social interactions, and science discoveries
- Representing inquiry reflections with a sense of aesthetics

The integration of play in nature and visual representation helps children develop a relationship with a wild place, and helps teachers and parents understand children's sense of that place. The naming of landmarks, mapping a plot of land, and representing details in a landscape are all activities that can help children think deeply about a place and then show their conception of that place to others. Children can discover a new palette of materials by learning the affordances of objects they find in nature. Giving children time to explore a place and then returning to it again and again allows children to develop questions and theories about the natural world and their place in it, and then to test their theories and try to learn the answers to those questions.

It doesn't take very much wild space to capture the interest of young children. My own two girls found hiding places, animals, room to play, and plenty of natural materials to build houses for the fairies in the alley behind our tiny city backyard. Our school was located in the basement of a church, which was situated on a triangular plot of land that was left to go wild. Thinking about a gathering place for children, families, and staff led to the forest just beyond the playground fence. It wasn't a particularly beautiful patch of ground to look at from afar, but the school was very lucky to have found it. The forest, as we called it, turned out to be a gathering place for families and the centerpiece of our curriculum for many years until we moved to a permanent home in a new location. Now the school inhabits a large campus next to a forested city park, once part of the same huge landholding. There are plenty of places to gather now including space for gardens, paths, and bird-filled brambles. Preschool parents and children have claimed "the hill," a steep place between a parking lot and large forested area. It's an embarrassment of gorgeous riches for a school once scratching for space.

Nevertheless, teachers realize that they have to work to consciously keep nature and time in the forest in the forefront as priorities. Faculty meetings are a place to talk through time constraints and fears and help each other accept the risks inherent in allowing children unstructured play in nature. Mentoring new teachers to see the importance of play in nature and to adopt the motto about there being no bad weather, just poorly chosen clothing helps teachers get into the spirit of visiting the forest year round. Activities such as climbing on boulders, playing with sticks and rocks, and wading in the small creek have many benefits, but also may lead to wet and muddy clothes, bee stings, bumps and bruises or a (rare) more serious injury. Suspending fear of risk is hard work that seems worthwhile when considering the way playing outside helps reserved children let loose, or kinesthetic children really move. Teachers help each other take on responsible risk and therefore see children learn the names of plants and insects, take on stewardship of the forest, and bond together over tasks that require strategy and true collaboration, like damming the creek.

Many families are attracted to the school because of the promise of lots of time in the forest. Parents come together in community with each other and with teachers as they collaborate over the children's experience. The forest is always available, but is scheduled, rain or shine, one day a week for each class from preschool through grade two. Older children spend an afternoon each week in the forest. Parents, grandparents and "special friends" help by taking turns accompanying their children's class on "forest walks." Families are important partners with the teachers in making forest days doable. The partnership includes families providing boots for all children, including donating outgrown boots to a free clothing and equipment swap. The families' help is crucial in many ways, from accepting the importance of risk to taking on the challenge of providing countless changes of dry, mud-free clothes.

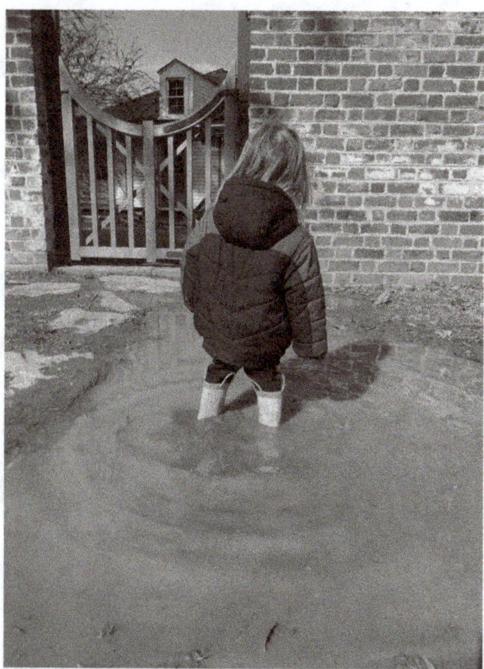

Figure 7.1 Leo wearing boots in a big puddle.

My own path into the forest came about from time spent in nature as a child as well as my occupation as an artist and a teacher. An artist/teacher in Reggio Emilia is called an Atelierista, a position designed to provide creative, out-of-the-box thinking. The Atelierista provides materials, strategies and documentation to fuel the children's exploration of ideas, to form and test hypotheses, and to collaborate in groups. In *Making learning visible* (2001), Vea Vecchi, Atelierista at the Diana School in Reggio Emilia, Italy, writes that children respond with vigor to tasks that fit within the context of their intentions (p. 180). In my role as the Atelierista at Sabot at Stony Point School, I have seen children become deeply engaged in representing the forest using many media because they first had time to joyously play and explore in it. Teachers at Sabot are in the habit of supplying sketchbooks, paper, and black felt markers for most activities that take place outside of the classroom. During forest explorations, children use these to record drawn observations. When they are away from the forest, the children work with media and materials such as drawing tools, blocks, woodworking, clay and embroidery to understand their encounters in nature. Time to play and materials to represent understandings formed in play – both factors are important.

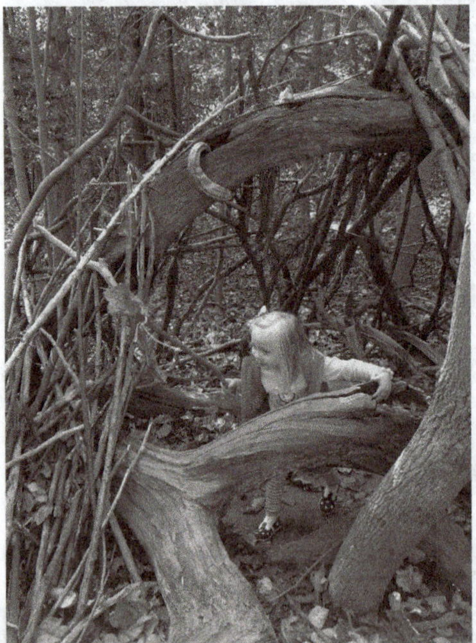

Figure 7.2 Tools for real work made from natural materials.

A kind of representation that may go unappreciated are earthworks made with natural materials. Earthworks are artwork that is site-specific and non-permanent. This work requires documentation through photography, written description, or drawing because it is likely to be gone due to wind, water or rearrangement. Children who have plenty of time to play in a wild space often build shelters, paths, or change water-courses with branches, sticks, stones, or anything they can find. When a class of 5-year-old preschoolers wanted to create an area to have circle in the forest, I had to think carefully about bringing them extra supplies from the art studio. I didn't want to alter their experience by bringing too much artificial stuff, but I knew they had trouble joining things together with what was available outside. A few lengths of hemp string and a pair of scissors seemed just helpful enough without interfering too much. In Figure 7.2 Caroline created a broom with a long stick, some leaves and a bit of string. This was a good tool to sweep an area so that other children could roll some stumps together to be seats for circle time.

Playing in wild space offers opportunity for understanding your own identity. Children, like adult mountain climbers, test themselves

Figure 7.3 Mask of natural materials.

against nature. For the children who wanted to have their circle meeting outside, there was a great sense of accomplishment once the logs were rolled into place and the center swept out neatly. There, well-loved songs sounded new when sung together surrounded by tall trees, breezes blowing through the leaves.

This same group of children who tamed a small area of wild space through hard physical work and practicality found magic in the forest as well. Robert MacFarlane writes, "What we bloodlessly call 'place' is to young children a wild compound of dream, spell and substance" (MacFarlane, 2016, p. 315). In the midst of sweeping and building of the meeting space, Zack found a triangular weathered piece of a tree and immediately held it to his face. He walked for a moment and then knelt and began to arrange leaves and other natural materials in the hollow of a nearby stump. He didn't want to talk about what he was doing, so I just took a few pictures and left him to his work. Small stories like Zack's happen all the time when children are in wild spaces. Documenting them allows adults to peek into the child's wild compound-sense of place. In the introduction to her book *Secret spaces of childhood*, Elizabeth Goodenough (2003) compares children's desire

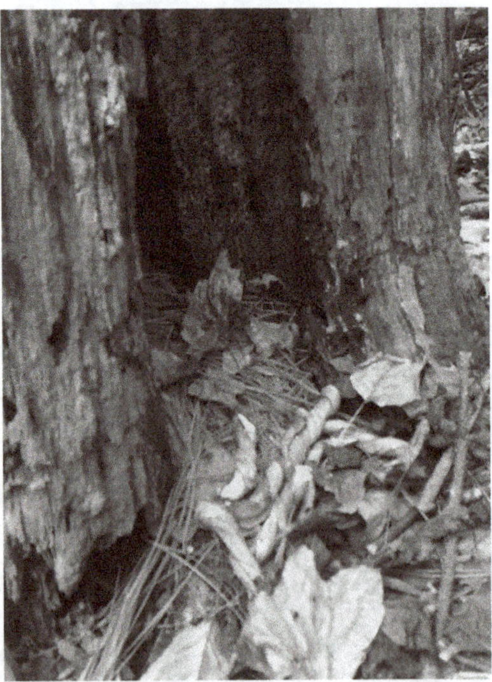

Figure 7.4 Fairy house constructed inside tree stump.

to find places that are magical (and all their own) with their creation of stories. "By assembling words – much like balancing twigs or arranging 'loose parts' for a little house," children "negotiate boundaries between what is real inside themselves and the world outside."

Documentation, in the sense in which the schools of Reggio Emilia use the word, is a form of "contextual curriculum" (Rinaldi, 2006, p. 206), or a daily practice of teachers observing the children's activity, documenting through some graphic media, reflecting on the notes and images, and interpreting the children's process and learning. My strategies for linking inquiry with nature exploration often start with careful observation of an experience. I record my observations by taking notes, photographs, or video, or by recording conversations using a small digital voice recorder. By reflecting on the observations, I try to determine a path toward some kind of learning goal that is true to the children's interest. Transcribing recordings takes time. So does reviewing photographs and cataloging them into useful groups. Since planning time is always at a premium, it is important to have a path for observations in mind beforehand; a few threads that are likely avenues for deeper exploration and learning. Then, when going through the photos, one can search for evidence of these. Over time, as the children revisit further experiences through documentation and

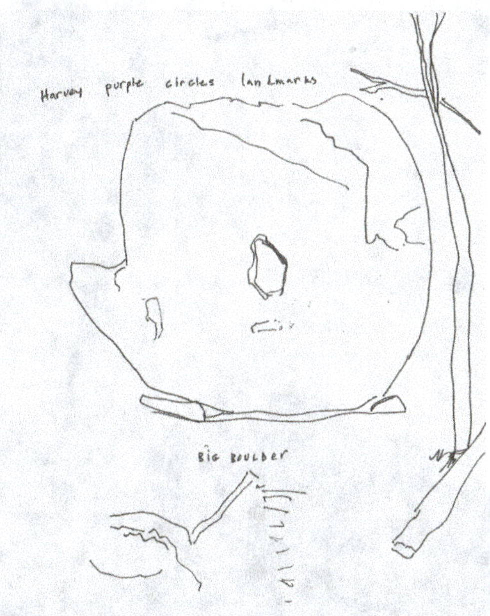

Figure 7.5 Harvey's drawing of landmarks along forest path.

discussion, and the teacher reflects on each succeeding interaction, a path for inquiry will emerge.

As described in Chapter 8, drawing maps is another way young children can define and represent their relationship to a natural place. Educational philosopher Jerome Bruner once wrote "knowing how something is put together is worth a thousand facts about it" (Bruner, 1983, p. 183). Child-made maps can help adults see children's perceptions of a place. Often the features of a landscape that are important to children are very different than those that adults see first. Part of this is because of scale – children are closer to the insects, fallen leaves, and rocks on the ground than adults are. Another part of it may be the nature of play in the forest. During our time outdoors children are not merely observing the scene but putting their arms around trees, lifting stones to look for bugs, and rolling down even the smallest hills. They also name things; the cave that is dark and spooky inside, the "spice-shop" where they've set up leaves, flowers, and grasses on a long-fallen tree trunk, the buffalo, a giant root ball from a hurricane-toppled tree. Through this play they form an intimate physical and linguistic knowledge of the place. Mapping can help weave these small parts together, expanding children's point of view and helping them form new understandings.

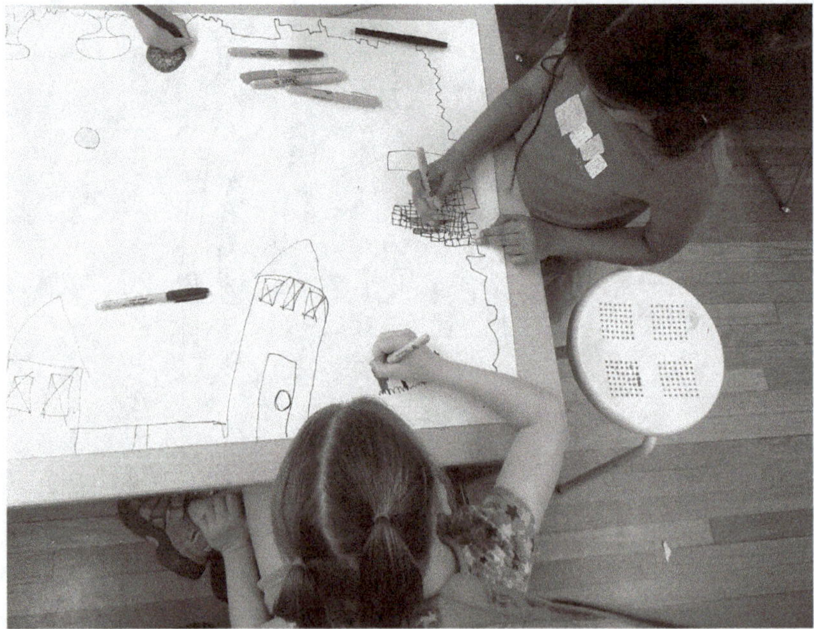

Figure 7.6 First grade 2019 children draw map of forest path.

Landmarks have proved to be a great place to start in asking children to take outdoor exploration into the representative and cognitive. Once, children argued with me when I implied that they follow a circular path through the forest, ending up a the same place they began, the "starting tree."

> I notice that when you draw the path on a long piece of paper you have to draw the starting tree twice-once at the beginning of the map and again at the end. If you use round paper, you could just draw it one time. Would you like to try it?

The girls agreed and worked for many days on a circular drawing, but it didn't solve their problem. Reflecting on the result, Poppy said,

> I think, see on here, because it's a circle, things that you put … see the (landmarks), they're kind of tipping. And then things will be upside down, things will be sideways. You know, if its a straight line, nothing is upside down.

In the end they explained to me that I was wrong, that the journey they were representing was best shown as a "bumpy square," which represented not only topographical features like dips and hills, but

Figure 7.7 Circular map – this representation was rejected as inaccurate.

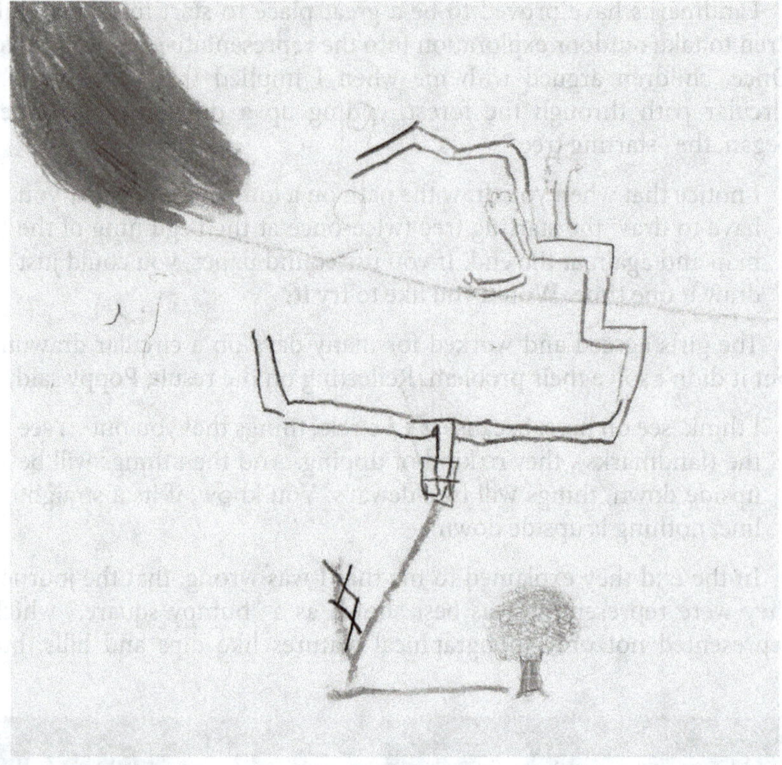

Figure 7.8 Map showing the path as a bumpy line.

which left room for everything to be drawn right side up. Isabel explained, "We can always make the square right, by bending it, see? The forest walk, it's not just a big circle. It's probably really squiggly. Can we do one in a bumpy square next?"

John Dewey (1934) wrote that learning comes from experience which is complete and powerful; when emotion is a significant part of it, and that true experience "moves and changes" (p. 43). Play in natural, untamed places has the characteristics of the best kind of learning experiences. Experiences with the forest have been powerful, moving and changing with the rhythms of the seasons and with the ebb and flow of the children's inquiry. Play in the forest unites children with common goals, perhaps because their bodies are small in comparison to tall trees and big spaces. Because I want to understand and share children's developing experience in the forest, my goal as a teacher has been for the children to form the habit of representing as an integral part of these interactions.

Since we wrote the first edition of this book, it has become established that children need time to play in natural places. This play has health and wellness benefits that are important. However it is not as well documented that play in nature has benefits for cognitive and social emotional learning as well. The outdoors is a vast and fruitful field for children's inquiry. Ungroomed, wild spaces in particular hold mysteries just waiting for a child to come along to discover. For young children, even a small patch of wildness yields plenty of interest in the insects, leaves, roots, and berries. There is plenty to see, touch, draw, imagine, and talk about. Tall trees, big stones, and bodies of water dwarf young children; however they learn that by banding together they can change some of the physical outlay of a wild space. Looking at the way children represent natural spaces through pretend play, magical thinking, visual representations, and discussion can help adults learn what children notice and what they want to learn. Guided by children's representations, teachers can then design provocations for further inquiry that will enhance children's emerging skills. Teachers can promote learning through sensitive and thoughtful documentation of children's interactions with nature. The key is plenty of time for children to play and develop a relationship with a place, and adults who are willing to step back and listen.

REFERENCES

Bruner, J. (1983). *In search of mind: Essays in Autobiography*. New York: Harper and Row.

Dewey, J. (1934). *Art as experience*. New York: Penguin.

Goodenough, E. (2003). *Secret spaces of childhood*. Ann Arbor, MI: University of Michigan Press.

MacFarlane, R. (2016). *Landmarks*. London: Penguin.

Rinaldi, C. (2006). *In dialogue with Reggio Emilia; listening, researching and learning* (pp. 53, 100, 206). New York: Routledge.

Vecchi, V. (2001). The curiosity to understand. In Project Zero and Reggio Children (eds.), *Making learning visible: Children as individual and group learners* (p. 180). Reggio Emilia, Italy: Reggio Children.

8

PUTTING THE FOREST ON THE MAP

Using Documentation to Further Natural Inquiry

Marty Gravett

Box 8.1 Key Science and Nature Elements

- Carefully constructed but open-ended invitations to notice, observe, and record ideas about the natural world beyond the classroom
- Creation of an interest-based small group to engage in more organized investigation of the forest area around the school
- The use of a guiding question, "How can we bring all of the children in the school to the forest," to guide the small group's inquiry
- The co-construction of meaning between the children and the teacher during the creation and revision of a map of the forest

Box 8.2 Key Inquiry Elements

- Design and use of viewing stations for children's nature observation
- Teacher-made plexiglass windows for nature observation
- Observational note-taking and audiotaping of children's nature conversations and "rich concepts"

- Analysis of the purposes and forms of mapmaking of children's forest travels

In the forest, children can show us things we adults cannot see. And they can lead us to understandings that will transform our practice. If we observe and listen carefully with our minds and our hearts (Rinaldi, 2011), we can catch glimpses through the lens the child uses in the natural world and find new ways to view the natural world ourselves.

As adults in our society many of us find ourselves separated from nature. And even for those of us teachers who have found a way to stay connected to the natural world, the overlay of an adult-centric and litigious society guides our professional decisions around children and nature. When arranging for children to come into contact with wild spaces, the guiding paradigm is often comprised equally of a didactic desire to lecture and considerable apprehension about the dangers, fearing the worst in terms of the children's safety. What I hope to do here is give a glimpse of a different paradigm and to reveal its value.

What follows is the story of my own first attempt to document provoking young children to attend to the nature around them and of what I learned from the experience that has since informed my practice. While I had previously found ways to bring young children to nature in other settings – even in an asphalt-laden urban environment – I had never before documented the experience. It was observing and listening closely enough to document children in nature, and later, reflecting deeply on what I had recorded that helped me see what children offered my practice. The act of documenting and its correlative of listening deeply was transformative.

This story illuminates the ways that children have an intuitive sense in experiencing nature, a natural approach to the wild that will reveal their understandings if we adults can listen deeply. From this larger observation I distilled two lessons. The first is that not only do children impart significance and meaning to elements of wild places, they are also capable of representing that significance. The second is that children are capable of addressing their fears about natural places and can act as models for adults on how to address our own fears in the same context.

FAILING TO SEE THE FOREST FOR THE TREES

More than an acre of forest embraced two sides of our small preschool; pine, gum, and oak edged the pathway from the carpool to the school. The trees were tall, 50, 60, 70 feet, and yet the children never mentioned the trees. In fact, every day the children made the decision to pass to the right or left of a huge pine that stood squarely in the middle of the entrance pathway; sometimes they even played a bit of a hide-and seek, waiting for a moment behind the tree to see if the adult greeting them on the path would notice their absence, and then they would peer around and laugh and perhaps play the game a second time. But still they did not name the trees, refer to them, or speak of them. And for children who were encouraged to draw their understandings of the world, to draw what was around them, nary a tree showed up in any but the most iconic pictures of the five year olds – you know the sort, the house, the tree, the sun, and rainbow. But none of the particular trees in our forest – or the forest itself – seemed present to the children.

The children appeared to be taking nature for granted as they passed the forest daily. Were the trees just too huge to come into their range of view? Were their interests subdued by the ways adults framed the children's experience? Did the physical challenge of the pathway and the relationships of carpools leave too little attention for the forest and the trees? Yes, probably, to all the questions, and understandably so for children who were only two-to-five-years-old. But did it make sense for these young children to traipse year after year past these magnificent conifers and deciduous giants ignoring them? We thought not. What was the cost to the children? To this small but lovely urban woodland? To the larger environment? To all of us?

WINDOWS ON THE FOREST: THE FIRST WINDOW

In our program, guided by inspiration from the preschools of Reggio Emilia, Italy, the emergence of children's interest is a necessary aspect of any inquiry. And so we took on the question of how to provoke children's interest in the forest; how to make the trees and woodland visible to the children.

Our first step was a literal one; where windows in the classroom looked out on the forest, we set up viewing stations with step stools, inviting children to step up and look out. We also put binoculars on the wide window sills, inviting them to notice in greater detail that the school environment included something beyond the classroom. Hypothesizing the children would be intrigued by familiar objects in an unfamiliar context, we placed small, surprising objects successively deeper into the forest – a plastic giraffe, a bright red ball. We also placed clipboards filled with white drawing paper and drawing pens on the window sills at the ready.

And children began to notice, to exclaim, to draw. At first the playground equipment shed was drawn more often than trees. We switched the objects – and planted new ones. The children looked deeper into the forest and eventually the objects became of less interest than the trees.

WINDOWS ON THE FOREST: ANOTHER WINDOW

Trying to give the forest even greater visibility, the teachers and parents collaborated to design and install a Plexiglas panel to replace a six-foot section of the playground fence which was adjacent to the forest. Hence, another window on the forest, more provocative and even closer to the trees, was created.

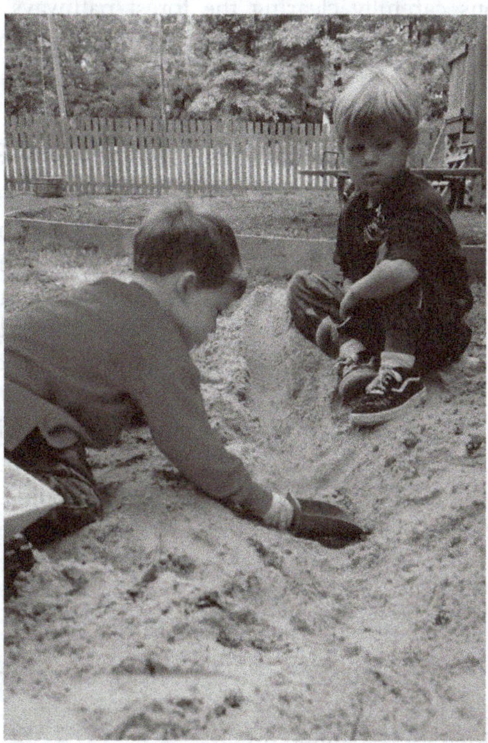

Figure 8.1 Creating a feature of the forest – a ravine the children call "the big hole" – in the sandbox.

Almost immediately we noticed children creating representations of the natural space outside the playground window. A small group worked industriously in the sandbox adjacent to the window constructing a model of the ravine or what they came to call "the big hole." From their viewpoint, the big hole was the closest feature of the forest.

We were delighted by their interest and used it as an opportunity to form a small group for further inquiry. The group was comprised of the three sandbox ravine builders and another child who had demonstrated a natural proclivity toward the outdoors, including (of her own accord) carefully observing and drawing wild mushrooms growing on the playground. We proposed to the group they explore the edges of the ravine and the interior of the forest and – as we were just learning to do – we provoked their interest further with a question to carry with them, asking, "How can we bring all of the children in the school to the forest?"

Meanwhile, I had been struggling with my own reluctance to go into the forest. Our urban woodland was rife with poison ivy and I was seriously allergic. Since childhood I learned to spy it from 30 paces. Since it was truly difficult to take a step without stepping in or on it – I spent afternoons carefully clearing the forest pathways closest to the school and used some small group time orienting the children to "the leaves of three."

FINALLY: THE FOREST AND ITS FEATURES

By the spring the pathways were clear, the Plexiglas window was in place and the group of children building in the sand had wowed us with their observations and their ability to represent them. I decided to take this group into the forest. Armed with clipboards and pencils they walked into the forest then stopped to draw. Their drawings were inventories of the forest matter – grass, mushrooms, rocks, and landmarks – particular trees, the wide pool of the creek.

But the highlight of this first foray was an encounter with a huge tree that had uprooted and fallen across the banks of the small stream that bisected the woodland. The portion the children could see from their vantage on the bank's edge was the tree's root system, the root ball, still covered in dirt and stones – so large that it loomed over the children.

In the first moments of discovery they seemed amazed and struggled to understand and describe this curious feature:

Hannah: I found a bridge. No I didn't. It's a tree fallen down.
Hunter: It's a tree bridge.
Hannah: No, it's a tree fallen down.
Eric: It's like a bridge.

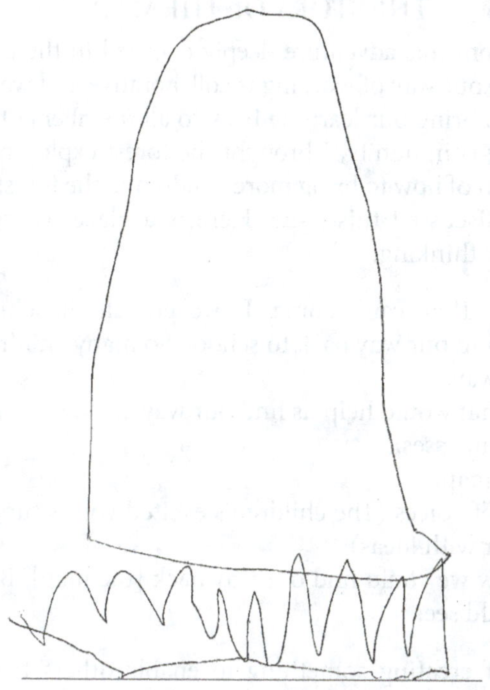

Figure 8.2 Drawing of the root ball of a huge fallen tree, which the children come to call the Mountain.

They decided to draw it and Hunter called it "the Mountain," a name that stuck.

As they explored it further, climbing and digging out stones and clods, they hypothesized about its composition and use. Here is an excerpt from that conversation:

Eric: It's a tree.
Hannah: I kicked it, it felt like a rock.
Hunter: I think the animals come and eat the leaves.
Hannah: No animals. They're scared of you.
A crowd of voices chime in together: Tree trunks are stuck to the rock. This [dirt] covers all snakes, lizards and bugs.

What rich concepts the children explored. Is the mountain inanimate – a rock? Is it living – with leaves to feed animals? Or is it some cross between the two – a tree melded to rock? A habitat for reptiles and insects? Their observations, testing, conjecturing, and comparing knowledge led all of us deeper into a relationship with the Mountain.

THE STORY OF THE MAP

We returned from this adventure deeply engaged in the exploration of the forest. Since our way of working is collaborative and we always feel a responsibility to bring our learning back to all members of our school's greater learning community, I brought the forest explorers back to the original question of how to bring more children to the forest.

The group discussed this issue. Here is a place where they move forward in their thinking:

> *Hunter:* No. They can't come. If we got all the children, we couldn't find our way back to school. So many children, they'd be in the way.
> *Teacher:* What would help us find our way back?
> *Hunter:* Compasses.
> *Hannah:* A map.
> A crowd of voices (The children's excited voices tumbled over each other with ideas):
> That's how we could find our way back [the map]. Binoculars! So we could see.

The concept of creating something to enable others to visit excited their interest. My colleagues reflected with me on the ideas that had emerged in the children's conversations and we decided making a map would present an exciting level of challenge to these children – collaborative and engaging.

I offered this provocation, and the children eagerly took on the task of mapmaking. In preparation for this small group, I made copies of the various natural objects and features they had drawn on their first forest foray, backed them with cardboard so they could more easily manipulate them, and also offered them a very large sheet of paper and drawing pens. I imagined they would discuss and negotiate the placement of the features, but was interested to see that instead, without any conflict, they excitedly placed the landmarks on the paper and taped them in place, in what then seemed to me a random fashion. Then they eagerly drew winding pathways between and around the features. They included the Mountain, the ravine, trees, grass, and even the footprints they had drawn in their forest inventories.

When they were satisfied with the map they had created, we returned to the forest. I proposed verifying the map's accuracy by orienting the map and ourselves to the playground and the school. As we walked, my intention was for the group to match natural features to the features they had placed on the map. We located the first major

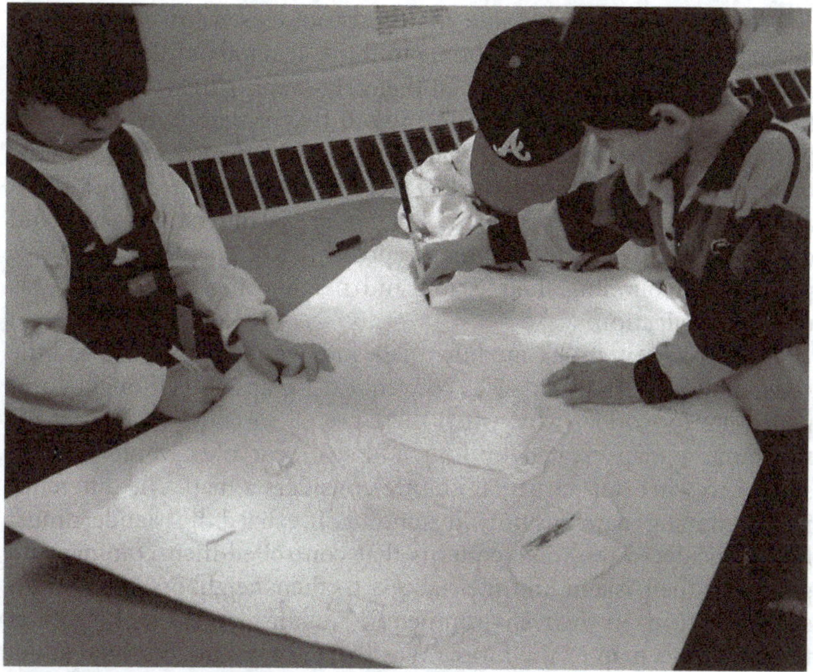

Figure 8.3 A small group creating a map of the forest.

feature, "the big hole" and started from there. But soon, following the path and the map we reached a stopping point – a fork in the path. In the dead center of their map is such a fork. On the map I pointed out to the children they had placed the Mountain at the fork but invited them to look and see instead a tree in front of us – the Mountain was not visible from where we stood. They conceded that the map did not read properly and decided to replace the Mountain with a drawing of a tree. When I asked where the Mountain should now be placed they all pointed to the right of the tree. We changed the Mountain on the map and then followed the path of the map to the right of center, and there, exactly where they knew it to be, was the Mountain.

In several more sessions, the children refined the map and then moved through a process to create a large sign reading, "No Falling in the Water" accompanied by a drawing of children standing on the tree bridge portion of the Mountain. By the time this work was finished, the preschool was ending for the year. So in a final visit, satisfied that with the map as a resource others would be safe, the group invited more children to accompany them and we headed into the forest and posted the sign in a little clearing near the Mountain.

When summer arrived and the preschool closed for the season, I had occasion one evening at home to think again about the Mountain and its placement on the map. In the early evening light I entered the living room and saw my husband and our two primary aged daughters poring over a *National Geographic* magazine. I peered over my husband's shoulder and saw that they were studying a picture of a shell-and-fiber map constructed by Polynesian islanders. My husband explained that the islanders' map represented the predominant wave patterns surrounding their island and neighboring islands and was used for navigation.

As I looked, it struck me how these indigenous maps bore so little resemblance to what I knew as conventional maps. This thought compelled me to wonder why, when there are all sorts of possibilities for mapping, a map created by four and five year olds would look so similar to what our particular culture considers a map. The difference in mapmaking materials notwithstanding, I realized the islanders must have considered the wave patterns that controlled their comings and goings to their island and their access to their neighbors as the most salient features in their environment. I was inspired to look again at the children's map of the forest. Was there something essential about mapmaking I was missing?

When I returned to the children's map I noticed (with chills I might add) the ghost of a shape of the Mountain in the dead center of the map. It was the first time I had noticed it, and it came to me then that when the children created the map, one of them had taped the cut-out shape of the Mountain on the paper, in the exact center. While it was there children drew around it again and again indicating paths coming and going all over the map. Then, after our trip back into the forest, when I had drawn their attention to the Mountain's "real" placement, the Mountain feature was "correctly" reset according to our system of orienting "properly" to the school building, and the children had moved the Mountain feature on the map. But evidence of the original placement remained in those tracings around the now-relocated Mountain. Staring at the outline of the Mountain, I suddenly realized that the children's original placement of their favorite landmark in the exact center of the map indicated its significance, its prominence in their view, in this wild place.

A year or so later, reading Nabhan and Trimble's *The geography of childhood* (1994), I confirmed my understanding; landmarks are the first thing children identify in the forest. "Children and adults begin their descriptions of environments with landmarks. Recognizing landmarks comes, on average, with the full development of the brain after

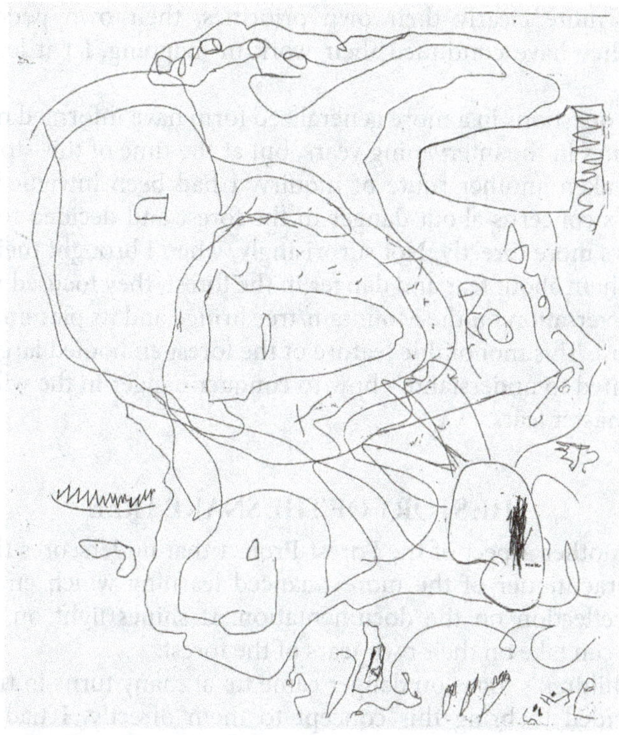

Figure 8.4 The "corrected" map with the ghost shape of the Mountain in the center.

about four years of age" (Nabhan & Trimble, 1994). What I had been calling features are the landmarks that helped them distinguish one part of the forest from another. Arguably, from the first moment they entered the forest they were mapping their way; and later they were intuitive about what we were asking of them, to map an unknown space, a natural space – the forest. Intuitively, they placed at the center of the map the thing about the forest that was central to their view of it. In my effort to help get the map corrected, I had not seen what it conveyed.

Mapping had been exciting and motivating to the children, but I couldn't help but wonder what the map would have looked like had I not set up the orientation exercise for the children. What more could I have learned about their thinking, about their understanding of the forest if I had fully seen this first schema? If I had noticed and honored their intention immediately, would they have started at the Mountain and mapped their way out of the forest? Would the map have made more sense to them, given them a greater sense of ownership if it had reflected more clearly their own priorities, their own perspective? Would they have continued their work in mapping, let it lead them further?

These questions in a more generalized form have informed my work many times in the intervening years, but at the time of this story I had already taken another route of inquiry. I had been intrigued by the children's concerns about danger in the forest and decided to pursue their fears more directly. Not surprisingly, when I brought their words back to them about fear and danger in the forest, they focused much of their conversation on the Mountain/tree bridge and its placement over the stream. This monolithic feature of the forest embodied large things they wanted to understand – how to conquer danger in the wild place, how to master fear.

THE STORY OF THE SNAKE TREE

This is another aspect of the Forest Project that underscores the value to the practitioner of the more nuanced learning which emerges in careful reflection on the documentation. It shines light on the way teachers can take on their own fears of the forest.

The children's focus on danger came up at many turns in the forest so I decided to bring this concept to them directly. I had learned enough to bring their words back to them: the words that seemed to have the most force or importance in order to relaunch their interest; the words with the greatest confusion or possibility for learning to stimulate further inquiry. So I read the group their own words that included expressions of fears such as the fear that having too many children in the forest would cause them to lose their way. But most of their fears centered on the Mountain/tree bridge and their worries about falling off the tree bridge into the stream below. Hannah said, "People wouldn't understand [that it is dangerous to cross the tree bridge] if we weren't back there. They'd dive into water, sink down. Help! Help!" (She acts out the need for assistance.)

Reviewing the tape of this dialogue, I heard a crowd of excited voices and an anonymous suggestion to make a sign saying, "The Water is Dangerous." This idea of a sign took hold of the group and, as they talked, a revised text was agreed upon – "No Going in the Water."

The group created drawings of children crossing the tree bridge then sought the help of a peer, Graceann, who was skilled at letter making. This new group member also provided leadership in an unexpected way. From the earliest days Hunter had been convinced snakes were in the forest. It was easy to see in retrospect that although he

Figure 8.5 The children post their sign in the clearing next to the Mountain. It reads, "No Going in the Water."

often brought up the subject of snakes in the forest and the problems they would cause, he was determined not to let this fear overtake him because he brought it back again and again to the group, seeking a way to address it. When we entered the forest with the sign team, which now included Graceann, a child suggested a particular tree on which to post the sign, and Hunter countered, "Snakes live there and [when] the snake comes out their tongues will get all the crayons off." He was inferring that the tree was not a good place because the snakes would lick off all the letters and drawing from the sign.

And again he offered evidence of how fearful they should be when Graceann made a different tree proposal. This is part of the conversation that ensued:

Hunter: That's a snake tree.
Teacher: You think the snake will bother the sign?
Hunter: Yeah. Cause he has sharp teeth.
Hannah: Only rattlesnakes have sharp teeth.
Hunter: That's what I mean 'cause that's a rattlesnake tree.

Hunter continued to counter others' suggestions and proposed a thorn bush because "if snakes come up there those things (thorns) will get stuck on him, they try to get him."

And then a moment later:

Hunter: All of this is snake stuff except for those prickly things.
Teacher: Hunter is concerned about snakes.
Hannah: And even that big rock?
Hunter: Even the rock has snakes on it.
Graceann: I don't believe Hunter. (She turns to others.) Do you believe Hunter? (She then proposes:) We could get a stick and tape it on to a stick.

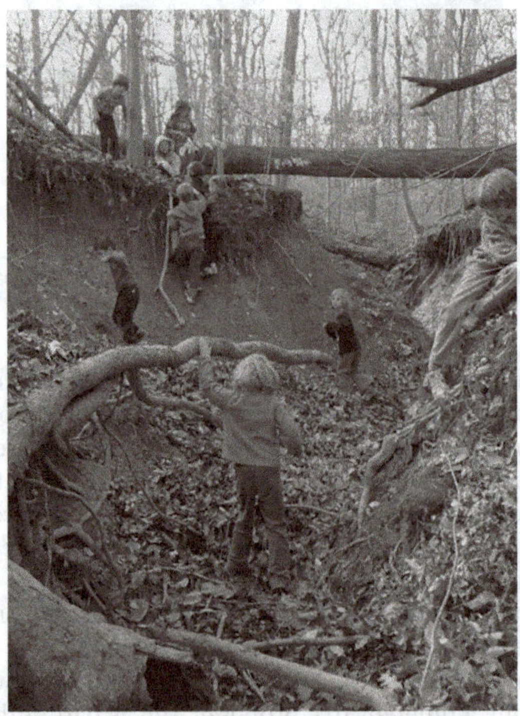

Figure 8.6 Later generations of children in the school take on even-greater challenges in the forest.

In the face of Graceann's disbelief Hunter changes his position slightly.

Hannah: Marty where is the snake?
Teacher: Graceann says she doesn't believe there are snakes.
Hunter: Yes there are. Well, they're sleeping.

Hunter seems to be (literally) proposing putting the snakes to rest. And metaphorically they seem to be put to rest as well because he does not bring them up again. Why is this? Do they seem less dangerous to him when Graceann refuses to worry about them? It appears Graceann's confidence mentored a new level of comfort for Hunter in this wild place. She loaned him her confidence. The presence of danger was, in large part, a point of view and Graceann co-constructed with Hunter a new point of view on the forest, a more benign perspective.

It has not been easy for us, as teachers, to fully trust the children or ourselves in this forest place. But interestingly, once I became fully awake to the children in the Forest Project, re-examining the documentation and noting how they took on danger and moved past fears, I saw Hunter and Graceann modeling how this can be done in a way that my colleagues and I could have used as we muddled through our own fears exploring the much larger forest that surrounds our school's new location. The simple answer is: let the fearless lead.

IN CLOSING

This brings us to the question that often comes to those of us who try to work in new ways with children – can we teach in ways we were never taught? And if not, how do we address this in our practice?

To this end, teachers in my school have joined forces, the intrepid with the fearful, the adventurous and the timid and even those who need to (figuratively) hold one another's hand, and have undertaken their own education in nature. In our case, group after group of teachers have made forays into the forest. On their own, without children, with time to startle at scary things, to examine the strange, to feel their own insignificance and fragility in the arboreal vastness, teachers tramp through the wild places, exploring with one another. And in doing so, teacher after teacher has come to terms with insistent inner objections and anxieties. This tramping about with their colleagues gives them the time they need to dampen their own fears and replace them with knowledge and delight. They spend this time reframing their experience and return to children with anxieties in check. In this process that presages what they will later offer the children they accompany to the forest, they come to expect the unexpected and to appreciate the untamed gifts of the wild.

In the years that have followed what we came to call the Forest Project, my colleagues have taken on far more daunting challenges in the forest than this seminal effort. One intrepid teacher spent every day for a year in the forest, all morning long, rain or shine, even on the coldest days with a group of three year olds. We learned from them that children can use the loose parts of the woodlands to create new challenges for themselves and they create new friendships to help them in their efforts.

Meanwhile, we have moved our school to 28 acres of land contiguous with a 100-acre wild city park. Finding a new setting steeped in nature was a strategic aspect of our move, an outgrowth of our first intentions to call the children's attention to the trees around them. Now, some dozen years after this first forest foray, we are a preschool through eighth grade and all of the students spend time in the forest, every single week. They splash stones in woodland pools, construct natural dwellings, build dams or bridges in the creek. They even take on take on math challenges and writing challenges. The children return again and again to test themselves in a vast canyon, to learn to jump streams and to crawl across logs and to climb the root balls of fallen trees three times their height.

These early lessons of the forest were not easily learned. They lay as dormant possibilities and only later, when we committed to serious reflection on our documentation did they emerge to guide our thinking. These metacognitive gains arrived too late to benefit the children whose stories we have shared here, but the documentation of those early explorations of the forest – those photos, audio recordings, and transcripts – have transformed our practice. When teaching is allowed to evolve from the active engagement and research of all of the members of the learning community, new learnings and best practices emerge. And so I honor the intuitive young children and the intrepid teachers of these forest stories not only as guides, but also as significant contributors to the ever growing practice of learning in the wild.

REFERENCES

Larsen, R. (2009). *The selected works of T.S. Spivet*. New York: The Penguin Press.

Nabhan, G. P., & Trimble, S. (1994). *The geography of childhood*. Boston, MA: Beacon Press.

Rinaldi, C. (2011). The pedagogy of listening: The listening perspective from Reggio Emilia. In Edwards, C., Gandini, L., & Forman, G. (eds.), *The hundred languages of children: The Reggio Emilia experience in transformation*, 3rd ed. (pp. 233–246). Santa Barbara, CA: Praeger.

9

NATURE EDUCATION AND THE PROJECT APPROACH

Jean A. Mendoza and Lilian G. Katz

Box 9.1 Key Science and Nature Elements

- Long-term, in-depth investigations of ideas that incorporate not only science concepts but also art, language, math, and other curricular areas
- Selection of topics that are personally relevant and amenable to first-hand investigation in the context of specific groups of children
- Development of teacher-mediated, broad guiding questions to focus early investigations
- Cycle of data collection, analysis, and reporting using tools and practices of scientists

Box 9.2 Key Inquiry Elements

- Collaborative and team approach to observing and recording children's project-based learning
- Collection of work and play samples on a regular basis
- Photographs of children's learning within and across the project approach phases

- Use of documentation displays to show children's work and learning
- Use of question tables to record and extend children's questions and discoveries

PROJECT APPROACH OVERVIEW

One of the major goals of early childhood nature education is to help children make deeper sense of their experiences of their natural environments and of their place in those environments. Most young children readily engage with natural phenomena around them such as animals, plants, and the weather. As John Dewey (1996) suggested long ago, adults play a key role in supporting and guiding children's interests. We can help children begin a lifelong interest in nature and the disposition to appreciate and understand important natural phenomena in their daily experiences and environments.

In fact, preschoolers may be most curious about things that, to adults, are familiar to the point of boredom – the spider in the hallway, the unusual leaf on the sidewalk, the puddle around a blocked storm drain on the playground. That spider, that leaf, or the puddle might become the basis for an in-depth investigation that could lead them on into many more topics worthy of study (see Figure 9.1).

Figure 9.1 A child's interest in an unusual leaf might launch a project on trees.

In the project approach (Katz & Chard, 2000), projects are a central part of the curriculum in which a group of children, or sometimes an individual child, conduct an extended in-depth investigation of a particular topic. Most activities directly related to a project also involve language arts, mathematics, and other curriculum areas. As a project progresses, teachers may often share books related to the project topic during story time. Teachers might also introduce a variety of music experiences (e.g., singing songs, listening to music, playing instruments) connected to the topic. Project work also provides opportunities for teachers to support children's social interactions with peers and adults.

Nature-related projects can be guided by lead teachers alone, or in cooperation with teaching assistants, working as a team. Some teachers have reported positive experiences with collaborations when two or more classrooms in a program investigate a topic at the same time. Teachers in half-day programs are sometimes able to engage both morning and afternoon classes in the same project, which can provide opportunities for children in the classes to share materials, artifacts, and information with each other.

Project work provides a very wide range of benefits for all of the participating children. Central questions for the teachers when planning any learning activities include: What should be learned? What should be learned by all of the participating children, by most of them, one or two of them in particular? Answers to these questions can be conceptualized in terms of four types of learning goals:

1. Knowledge and understanding
2. Skills
3. Dispositions
4. Feelings

Any extended in-depth investigation can be expected to deepen the participating children's knowledge and understanding of a wide range of related topics (Katz, 2010). The processes of gathering and representing the data encourage children to use many skills such as drawing, writing, measuring, model making, and interviewing. Incorporating project work in the curriculum supports a number of dispositions (or habits of mind) in young children, such as their natural "nosiness" – children's motivation and interest to find out about things around them and understand them more deeply (Katz, 2015). Project work offers many opportunities for children to contribute significantly to the investigation through collaboration and through individual work, which may promote such positive feelings as self-efficacy, a sense of belonging to the classroom community, heightened interest in things and people around them, and satisfaction with what they have learned and created.

Teachers who undertake project work with young children in the context of the current emphasis on standards and testing might wish to consider the distinctions between the *academic* versus *intellectual* goals of education. Academic goals are those concerned with acquiring small discrete elements information, usually related to pre-literacy or arithmetic skills that must be practiced in drills or worksheets, and other kinds of exercises designed to prepare them for later literacy and numeracy learning. Academic elements of the curriculum are those that require correct answers, and that rely on memorization and the learners' application of standard procedures versus demonstrations of understanding. The activities consist largely of giving the teacher the correct answers that the children know she awaits. Although one of the traditional meanings of the term *academic* is "of little practical value" these kinds of information are essential components of reading and other academic competences (Katz, 2010).

Intellectual goals and their related activities, on the other hand, address the life of the mind in its fullest sense. The formal definition of the concept of *intellectual* emphasizes reasoning, hypothesizing, predicting, conjecturing, raising questions, the development and analysis of ideas, and the quest for understanding. Project work provides rich contexts for children's inborn dispositions to make the best sense they can of their own observations, experiences, and environments and all of the intellectual dispositions listed above.

Both academic and intellectual goals must be taken seriously. Teachers who implement the project approach frequently report how much the children become motivated to master basic academic skills, e.g., beginning literacy and numeracy skills, *in the service of their intellectual pursuits.* In the context of project work the children seem easily able to sense the purposes and usefulness of mastering a variety of academic skills (Katz, 2010).

Documentation in project work refers to the processes of keeping records and work samples, in order to show the children's experiences and their findings. During a tree project, documentation might include children's field sketches or photographs of trees, their field notes, a tally chart recording the number of trees they counted in different locations, drawings or notes depicting what they learned from a visiting arborist, clay models of various tree seeds, and a report dictated to a teacher by several children telling the story of their field trip to a park. In addition to enabling children to record and share the data they have collected, documentation during a nature-related project sharpens teachers' awareness of what children understand about nature and the academic skills children use in their work. On the basis of the rich data made available through documentation, teachers are able to make well-informed decisions about how best to support each child's development and learning. Careful examination of the project documentation provides insights into aspects of children's progress that are not demonstrated by the formal standardized tests commonly employed by schools (Katz & Chard, 2000) and which may have very little to do with understandings of nature.

LAUNCHING NATURE-RELATED PROJECTS WITH YOUNG CHILDREN

Choosing a Topic for a Nature-Related Project

When helping young children select a project topic, teachers usually find it best to focus on potentially familiar local phenomena because of the opportunities for first-hand experiences. A project on tide pools might be appropriate for preschoolers living in a coastal town, but not for children in a Rocky Mountain community. Tropical storms may not be immediately relevant to a class in rural Alaska, but children in Louisiana who have lived through a Category 5 storm will have personal knowledge to draw upon during a hurricane project. Nature-related topics with more distant foci (dinosaurs, the Arctic) are better suited for older children with more mature understandings of geography and time. (Of course it does not harm young children to learn about places and phenomena that they cannot investigate first-hand, but such studies are not appropriate for projects, by our definition.)

Teachers from a wide variety of locales have reported to us about nature-related projects on a range of topics, including Mollusks in the River, Box Turtles and their Relatives, Fish and Fishing, Squirrels on the Playground, Worm Composting, the School Garden, and The Ravine Behind Our School.

Fortunately for teachers who would like more specific information about nature-related projects that have been undertaken with young children, a number of reports on such projects are available on the Web. We want to emphasize that the teachers who facilitated these projects were not experts on the topics. As is so often the case with project work, the teachers learned alongside the children and both became more knowledgeable about their topics.

THE THREE PHASES OF PROJECT WORK

Most teachers find it helpful to plan project work in terms of three successive phases. We now refer to a trees project to illustrate what occurs during the phases.

Phase 1 – Getting Started

The first phase of a project includes selecting the topic to be investigated. Typically, children and their teachers arrive at an agreement on the general topic following some discussion. A good topic is one that is of some interest, or at least potentially of interest, to most of the children, and that can be investigated through first-hand experience. A project on trees, for example, would be appropriate in many, but not all, parts of North America.

During Phase 1, the teachers invite the children to revisit their previous experiences related to the topic. Teachers may arrange some introductory event such as hearing a relevant story, going on a field trip, exploring related artifacts, or watching an appropriate video, particularly if the children do not seem to be familiar with the topic. During a tree project, for example, the teachers might bring in acorns, a pine cone, a twig with some leaves or needles, a photograph of a fallen tree, or other tree-related artifacts and, during group time, solicit the children's recollections of their own experiences related to the objects. The teachers might then suggest that the children draw or paint representations of their recollections related to trees. Children can share with their classmates the stories represented in their memory drawings.

As Phase 1 progresses, the teacher guides the children's discussion toward summarizing, representing, and recording what they already know and understand about the topic. Many teachers construct a "topic web" with the children's input to record and organize their knowledge and questions at the beginning of the project (see Figure 9.2.) Even children who are not yet reading benefit from seeing their ideas written on the topic web. The teacher posts the completed web where children can easily view it, and help them add to it throughout the project.

Phase 1 also includes generating a list of questions that the investigation will be designed to answer. Many teachers use a question table to help organize the children's questions in preparation for their field work, and to help teachers reflect on where children are in their understanding (see Figure 9.3).

It is usually not productive to ask preschool and kindergarten children what questions they have about the topic at the beginning of

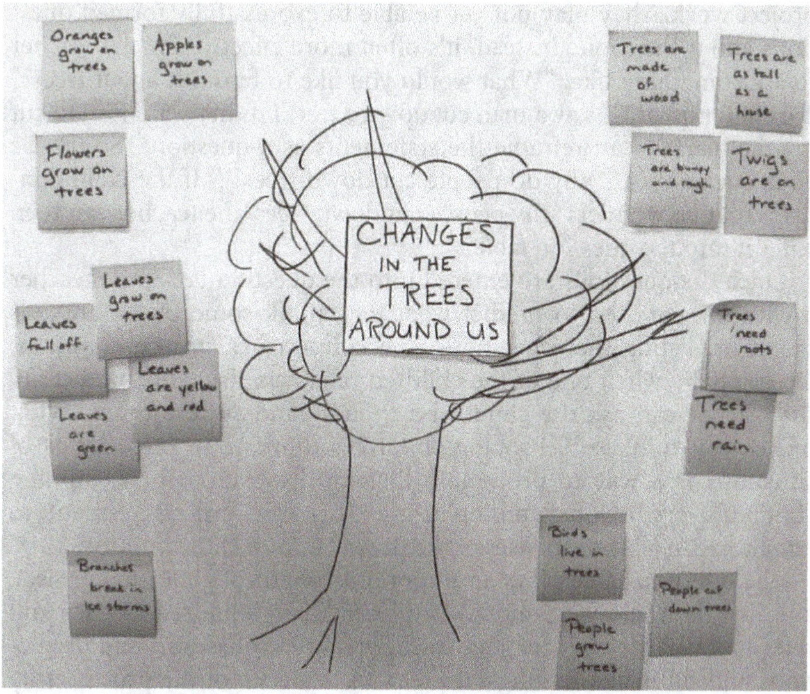

Figure 9.2 A children's topic web about trees is based on their knowledge of the topic at the beginning of the project.

Questions	Predictions	Findings
Why do people cut down trees?	Because they want to have logs for a campfire.	
Why do leaves on trees start out green and then turn brown?	Because someone didn't water the tree. Because something hurt the leaves.	
Are there flowers on trees?	Yes, because my tree has flowers on it. No, because flowers grow in the ground. Some trees have flowers and some don't.	

Figure 9.3 This sample excerpt from a question table about trees shows three questions and accompanying predictions.

project work. They may not yet be able to express fully formed questions about the topic. Instead, it's often more effective for the teacher to ask something like, "What would you like to find out about trees?" If a child replies, "I saw a man cut down a tree. I didn't want him to cut it," the teacher can reframe the statements as a question: "So maybe your question is, 'Why do people cut down trees?'" If the child confirms that he wonders why people cut down trees, the teacher can then enter it into the question table.

Once the questions are entered into the question table, the teacher invites the children to predict what they think some of the answers might be, listing the predictions in a column next to the questions. Occasionally when one of the children offers a reasonable prediction, the teacher can ask the child, in a friendly and sincere tone: "What makes you think so?" Probing children's thinking in these kinds of situations is a way to promote a lifelong disposition for examining children's predictions and opinions. This is a critical element to emphasize in all three phases of the project approach.

The question table plays an important role throughout the project, and like the topic web, should be placed where children can see and refer to it. As the children and teacher add new questions and predictions and fill in the findings, it provides evidence of the processes by which the children's understanding and knowledge are growing. Even if the children are not yet reading, they benefit from seeing their questions and ideas validated in print for the classroom community.

Once the children's initial questions and predictions are recorded, the teacher can ask them to how they think they might find the answers they are seeking. Where might they go? Whom could they ask?

These Phase 1 conversations related to children's memories, the topic web, and the question table will help the teacher become aware of what children know and understand, as well as what some of them misunderstand, about the topic.

Depending on the children's experience with Project work and their prior knowledge of the topic, Phase 1 usually lasts about a week or two.

Phase 2 – Gathering the Data

During Phase 2, the children collect the data they need to answer the questions developed in Phase 1. The teacher can help them form small groups that will focus on particular subtopics related to the overall topic of investigation. The groups are generally based on common interests reflected in their contributions to the topic web and the question table. For example, if two or three children have asked questions about animals that live in the nearby trees, they might form a group to find out more about those animals. A child who is curious about acorns might be part of a group investigating seeds, along with a child who likes to collect pinecones.

Phase 2 activities include site visits, making observational sketches and drawings of relevant phenomena, interviewing people with expertise related to the topic, conducting surveys, distributing questionnaires, and other ways of gathering and representing pertinent data. During a project on trees, for example, children might visit an orchard, an arboretum, a nearby park that has several types of trees, or some of the trees near the school. They could collect their data using the same equipment that adult scientists use – magnifiers, binoculars, measuring tools, specimen jars, and so on (see Figure 9.4.). They could sketch or photograph individual trees, leaves, fruit, bird nests, or tree-trimming tools.

They might interview a botanist, an arborist, or someone who creates sculptures using parts of trees. They could use surveys and questionnaires to gather data from their families, neighbors, and classmates, asking questions such as "Did you ever climb a tree?" or "How big around is the biggest tree in your yard?"

In their subgroups, children also organize and analyze their data during Phase 2, often with the teacher's help. Depending on the

Figure 9.4 Young children can use some of the same tools that scientists use to observe and to collect their data.

children's ages and experiences, and the resources available, they may use a variety of media and methods to document their findings, such as drawings and paintings, diagrams, models, graphs, music, pretend play, and verbal expression (see Figure 9.5.)

An entire class engaged in a tree project might keep nature journals in which they record observations of specific trees several times a week. Some of the children might make a graph comparing the circumferences of several trees they have measured. Others might create a diagram or a three-dimensional model depicting and labeling the key parts of a tree (crown, trunk, roots, etc.). Still others could collect a variety of leaves and name the trees they came from, using a field guide to identify them. Children who are interested in what arborists do might turn the dramatic play area into an arborists' workplace, complete with tree-trimming tools and a truck made from an appliance box.

Throughout Phase 2 the teacher helps the subtopic groups to report on their findings, and solicits suggestions and questions from their

Figure 9.5 This painting of a leaf by a four-year-old shows that she has noticed the midrib and veins.

classmates. Also during this phase of the project, the teacher guides the children in creating displays of their works in progress so that they and others can refer to their evolving learning. Displays can include a wide range of documentation, including sketches, models, photographs taken by the teacher or the children, transcripts of children's comments, and other representations of their findings and experiences. Phase 2 can last a few weeks or a few months, depending upon the topic, the depth of the investigation, the resources available to the children, the children's ages, and the extent of their experience with projects.

Occasionally the processes of data gathering lead to new subtopics that take over the originally planned project. Children who are studying trees, for example, may become so deeply interested in the insects, mammals, amphibians, birds, and reptiles that live in or near trees that the tree project becomes a project on one or more of those animals. As long as the new subtopic is a rich and useful one, shifting the topical focus of the project expands children's emergent nature learning.

Phase 3 – Bringing the Project to a Close

In the final phase of a project, children and teachers examine their findings and reflect upon what they have found out from their investigation (see Figure 9.6). Together, they revisit their topic web and the question chart to see if they have addressed all of their original questions. This is a critical element both for the children's inquiry learning and teachers' own reflections on what and how the children have learned.

Questions	Predictions	Findings
Why do people cut down trees?	Because they want to have logs for a campfire.	People cut down trees for a lot of reasons. Sometimes for firewood. Sometimes insects are hurting it, or it is sick or dead or in the way of a building or a power line.
Why do leaves on trees start out green and then turn brown?	Because someone didn't water the tree. Because something hurt the leaves.	Green leaves might turn brown when a tree is sick or dead. Leaves turn brown in the fall when they stop making food for the tree and the leaves dry out.
Do trees have flowers on them?	Yes, because my tree has flowers on it. No, because flowers grow in the ground. Some trees have flowers and some don't.	Some trees have flowers and some trees don't.

Figure 9.6 This excerpt from a question table shows that children have answered some of the initial questions they asked about trees.

Then, with guidance from the teacher, the children plan and conduct final presentations of their work to share with their families or with others in their school. A culminating event in Phase 3 usually constitutes the conclusion of the project. A culminating event may be as simple as the creation of a book about the project to be shared with families, or as complex as an open house to which families and other classrooms are invited. The type of culminating activity will depend on several factors: the ages and interests of the children, their own and their teacher's experience with project work, and the time and resources available.

An important part of Phase 3 is the completion of the documentation of the project – documentation that began in Phase 1 and continued throughout the project. By Phase 3, children's work can take many forms and include a variety of graphic representations, model building, notebooks, nature journals, collections of related artifacts, and albums and perhaps slide shows or videos. The teachers also typically have been documenting the investigation through photographs, videos, notes, and sketches of the children's activities.

The basic purpose of the documentation is to tell the story of the project: how it started, the main questions that guided the investigation, and the main activities involved in collecting and representing the data. Therefore, a documentation display should have a clear narrative quality to it, including the dates and times of events depicted. Phase 3 documentation might consist of a wall display outside of the classroom, as well as shelves that hold labeled models the children have built, books they have created of their pictures and reports, and other items that make it possible for them to revisit their experiences and share what they have learned with others. The completed question table can be included in the final documentation of the project. Children can also learn to take the role of guides, helping parents and other visitors view the story of their work as presented in the documentation, and answering visitors' questions about the project.

It is helpful for teachers to let the children know early in the project that the story of their investigation will be displayed for others to see. However, it is unlikely that there will be sufficient space for every piece of field work or all of the details of the project to be represented in the documentation displays. Some thoughtful selections must be made. Teachers can involve the children in a discussion of what they think would be of most interest to others who were not involved in the project. It is usually helpful to ask such questions as, "What do you especially want others (your parents or another class) to know about your study of trees?" and "What do you think might be especially interesting to (your father, your little sister, the principal, etc.)?"

As part of the culmination of a tree project, a subtopic group that has been studying animals that live in trees might decide to display a sketch of an ant, a photograph of a squirrel, and a model of a bird nest for visitors to see. They might also set up the display under a tree on the playground where they observed these things. Children in a subtopic group that studied leaves could set their leaf collection on a table and invite visitors to trace the leaves on paper. Every child can have a role in the culminating activities, although the roles may vary.

SPECIFIC BENEFITS AND CHALLENGES OF NATURE-RELATED PROJECTS

Benefits

Undertaking projects related to natural phenomena can have positive effects for children and teachers in addition to the general benefits of project work. Teachers who facilitate nature-related projects should keep in mind that they are not necessarily "introducing" the children to nature; rather, the project work may enable the children to gain new perspectives on phenomena they have already encountered. Even children who rarely go outdoors are likely to have some awareness of weather, plants, and animals; project work can deepen and broaden their nascent understandings of these and other natural phenomena. Depending on the topic, a nature-related project may enhance children's familiarity with basic scientific activities (observation, data collection, prediction, hypothesizing, analysis, interpretation) and with fundamental concepts of science: principles of classification, awareness of part-to-whole relationships, knowledge of structures and their functions, and recognition of patterns, cycles, and systems. During a project on trees, for example, children may come to better understand the structure of a tree and how parts of a tree such as roots and leaves keep the tree alive. They may gain insight into changes that occur in a tree over its life cycle, and the ways in which trees support the existence of other organisms.

It is in children's best interest to understand that natural phenomena are extremely complex. They may be awe-inspiringly large – a confluence of two great Western rivers, the Midwestern sky on a spring afternoon – or, like a pebble with shiny flecks of mica, small enough to hold in one's hand. A goal of doing nature-related projects is to have children recognize the importance of "nature," its role in human life, and their own potential role in caring for the places and the living things around them. The teacher must take care not to lead children to romanticize nature, although many of their nature experiences may be positive. Nor is it optimal to impart a sensationalist notion that natural phenomena are inherently "gross" or dangerous. Avalanches, toxic plants, and the smell of decay are parts of nature, but a child's perspective on nature that is limited to the unpleasant or frightening remains incomplete.

Other benefits of project work focusing on nature have been articulated in the literature on place-based education – an approach that considers the local community to be central to children's education, and local schools to be central to the life of the community. When children investigate what is nearby, they encounter situations, people, life forms, and phenomena that directly affect their lives. An ongoing tendency in our field to focus young children's attention on "long ago and far away" (dinosaurs, penguins, the rain forest) may contribute to their loss of "a sense of place" and a fuller understanding of the places they live. As they learn about the environment, culture, and history of their home communities, children may be better able to engage with challenges that those communities face, and may even participate in work to address those challenges. They become experts on their "home ground" and the basic understandings, knowledge, skills, and dispositions they gain can, as their experience broadens to make distant things more meaningful, be applied to their interactions with the world beyond their communities.

Some recent research suggests additional benefits to nature-related projects. Being outdoors for a variety of purposes may have significant cognitive and mental health benefits for children (see for example Faber Taylor & Kuo 2009, 2011; Faber Taylor, Kuo, & Sullivan 2002). It seems reasonable to assume that doing field work and related activities outdoors offer some of those benefits. In addition, outdoor field work can involve walking and similar physical activity which can support children's physical health and counteract lengthy sessions of sitting at desks.

Challenges

Teachers we talk to have identified some specific challenges to their efforts to engage children in nature-related projects. Some teachers are not able to take children off the school grounds, severely limiting their contact with what we typically call "nature." In some cases, school policies and transportation costs preclude doing field work away from school. Even when safety is not an issue, teachers in programs located in heavily paved urban areas with many buildings and little green space report that they must make concerted efforts to engage children with nature. In such situations, projects that help children learn more about the natural environment are still possible. Most playgrounds and even school buildings are home to a surprising number of life forms – ants, dandelions, birds, and so on. Container gardens and even house plants could be at the center of nature-related project topics. If live animals are permitted in the school, children might investigate beetles, earthworms, fish, rabbits, chickens, or other small creatures.

Some research suggests that young children in the early twenty-first century spend far less time outdoors than did any previous generation. Experience indicates that nature study (and in fact, much general science experience) even in the preschool years is being set aside in favor of added direct instruction in literacy and math. As a result, some teachers are finding that before they begin project work on a nature-related topic, children may need time just to explore the natural world – walking on unpaved surfaces, touching rocks and plants, looking for evidence of animal life, listening to birds and insects, watching clouds overhead (see Figure 9.7).

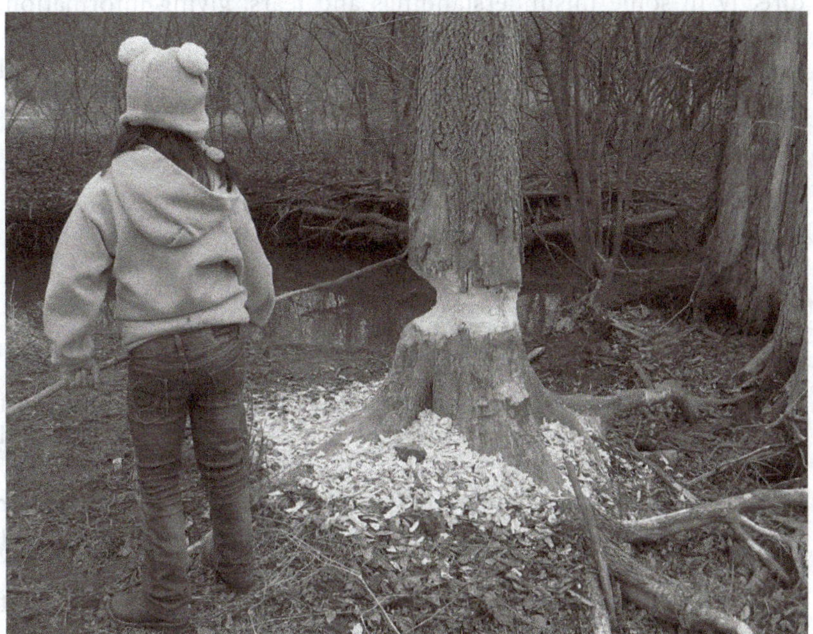

Figure 9.7 A child examines a tree chewed by a beaver. Children may need time just to explore the natural world before beginning project work.

After they have such basic experiences, they are better able to develop interests and formulate questions that are important to project work. We understand that some adults, including teachers, may feel that they do not know enough about natural phenomena to facilitate a project, or even to keep children safe when exploring outdoors. Teachers may want to arrange more exposure to nature for themselves, just as they would for children who have not had encounters with nature.

Lack of familiarity also contributes to another challenge teachers have reported: the fact that children – and even parents – may harbor misunderstandings and fears of what might be found "in nature." They may believe that butterflies bite, or that serious dangers lurk among the trees of a city park. The teacher may want to solicit from family members any concerns they may have about their children's involvement in a nature-related project. It's also a good idea to listen closely to the children's questions and concerns about natural phenomena. Do they imagine that trees will reach their branches down and grab unsuspecting children? Do they think they can drink directly from the stream in the park? Do they think dragonflies are flying dragons that shoot fire? The teacher may intervene directly in some misunderstandings and fears, giving information, guidance, or reassurance; he or she might also turn these misconceptions and concerns into opportunities to inspire the children to find answers:

> No, trees don't really grab people. That's only in movies.
>
> No, stream water is not safe to drink. You may *not* taste it just once to see if you get ill or stay healthy. But I'll try to find someone who can tell us what is in the stream water that might make people sick.
>
> What could you do to find out if a dragonfly is actually a dragon?

Projects about natural phenomena can address the dual problem of ignorance about and fear of nature. During a project, teachers and parents often learn alongside the children; as they do so, any fears they have based on misinformation can be replaced by informed respect for their environment. There are reasons to be cautious with nature, but fear need not overwhelm understanding and enjoyment.

In this chapter we have described why and how teachers might engage young children with nature through the project approach. A teacher need not be a naturalist to facilitate such projects successfully. In fact, one of the benefits of nature-related projects that teachers report is that often they learn as much as the children do. We hope that readers of this chapter and volume will experience for themselves the positive effects of engaging children's minds in long-term projects investigating the natural world.

REFERENCES

Dewey, J. (1996). Three years of the University Elementary School. In Paciorek, K. M. & Munro, J. H. (eds.), *Sources: Notable selections in early childhood education* (pp. 150–155). Guildford, CT: Dushkin Publishing Group.

Faber Taylor, A., & Kuo, F. E. (2009). Children with attention deficits concentrate better after walk in the park. *Journal of Attention Disorders, 12*, 402–409.

Faber Taylor, A., & Kuo F.E. (2011). Could exposure to everyday green spaces help treat ADHD? Evidence from children's play settings. *Applied Psychology: Health and Well-Being, 3*(3), 281–303.

Faber Taylor, A., Kuo, F. E., & Sullivan, W. C. (2002). Views of nature and self-discipline: Evidence from inner-city children. *Journal of Environmental Psychology, 22*, 49–63.

Katz, L. G. (2010). STEM in the early years. Collected papers from the SEED Conference, Fall 2010. Retrieved from http://ecrp.illinois.edu/beyond/seed/katz.html on April 4, 2019.

Katz, L. G. (2015). Lively minds: Distinctions between academic vs. intellectual goals for young children. Retrieved from https://deyproject.files.wordpress.com/2015/04/dey-lively-minds-4-8-15.pdf on April 4, 2019.

Katz, L. G., & Chard, S. C. (2000). The contribution of documentation to the quality of early childhood education. Retrieved from https://files.eric.ed.gov/fulltext/ED393608.pdf on April 4, 2019.

10

NATURE-BASED EXPLORATION TO SUPPORT LANGUAGE DEVELOPMENT AND INQUIRY WITH PRESCHOOL DUAL LANGUAGE LEARNERS

Isauro M. Escamilla, Sahara Gonzalez-Garcia, and Alicia Alvarez

Box 10.1 Key Science and Nature Elements

- Diet and life cycle of turtles
- Identification of anatomy and body parts of a turtle
- Content knowledge and understanding that emerges from long-term, repeated exposure to a small, child-accessible, natural garden area
- The development and use of sophisticated vocabulary that emerges naturally in two languages as children need new words to describe their understandings

Box 10.2 Key Inquiry Elements

- Capturing children's conversations in their first language and second languages
- Guiding children to make observational drawings to represent their nature engagement and learning
- Recording children's dual language conversations via written notes, audiotaping, and videotaping

- Use of Learning Stories to document and share children's nature learning, development, and collaboration
- Using selected research literature on teacher inquiry and emergent curriculum to understand children's nature learning

Our role as early childhood educators working with young children is a demanding job. In the last few years we have experienced a constant pressure to adapt an academic curriculum traditionally reserved only for kindergarten. Letter recognition, pre-writing skills, rhyming, and phonological awareness are important skills, but so are children's right to play and for preschools that prepare children for school readiness to include the development of children's fine motor and socioemotional skills, preferably outside of the classroom where children have more space to be active and connect with nature. According to Richard Louv (2008), many schools continue to shortchange the arts and fail to offer anything resembling hands-on experiences with nature outside the classroom. In our case, when we took a closer look at our daily schedule we realized that we usually spend much more time indoors than outdoors. In a 10-hour day we spend an average of 2.5 hours in the school yard of our public preschool. Perhaps, as a society we don't value nature education with young children as much as we should. For example, in a recent visit by a CLASS (Classroom Scoring Assessment Survey) assessor for a standardized evaluation of teachers' performance, the evaluator made it clear that anything taking place outside the classroom would not count as part of the observation. Too bad, because children actually have multiple opportunities to explore, discover, and learn when they are outdoors.

Access to immediate green spaces and natural elements such as sand, water, plants, flowers, birds, and insects, should be considered when rating a high-quality program for young children. The school yard garden in the urban preschool where we work, teach, and learn offers our young children multiple opportunities to encounter the wonders of a spider making a web, a morning dove nesting above the door frame, a colony of ants devouring cookie crumbs, or a humming bird swirling around a lavender bush.

Sometimes, the children have chance encounters with natural phenomena. For example, when they dig in the planter boxes and discover a "family" of roly-polies. At other times, teachers are more intentional, for example by bringing into the classroom a bag of pinecones collected on a weekend walk, a caterpillar, a snail, or even a small turtle. A small turtle roaming among the plants in the planter boxes is an example of a spontaneous encounter between the children and the turtle. When children show interest in something and teachers are genuinely curious about children's interests, this duality can serve as a springboard to generate increasing awareness of nature-related topics and the subsequent emergent inquiry. Later in this chapter, we describe a Learning Story about the children's interest in and learning from the turtle.

When children play outdoors, we try to support them as much as we do indoors, in many ways we humbly consider our school yard an extension of the indoors classroom and perhaps it might even be considered an example of an outdoors classroom. Although we feel pressured to prepare our young students for academic success, we understand the importance of and are committed to support them as much as we can in their social and emotional development and quite often, our schoolyard garden offers multiple opportunities and possibilities to accomplish these goals.

OUR SCHOOL

Our preschool is located in the Mission District of San Francisco and is part of the San Francisco Unified School District's Early Education Department (SFUSD EED). When children first enter the preschool program, very few speak English and the majority prefers to speak their home language, resulting in Spanish, Cantonese, and Mandarin as the most common spoken languages in the school community, which has resulted in a recent initiative to offer Dual Language Learning (DLL) education at the preschool level with an emphasis on biliteracy in Spanish/English and Cantonese/English. An important goal of the preschool dual language programs is to support the children's home or ancestral culture and language through immersion in Spanish or Cantonese. Of 36 preschools that make up the SFUSD EED, six schools offer dual language programs for children aged three to five years' old in Spanish/English and four schools have dual language programs in Cantonese/English. In DLL preschools teachers speak and teach in Spanish or Cantonese most of the day (80 percent in Spanish or Cantonese and 20 percent in English). These DLL programs accept all students, even if they do not speak Spanish or Cantonese. Some of these children might continue their DLL experience by enrolling in the Spanish or Cantonese pathways in elementary schools of the school district.

In our preschool program, nature-related experiences do not come from a prescribed curriculum. Instead, we rely on children's interests and our own awareness in bringing children's attention to a bird building or a nest in a tree in the school yard, the capricious shapes of clouds in the sky, the sour taste of oranges at lunch time, or the sound of rain during spring showers at nap time. As much as possible, we try to build upon children's knowledge of the natural world as well as their cultural and linguistic assets or *funds of knowledge* (González, Moll, & Amanti, 2006). Depending on the children's level of interest and our curiosity, we identify additional resources to extend children's learning through their senses and by planning activities that usually include reading fiction and nonfiction books, singing songs in Spanish and English, fieldtrips the local library, a walk in the neighborhood, observational drawings, sculpting with playdough, building with recycled materials, or painting with acrylic paints. All of this, as much as possible, is conducted in the children's home languages, making pedagogical spaces where children can access prior knowledge as a bridge to make connections to new science, scientific, and/or nature words or concepts.

INQUIRY AND LEARNING STORIES

The California Preschool Learning Foundations (California Department of Education, 2008) states that given the importance of direct experience for young preschoolers' interests in and understanding of the natural world, the ways that young children learn about the natural world will vary depending on the ecological context in which each child lives. Children in rural areas might have more opportunities to interact with the natural world, but for children living in urban environments, it is crucial that early childhood educators find ways to encourage children to familiarize themselves with nature and life science concepts and to use those moments to build on children's innate curiosity and ability to role-play. Pretending to be a scientist is something that perhaps children are naturally inclined to do. Thinking like a scientist implies that young children engage in inquiry practices and these practices require specific dispositions, knowledge, and skills. These practices and skills include but are not limited to the following (Hamlin & Wisneski, 2013):

- observing;
- asking questions;
- describing;
- predicting;
- providing explanations;
- using tools to extend the senses;
- planning investigations;

- recording what happens during these investigations;
- communicating and sharing ideas.

We try to integrate these practices and skills in our nature curriculum, and we often find that following the children's interests and lead shows us where and how these skills are best extended and supported.

THE VALUE FOR IMPROVING NATURE EDUCATION FROM A HOLISTIC PERSPECTIVE

A review of selected literature (Carr & Lee, 2012; Lee, Carr, Soutar, & Mitchell, 2013) provides evidence that the Learning Stories approach holds great potential for children in early childhood settings in Western countries modeled on the experience in the Maori experience in Aotearoa/New Zealand. New Zealand's early childhood curriculum is built from a Maori and social constructionist perspective that views knowledge as situated within culture, history, and society and regards the connection between the child and family as integral, relational, and irrevocable. For example, the newly republished *Te Whāriki*, the New Zealand early childhood curriculum document (Te Whāriki, 2017) presents a framework for working with young children based on four principles that California early childhood educators find particularly appealing for its inclusive worldview:

1. *Whakamana* – Empowerment: The early childhood curriculum empowers the child to learn and grow.
2. *Kotahitanga* – Holistic Development: The early childhood curriculum reflects the holistic way children learn and grow.
3. *Whānau Tangata* – Family and Community: The wider world of family and community is an integral part of the early childhood curriculum.
4. *Ngā Hononga* – Relationships: Children learn through responsive and reciprocal relationships with people, places, and things.

Given that California is home to many immigrants from Central America and Mexico, and young Latinx children (ages 0–5 years) with diverse linguistic and cultural backgrounds are also the largest and fastest growing ethnic minority population in the United States, it is imperative to explore innovative ways of facilitating and teaching Spanish and English to these young children. Most of these immigrant families rely on public preschools for their children's early education. Yet the majority of these children in urban environments do not receive a preschool education that provides a solid foundation to help them become bicultural and bilingual, and have more than basic knowledge in the natural sciences.

In this chapter, we explore the potential rewards and challenges of using children's individual and collective stories in dual language preschool settings to move teaching practices and observation and assessment of dual language learners toward a more strength-based approach. The suggested structure to create and write a Learning Story helps us organize fleeting ideas into a coherent narrative to make sense of specific children's experiences. More importantly, the writing of Learning Stories encourages us to showcase young dual language children as competent nature explorers and linguistic learners in familiar settings at any given moment during the school day. When a teacher writes a story to the child the purpose is not to test a hypothesis or to evaluate. At the root of writing a Learning Story is a genuine interest in understanding children's lived experiences and the meaning teachers, families, and children themselves make of those experiences.

As teachers in a dual language public preschool we are required to conduct ongoing classroom observations to assess children's learning. This has led us to explore the following questions: How can early childhood educators support and make visible children's emergent linguistic identities? And within this process, how can teachers embed story and narrative to document children's growth and strengthen parents' participation in their children's education? We are exploring the use of an authentic assessment approach in the form of Learning Stories (Carr & Lee, 2012), a narrative-based formative assessment and mode of inquiry created by New Zealand early childhood education leaders to highlight children's strengths and improve instruction based on the interests, abilities, and expertise of children and their families. The Learning Story journey starts by honoring and respecting the process of observing, listening, reflecting, and sharing. When we engage in writing and reading stories – stories where the children make discoveries about the natural world – we uncover who we are as a learning community and, in the process, we deepen and broaden our appreciation and understanding of children's actions, play, and behaviors at any given time, which we try to capture within a Learning Story.

CAPTURING CHILDREN'S LEARNING THROUGH LEARNING STORIES

We were first exposed to Learning Stories in the spring of 2017 when Isauro visited New Zealand on a study tour to learn about their early childhood education systems. Later, in the fall of the same year, he attended the national Learning Stories conference in Auckland, New Zealand, where Margaret Carr was the keynote speaker and where he learned how intertwined nature is with everyday life in New Zealand. In most schools that Escamilla visited, when the children and teachers introduced themselves, they made evident that, for the Maori, the relationships with place were as important as relationships with people, and shared where they came from including where their *whenua* (land), *awa* (river) or *maunga* (mountain) are.

Learning Stories, as a philosophical approach, emerged around two decades ago, as a pedagogical tool to assess children's development and to help educators reflect on their roles in the complex processes of teaching and learning (Carr & Lee, 2012; Carter, 2017). A Learning Story is first and foremost a story. It tells a tale written to the child that is meant to be shared with the family (Carr & Lee, 2012). Learning Stories are records of children's lives in the school community and, to some extent, mirror the professional lives of educators based on daily observations of children at play engaged in their immediate environment.

Learning Stories are visual and written narratives about children's growth created by teachers from a strength-based perspective. These are the foundational components of a Learning Story (Carr & Lee, 2012; Carter, 2010, 2017):

- an observation with accompanying photographs or short videos of children in action, engaged with materials; interacting with people, places, or objects;
- a pedagogical analysis of the observation;
- a plan to extend children's learning by planning specific activities;
- the families' perspective on their child's learning experience; and
- links to specific evaluative measures, which in our case in the Desired Results Developmental Profile (DRDP-R 2015).

The suggested format for creating and writing a Learning Story can be accomplished individually, but we have found that sometimes it is a less challenging and a much more enjoyable task when the process becomes a collaborative effort shared between teachers who work in the same classroom. Believing that everyone has a story to tell, we teachers support one another by sharing photographs, short videos, and vignettes of what children did, said, discovered, or accomplished during the school day. This exchange of ideas and images where we try to explain what we saw, heard, photographed, or captured in videos is what leads us to find meaning in our ephemeral thoughts. Sometimes one of us types on an iPad while the other describes and narrates what happened. At other times, one of us asks questions while the other elaborates and recalls specific information and details to recreate the events that took place, going back to the photos, videos, or anecdotal notes as reference.

We have found that narrative in a Learning Story format provides us with an alternative method to structure our individual observations and, in the process of sharing with our colleagues, we find delight in what children discover, wonder about, and naturally do in their everyday play. We realize that quite often our observations happen at any given time, since children are constantly discovering something new or making new connections in their interactions with other children, materials, or the natural environment, and we try to be ready to create a record of what catches our attention. By creating a record, we mean taking a photograph, making a 5-minute-long video, or jotting down what children say or do, the way they react, or behave in their everyday play in our school yard garden.

NATURE-RELATED MEMORIES IN FAMILIES' HERITAGE LANGUAGE

Educational nature-based activities with emergent preschool dual language children should be based on daily observations of children at play both in the classroom and outdoors, including teachers' reflections and, as much as possible, the input of families. Besides the dual language focus of our program, parents report that the schoolyard garden is a strong incentive to enroll their children in our preschool. Quite a few parents claim that the trees, wild flowers, the sandbox and bees, butterflies, ants, and birds in the schoolyard garden help children feel calmer and more focused.

Early in the school year, we make it a habit of asking parents what languages they know, where and how they learned their languages, and their perceptions about monolingualism and bilingualism. We ask them what they miss about their home countries, what traditions or celebrations they miss the most, and how we could fill that void, if at all. In a memorable parents' meeting hosted by the Bay Area Discovery Museum at our school, parents and teachers were invited to share a childhood memory related to nature and most of us recalled that we did not need any fancy toys to have fun. Many of us remembered playing in puddles after a rainy day, walking barefoot on sand dunes, or the cacophony of cicadas on a hot and humid summer day. The main point was for families and teachers to make connections between nature and play and reflect on the importance of accessing and maintaining green spaces for young children, especially for children of color growing up in tiny studio apartments in such an urban and expensive city as San Francisco.

A LEARNING STORY – AZEL AND THE TURTLE

The activities that we now describe started with a Learning Story written by Sahara Gonzalez-Garcia and later enhanced by Alicia and Isauro.

Most of our children are emergent bilinguals, since we teach in a Spanish/English dual language program. Out of 24 students, two children are native English-language speakers and four receive speech and language therapy services on site. Children who are learning two languages often benefit from emotional support from a caring adult in times of distress. One of those instances took place one morning outside in the school yard when the children were trying to see our recently adopted school pet, a small tortoise that the teacher next door, Edwin, had found wandering on the street and, since he almost ran over it, decided to rescue it and bring it to school for the children to feed and take care of. They named her Tatiana, in honor of the old turtle and main character of a song in our Spanish-scripted curriculum, which we had been singing to practice the beginning sound /t/.

Almost at the same time that Tatiana the turtle became our school pet, we had been experimenting with a new way of documenting children's learning known as *Learning Stories*. The following is a Learning Story we wrote based on our collective observations, photographs, and discussions in collaboration with the children's parents and with the ongoing support of our instructional coaches and Daniel Meier, who participate in our monthly, school-wide inquiry group meetings.

Azel and Tatiana the Turtle
February 17, 2018

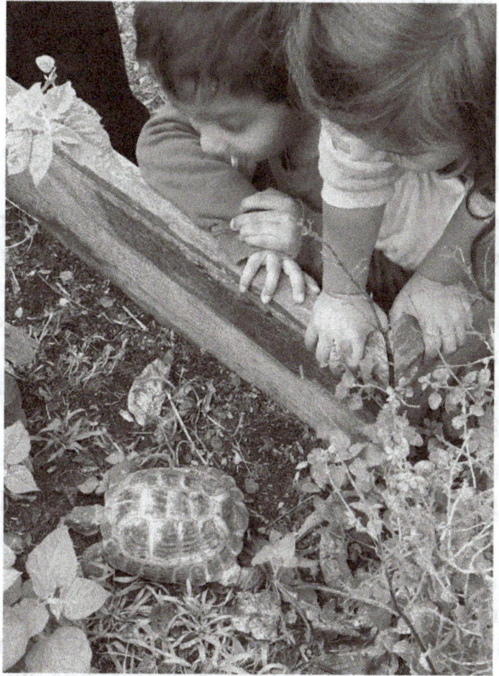

Figure 10.1 Azel observing the turtle in the garden.

WHAT HAPPENED? WHAT IS THE HISTORY?

Azel, this afternoon when we went out to the patio, you came to me very sad. You tried to tell me something. I asked you, what happened? You did not answer me, you took me by the hand and you took me to where some children were in the garden. One girl explained to me that you wanted to see the turtle but that the children would not let you see it. I asked you if you wanted to see the turtle and you moved your head saying yes. I told you, "We're going to ask the children to make room for you to see the turtle." We asked for a turn to see her. The children moved and made a space for you to see her up close. You stayed watching the turtle for a few minutes. Later, a girl offered you some pieces of carrot that were in the garden to feed the turtle. You placed the carrot bits in front of the turtle to eat. You were there for several minutes, very patiently watching how the turtle moved slowly.

After a while, the turtle hid among the plants. "Sleep, mom, dad." You said. I answered, "Yes, she's going to sleep." I understood that you were trying to tell me that the turtle was already going to sleep. Glad to have been with the turtle for a while, you went to play in the playground.

Teacher Sahara Gonzalez-Garcia

WHAT DOES THIS ACTION OR ACTIVITY MEAN?

Over time, the interest that Azel showed in the turtle sparked the other children's interest too. One of the first activities we carried out following the educational theory based on projects by Lilian Katz and Sylvia Chard (2000) was to give children ample time to explore and observe something concrete around them. The children observed the turtle, which we named Tatiana, inspired by the name of the turtle in a song from our songbook in Spanish.

OPPORTUNITIES AND POSSIBILITIES TO EXTEND THE ACTIVITY?

Mrs. Ana, Azel's mother, suggested some ideas to support her son Azel and the other children in the class to participate in the study of the turtle. Some ideas were that children take turns taking the turtle home on weekends to take care of it and feed it. Mrs. Ana, like the teachers, also thought about getting informative books about turtles to learn more about them.

Mrs. Ana and her son Azel formulated the following questions:

What kind of turtle is it?
How old is it?
How big is it?
How much more can it grow?

Other ideas that emerged from the children and teachers were:

- obtaining fiction and nonfiction books about turtles from our local library;
- sculpting turtles with play dough;
- naming the body parts of the turtle;
- making turtles with recycling materials;
- learning a new song about turtles;
- offer paper, pencils, crayons, or markers to draw the turtle;
- painting with watercolors or acrylics;
- encouraging the care and maintenance of the turtle.

DESIRED RESULTS DEVELOPMENTAL PROFILE MEASURES (DRDP-R 2015)

- Curiosity and initiative in learning.
- Self-control of feelings and behavior.
- Shared use of space and materials.
- Relationship and social interaction with a familiar adult.

The first representations of the turtle Tatiana made by the children were based on direct observations during a small group activity in the garden. The children also had the opportunity to make drawings of the turtle when we brought her to visit the classroom. We put the turtle on a table so that the children could observe it closely and see the details of its shell and its movements. These are some of their comments:

"*The turtle walks very slowly*" – Brian.
"*The turtle has four legs*" – Luna
"*Tatiana's shell has figures that look like squares of various colors*" – Lucas

FROM OBSERVATION AND DISCUSSION TO REPRESENTATION

> Putting ideas into a form of graphic representation allows children to understand what their actions can communicate. It is an extraordinary discovery because it helps them to realize that to communicate, others must understand their graphics. From our point of view, the graphic representation is a communication tool much more simple and clear than words. Loris Malaguzzi. (Gandini, 2012, p. 66)

Malaguzzi (cited in Gandini, 2012) theorized that putting ideas into visual representation helps young children understand that their drawings can communicate what they might not be able yet to express only in spoken words. In this sense, for young children who are English language learners or dual language learners, graphic representation is a communication tool and a creative medium that is perhaps simpler than words, although the act of representation is in itself a complex process since it requires children to make important cognitive and scientific choices based on their observation abilities and previous representational experiences. The use of visuals during those experiences to represent scientific observation and learning is a critical option for emergent bilingual children, who are learning to speak about and understand science concepts in two languages.

This is why, in our place-based science curriculum, we cannot emphasize enough the value of drawing, sketching, and painting, which allows young dual language learners to produce visual representations to complement their emerging language skills in science and nature study. By revisiting their own work, we have discovered that children as young as four years old can actually become critical (thinkers) of their work and make changes to their initial renditions that best reflect their evolving understanding.

The following set of photographs and drawings depict our students in scientific practice, such as observing the complex anatomical exterior structure of a live turtle on a picnic table in our school yard garden.

Abigail and other children observed the turtle with extreme care and tried to capture the shape of the body and the expression of the face, and as their observations became more intentional their drawings became more detailed (Figures 10.2 and 10.3).

Nathalia made two drawings of the turtle trying to capture the details of the shell and limbs.

Nathalia made two drawings of the turtle trying to capture the details of the shell and the limbs, and her first drawing shows a highly detailed representation of the turtle (Figure 10.4).

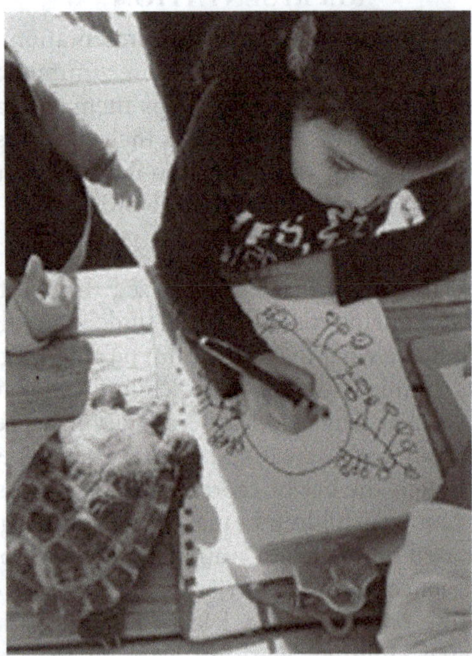

Figure 10.2 Abigail drawing the turtle from direct observation.

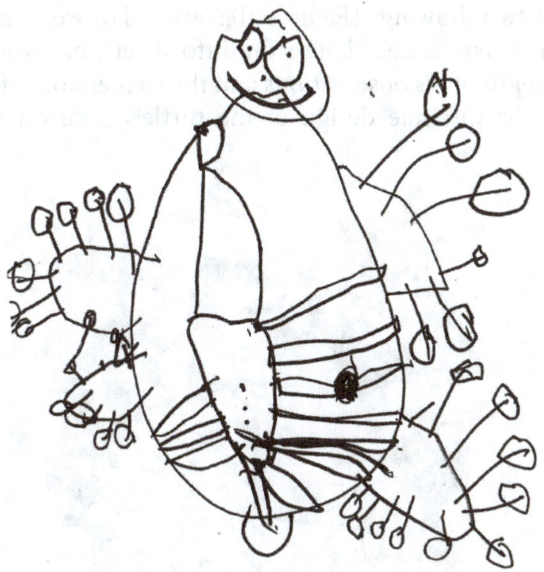

Figure 10.3 Drawing of Abigail's turtle.

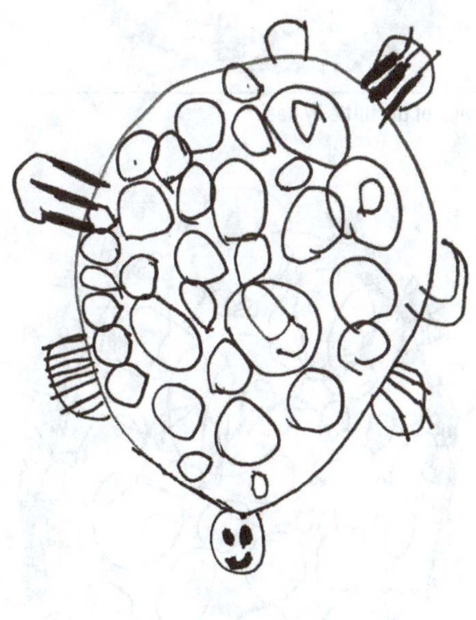

Figure 10.4 Sketch of the turtle by Nathalia.

The next two drawings (Figures 10.5 and 10.6) were made by Gael, who does not like to trace letters on ditto sheets, but whose drawings reveal the depth of his observations and the tremendous effort he made to capture the intricate design of the turtle's shell on two separate occasions.

Figure 10.5 First drawing of the turtle by Gael.

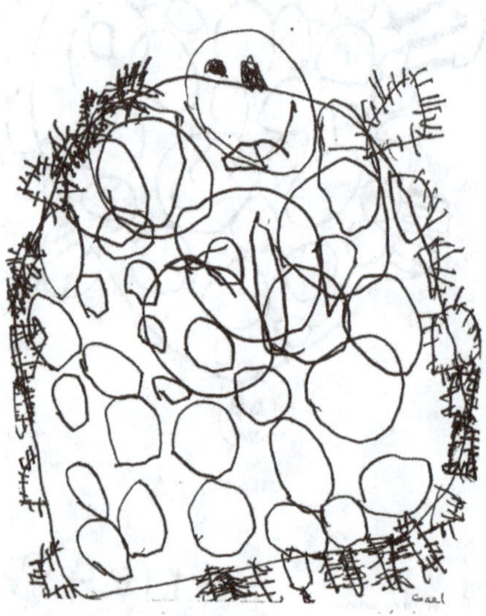

Figure 10.6 Second drawing of the turtle by Gael.

SCIENTIFIC INQUIRY AND YOUNG DUAL LANGUAGE LEARNERS

Crucial to the development of scientific inquiry is the children's ability to use language and as much as possible, the use of specific words and terms to describe what they observe and explore and to explain their ideas to peers or familiar adults. The use of language allows children to become aware of their thoughts and to express them in oral, written or signed words (California Department of Education, 2008). In our experience, young children who are dual language learners quite often have an understanding of the concepts being explored, but they might not have acquired the English-specific vocabulary to describe and explain what they have observed, explored, or learned. Iterative observations and hands-on investigations over a sustained period of time allows children to play with new words in their home language or English. In our case, we strongly encourage the children to use Spanish in their interactions during their play and work time both indoors and outdoors. Our dual language program follows a daily 80 percent Spanish–20 percent English model. It is in this context that the children in this story learned the meaning of the following nouns: *tortuga* (turtle), *reptile* (reptile), *caparazón* (shell); action verbs such as *explorar* (to explore), observar (to observe), dibujar (to draw); and adjectives derived from studying the turtle up close; such as *bonita* (pretty), *despacio* (slow), and *hervíboro* (herbivorous).

While some children drew, others looked for information about turtles in nonfiction books, showing interest in photographs such as Azel and Abigail, who were interested in "reading" on their own (see Figure 10.7).

In addition, Azel, although with some difficulty, also managed to paint a small turtle made with recycled cardboard that his mother had sent from home. The turtles made with recycled materials were put on a simple display on a shelf in the classroom.

AN UNEXPECTED END

Unfortunately, upon returning to school after a weekend, the children looked for the turtle in the garden and found it badly hurt. Perhaps a raccoon had attacked her, and although teacher Edwin had immediately taken her to the veterinary's office, the turtle Tatiana died the next day. The children were sad and some did not understand what was happening, or maybe they understood but could not express their feelings with words. After a brief discussion it was decided among the children and teachers that the turtle would be buried in the school garden next to our avocado tree.

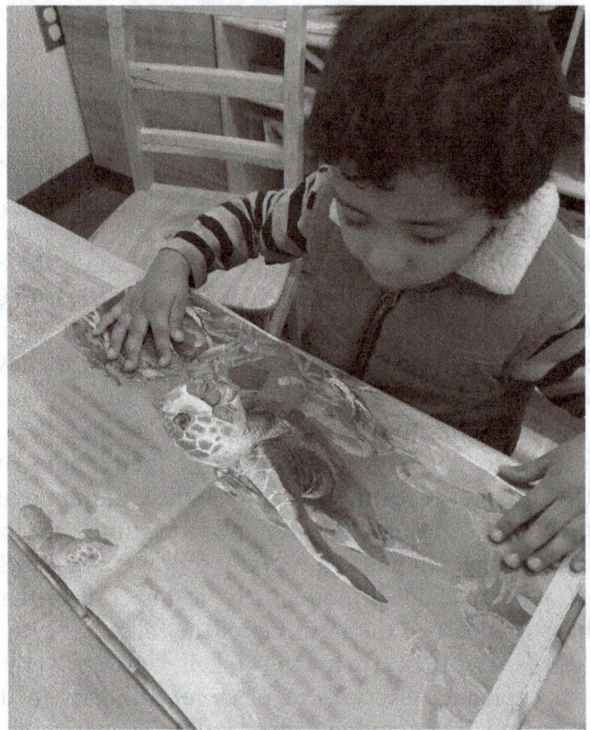

Figure 10.7 Azel "reading" a book about sea turtles.

Some children seemed to understand that they would no longer see the turtle when they saw teacher Edwin digging a hole where the turtle would stay forever, since she was no longer alive. Each child placed a flower around the turtle and made drawings with phrases expressing their love, which we hung on the garden's fence. In his message Enrique said that he would give the turtle some flowers and Abigail found a way to summarize in a sentence the collective feeling of the class: "I love you so much. I'll miss you in the garden. I liked you when you were happy and I always looked at you." It was a solemn moment when the children buried the turtle in the school garden by the avocado tree in the school yard (Figure 10.8).

The children no longer had the opportunity to take the turtle home on weekends as they did at the beginning of the investigation. Working with children and nature is working half with certainty and half with uncertainty. We learned that nature and place-based activities with young children should be based on the daily observations and reflections of children and teachers and the suggestions made by the parents.

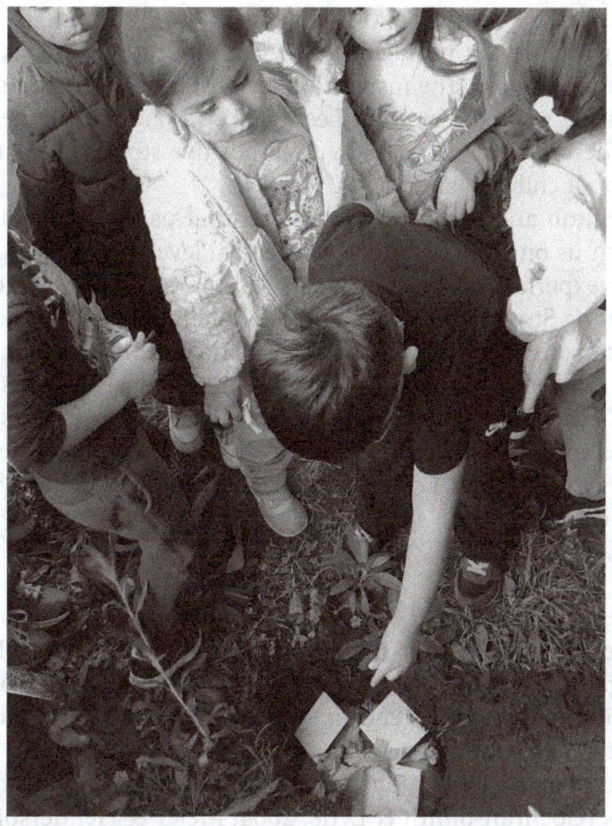

Figure 10.8 Children burying the turtle.

CLOSING AND FINAL REFLECTIONS

> A story is a train of thought that is told so that members of a culture learn or remember something. Stories are made accessible through words, and are reconstructed each time they are told or read. Stories contain common things in a culture – meaning of words, concepts, and the context of an experience. Stories show what a culture keeps and shares and what the brain processes and remembers. (Lewin-Benham, 2011, p. 96)

THE VALUE OF LEARNING STORIES

The beginning of this Learning Story began with the questions: What happened? What is the history? Teacher Sahara Gonzalez-Garcia answered those questions by writing directly to Azel and giving life to a story involving the protagonists – Azel, the turtle Tatiana, and the children in our class. The inspiration for writing this Learning Story is based on the work of Carr and Lee (2012), who argue for the value of detailed descriptive narratives that tell positive stories of learning and ability about children and adults.

Sisk-Hilton and Meier (2017) also remind us that well-told stories that touch us on a personal and intellectual level are frequently linked with our experiences, feelings, ideas, dreams, and hopes. In our case, the Learning Story that teacher Sahara wrote to and about Azel started a series of activities that were not pre-planned as in a prescribed curriculum, but emerged from observing and trying to understand the children's actions and behaviors, and their curiosity, frustration, and eagerness to make sense of a sequence of vignettes that when linked together gave life to a Learning Story based on our collective shared experiences at school.

TEACHER INQUIRY

We believe that the professional and pedagogical value of Learning Stories gains strength when integrated within the structure of regular teacher inquiry groups. Teacher inquiry and reflection involves the systematic collection and interpretation of classroom data to improve children's learning, teacher knowledge, and instructional practices (Cochran-Smith & Lytle, 2004; Meier & Henderson, 2007). The teachers at our school have regularly met at least ten times a year for the last seven years in what we call our inquiry group, a form of on-site professional development, to collaboratively reflect on our documentation techniques, dual language teaching strategies, and exploration of science and nature, among other topics. The regular use of inquiry and reflection provides a structured forum for early childhood professional discourse and engagement (Kroll & Meier, 2015; Rust, 2009), and thoughtful inquiry also often relies on the power of story to document, record, and make sense of teaching and learning. We began the integration of Learning Stories in our preschool classrooms two years ago, enticed by the power of narrative, inquiry, and stories as a promising form of documentation and formative assessment.

As educators with the dual responsibility of teaching and learning with young children, one of our most important roles is to support children with their ideas and interests. With the right support, guidance, and shared enthusiasm, those interests may be sustained for days and even weeks at a time. From our point of view, a curriculum for preschool children based on experiences in their daily lives makes more sense than a series of rigid activities planned days or weeks in advance by adults, detached from the true interests of children. We discovered that working with small groups of children gave us the time and space to observe and document their explorations and understanding of nature and science concepts.

These activities emerged from the children's innate curiosity and interests. Working with very small groups of two, three, or four children at a time provided ample opportunity for closer social interactions among the children and allowed us to see the evolution of our scientific knowledge as a community. We got to know the children better individually and developed a better understanding of our role in supporting their construction of scientific language and knowledge.

Using narratives in the form of Learning Stories as records of children's learning written mainly in Spanish has particular implications and potential benefits for US practitioners in the context of on-site inquiry groups. In this chapter, we have described how we took an inquiry stance to document the evolution of our teaching practices and record children's nature learning narratively and systematically. We look forward to becoming more reflective practitioners and, over time, deepen, broaden, and improve our instruction practices around nature, scientific inquiry, and the use of heritage languages such as Spanish or Cantonese in an academic setting. Ultimately, we hope to find more joy and meaning in our work.

REFERENCES

California Department of Education (2008). *California preschool learning foundations: History-social science. Science* (Vol. 3). Sacramento, CA: California Department of Child Development.

Carr, M., & Lee, W. (2012). *Learning stories: Constructing learner identities in early childhood education*. London: SAGE.

Carter, M. (2010). Using learning stories to strengthen teachers' relationships with children. *Exchange, 32*(6), 40–44.

Carter, M. (2017). Growing ourselves as leaders: A conversation with Annie White. *Exchange*, November/December, 46–51. *Cultural Studies, 21*(2–3), 240–270.

Cochran-Smith, S., & Lytle, S. L. (2004). *Inquiry as stance: Practitioner research in the next generation*. New York: Teachers College Press.

Gandini, L. (2012). History, ideas, and basic principles: An interview with Loris Malaguzzi in Edwards, C., Gandini, L., & Forman, G. (eds.), *The hundred languages of children: The Reggio Emilia experience in transformation*, 3rd ed. Santa Barbara, CA: Prager Press.

Hamlin, M., & Wisneski, D. B. (2013). Supporting the scientific thinking and inquiry of toddlers and preschoolers. In Shillady, A., *Spotlight on young children: Exploring science*. Washington, DC: National Association for the Education of Young Children.

Katz, L., & Chard, S. (2000). *Engaging children's minds: The project approach*. Stamford, CT: Ablex.

Kroll, L. K., & Meier, D. R. (2017). *Documentation and inquiry in the early childhood classroom: Research stories of engaged practitioners in urban centers and schools*. New York: Routledge.

Lee, W., Carr, M., Soutar, B., & Mitchell, L. (2013). *Understanding the Te Whariki approach: Early years education in practice*. New York: Routledge.

Lewin-Benham, A. (2011). *Twelve best practices for early childhood education: Integrating Reggio and other inspired approaches*. New York and London: Teachers College Press.

Louv, R. (2008). *Last child in the woods: Saving our children from nature-deficit disorder*. Chapel Hill, NC: Algonquin Books.

Meier, D. R., & Henderson, B. (2007). *Learning from young children in the classroom: The art and science of teacher research*. New York: Teachers College Press.

González, N., Moll, L. C., & Amanti, C. (Eds.). (2006). *Funds of knowledge: Theorizing practices in households, communities, and classrooms*. New York, NY: Routledge.

Rust, F. (2009). Teacher research and the problem of practice. *Teachers College Record, 111*(8), 1882–1893.

Sisk-Hilton, S., & Meier, D. R. (2017). *Narrative inquiry in early childhood and elementary school: Learning to teach, teaching well*. New York: Routledge.

Te Whāriki (2017). *Early childhood curriculum*. Wellington, New Zealand: The Ministry of Education

Part IV

Child Agency in Nature Education

11

PROMOTING NATURE STUDY FOR TODDLERS

Mabel Young

Box 11.1 Key Science and Nature Elements

- The importance of developing comfort with nature and living things as a precursor to building knowledge and understanding
- The ways in which even young toddlers collaborate to build understanding (showing each other objects and creatures up close, working on words together)
- The remarkable change in children's ability to represent natural objects after months of study and observation

Box 11.2 Key Inquiry Elements

- Brainstorming with colleagues to ask such questions as "What caught the children's attention on our nature walks?" and "How much did they comprehend when we started to introduce specimens from the trails?"
- Interviewing and audiotaping toddlers as they examine specimens and noting the level of detail in their descriptions
- Teacher journaling to record children's actions and conversations during nature walk
- Focusing on individual children and looking for key "turning points" in their nature understanding

- Photographing children on nature walks and their clay replicas of banana slugs, worms, and spiders

A TODDLER FOLLOWS A SPIDER'S DAINTY movement along the web with her eyes. The teacher walks over to the toddler and asks, "What are you looking at?" The toddler gently lifts her index finger to the spider's web. Instantly, the teacher grabs a plastic toy nearby and smashes the spider. The toddler analyzes the balled-up spider while the teacher shakes off her fear.

Growing up in the heart of San Francisco's Chinatown, I never recall the experiences of running through an open patch of grass or even smelling freshly mowed grass. My parents worked long hours six days a week, and there were not any other grownups to take my siblings and me to the park. However, when I was four years old I went to a neighborhood day camp, and we went to Golden Gate Park. I felt so out of place. Even when exposed to the many trees and wild flowers, I simply did not appreciate it because the park and shaded trails felt foreign.

In my first public preschool teaching position, our playground was paved in concrete and cement. One of my first science projects was a sink and float project, which even then I did not consider a true science project. I always thought of "science" as being alive – having a life cycle so to speak. But I did not have a lot of knowledge about how to change and expand my science teaching. Our school then moved to San Francisco's Presidio National Park, an urban oasis filled with acres of trees, grass, flowers, soil, water, open space, and sunlight.

The odd sounding chirps, quick low hums, and rustling of the nearby eucalyptus trees intrigued me, but I did not want to explore the Presidio's trails by myself, and so I decided to explore them with my students. So over the last 15 years, I have shared with the children treks to Crissy Field by the bay and even to the Golden Gate Bridge. We have thrown pebbles along the shores, built sandcastles, fed and ridden on the United States Park Police horse, looked for worms, encountered spider webs, found bird nests, and collected eucalyptus pods, leaves, berries, pinecones, feathers, and calla lilies.

I have transformed from a "city" person to a naturalist. Though the change has been slow and steady, the passion of wanting to discover with the students was a priority for me. I know that each time we introduce something in nature to each other, we give each other the satisfaction of "awe" and "wonderment." I have not ever had a child who was not interested in the banana slug slithering among the fallen rotting leaves or watching the ducklings swimming to the mother duck. While many toddlers see what adults point out, they ask many of their own questions, "Why are the blackberries so small?" "How come the grass is so wet?" "Why do the flowers only open in the sun?" "Where do the worms sleep?" They want to make sense of their surroundings, and our responses and experiences can add to their scientific theories.

Through our expert guidance, we build on children's spontaneous exploration and questions, gradually guiding children to become more focused and systematic in their observations and investigations (Worth & Grollman, 2003). Ten years ago when our school changed to a Reggio-inspired curriculum and philosophy, I was elated for the change because I saw my role as teacher changing as well as my image of the children. I learned to see them as competent, full of potential and active in constructing their knowledge through interactions with others. This became the foundation for my nature study with my children.

Susie and Stephanie, my co-teachers, our group of toddlers, and I take daily walks on the Ecology Trail, Golden Gate Promenade, and the Presidio Promenade. We have similar philosophies for introducing nature – to give children first-hand experience through outdoor field excursions and elevate children's comfort level and familiarity with the natural world (Danoff-Burg, 2002; Kupetz & Twiest, 2000). Our goals for the toddlers include the following:

- For the children to observe, hear, touch, smell, and interact with the natural environment, and develop a sense of wonder and joy for the natural world.
- To collect outdoor materials to be moved to an indoor setting for further investigation.
- To challenge themselves physically. We encourage children to grow confident by physically interacting with their environment – running, climbing, jumping, walking, and noticing.
- For children to develop theories and test their ideas about the natural world through active investigation.
- For the children to develop a sense of belonging, influence, usefulness, respect, and competence through our explorations and excursions both inside and outside our school.

OUR NATURE WALKS

The heart of our almost daily nature walks involve slowing down time, and allowing the toddlers to observe, experience, and talk about what they see, hear and touch. Toddlers are just starting their formal schooling years and I want their first school experiences with nature to be based on their spontaneous interests on our nature walks. From September on into November, the children were tentative and hesitant on our nature walks. For example, they would coil away from wanting to look at a banana slug close up, but after repeated exposure to these large slimy slugs, the children's interest and ease increased. After a few months, the children became accustomed to our natural surroundings, our observations of the natural environment, and our questions and theory-probing.

SENSES AND EXPLORATION OF BANANA SLUGS

One winter morning, Susie and I took six toddlers on a walk along the Ecology Trail, located in the Presidio Park's largest watershed and overlooking Inspiration Point, from which we can see eucalyptus groves and the San Francisco Bay (see Figure 11.1). On our way to the Ecology Trail, the children felt confident to walk and explore the trail on their own. This newfound assertiveness unfolded as we took more focused nature walks.

Keala crawled under bushes to find something alive to investigate. She picked the blackberry vines away from her face and searched through the damp underbrush. Her perseverance paid off when she spotted a banana slug moving along a thin piece of rotting twig. She squatted lower to

Figure 11.1 Ecology trail.

catch a better view of the crawling specimen. Andrew used a thick branch to carry the slug out and lay it on the trail. All the children squatted about two inches above the dirt trail to investigate the banana slug's every movement. Dylan and Andrew, who once could not stand the sight of a banana slug, tore a piece of green leaf and held it toward the front of the banana slug, perhaps offering it a snack.

Andrew pulled out a plastic bag from his hood and handed it to me. He was still uneasy putting the banana slug in a bag. We would bring plastic bags as temporary storage so that we could bring the specimens back to school for further investigation. (We returned the slugs later to the trail.) I told him to try to capture the banana slug himself, but he pushed the plastic bag into my hand. I gently pushed the bag back to him because I wanted him to figure how to put the specimen in it himself. I reminded him of all the times he had seen Susie, Stephanie, and I collect specimens in the past. Since toddlers have less experience than adults, they often cannot automatically understand a new situation. Thus, they must problem-solve and bring their knowledge and skills to a particular problem and attempt to solve it (Flavell, Miller, & Miller, 2001). My recounting of past examples of how to place the slug in the bag helped Andrew accomplish his solution. He placed his hand in the bag, and held it over the banana slug. He touched the banana slug with the bag and turned the bag inside out to tote it back to school.

That was the first day Andrew ever collected a specimen and he could not have been more pleased with himself. True scientific inquiry is instilled with excitement, creativity, and wonder and also encourages children and adults to take risks and pursue new challenges (Worth & Grollman, 2003). When we reached the classroom, Andrew confidently and gently lay the banana slug from the plastic bag into the container for the first time.

FIRST TOUCH

Later, Andrew dug through the mass of fallen dirt from underneath the planters. He found several dirt-covered worms and small half-inch garden-variety slugs. He picked them up with a shovel and dropped them into the banana slug's container. When he came to the biggest slug, he used the shovel and picked it up so he could study how the slug's eye stalks retract in and out of its body. While I noticed that he used his shovel, when Keala came over she picked up the slugs with her fingers. That was the first time I had ever seen her handle a slug. She did not care that it slithered up her sleeve. Minutes passed before I noticed Keala stroking the four-inch banana slug (Figure 11.2). Keala

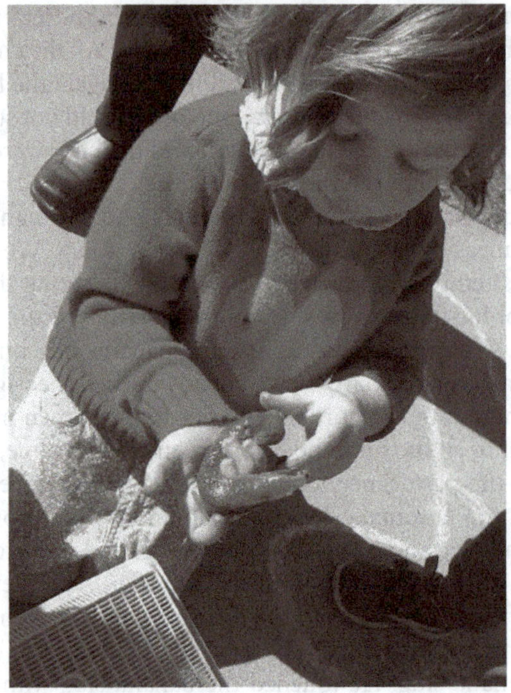

Figure 11.2 Holding banana slug.

kept comparing the antennae and sizes of the garden slug and the banana slugs. She even encouraged Jose to hold the banana slug. Surprisingly, he touched it willingly.

Once Stephanie, Susie, and I introduced a nature activity to the children, it was vital to allow the toddlers opportunities to continue to work with the materials and ideas. We documented the children's progress so we would know what they understood and how we could deepen their learning (Williams, Rockwood, & Sherman, 1987). I especially wanted to encourage the children to reflect on, represent, and document their own experiences primarily through graphic representation and sculpting (Worth & Grollman, 2003). While the children were napping, I set up our art studio with materials that the children could use to represent their banana slugs. They knew that our studio was another environment where they could have the opportunities to study the banana slugs, snails, or worms.

I often leave out paper, paint, and markers on the table or place a huge chunk of clay in the middle of the table. Off to one side, I display books of slugs, spiders, or worms so the children have opportunities to study and analyze the colorful pictures while they draw and sculpt. The range of materials and open setting provide children with choices for how they might represent the creatures. Children learn best when they can recreate an idea in multiple modalities. Thus, by encouraging children to recreate in a construction what they have observed in real life, we promote learning of abstract concepts (Danoff-Burg, 2002).

TIPPING OVER THE FLOWER PLANTERS

One month after going on more focused and intense nature walks, I observed some remarkable changes in Andrew's behavior while he was out in the toddler yard. Before I used to see him wander alone in the yard aimlessly, now I saw him more relaxed while he explored living creatures on his own. The outdoor setting provides less structure than a classroom, offers a wide array of opportunities for individual exploration, and is conducive to a discovery-oriented and approach to learning.

Exploratory play is about finding out. Andrew actively found his own specimens. When I walked out into the yard, I saw Susie had tipped over one of the octagon-shaped flower planters to look for something underneath. From a distance, I saw Andrew near her as she squatted to what appeared to be material scraped off from the bottom of the planter. As I walked closer, I saw Andrew staring inside the orange plastic container. I then saw five slugs who had slithered up along the sides and on the bottom. He did not pick them up, but simply observed them. In this case, Susie supported, guided, and challenged him to pursue questions and ideas and focus on new ones (Worth & Grollman, 2003).

Out of the corner of my eye, I then saw Keala running to Andrew. She gently pulled his forearm away from the container so she could get a better glimpse of the contents. "Baby banana slugs," she squealed. "A NANNA A NANNA," Andrew repeated. Both of them looked at the specimen before I asked, "Are those baby banana slugs?" When showing new materials, I want my children to take time for exploration. I had learned that they were more willing to listen to my line of questioning if they first satisfy their curiosity (Williams et al., 1987).

After a few minutes, Susie left Andrew alone as he probed the slugs. He put down the container by another flower planter. He squatted and used his upper body strength to tip over the flower planter. He was determined as he took the initiative to find for more slugs (see Figure 11.3). I stood there speechless because in the past when Andrew wanted a specimen, he dragged an adult's hand to retrieve it for him.

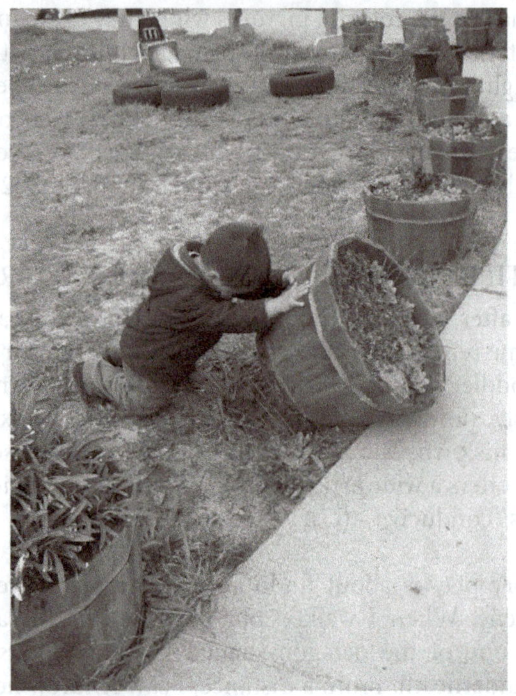

Figure 11.3 Tipping over planter.

This was the first time I saw him take the plunge to collect the slugs himself. After a few hefty pushes, he tipped the planter over.

Keala ran over and together they pored over the bottom of the planter. As I walked closer to see what they were doing, I saw her holding one small garden slug on her palm. She held it right in front of Andrew's face so both of them could see the slug's eyes pop up. Keala had taken the initiative to use her sense of touch, and therefore, became more deeply involved, magnifying the learning experience for both of them (Sisson, 1982).

REPRESENTATION OF THE BANANA SLUGS – POWER OF GRAPHIC EXPRESSION

Back in early January, Keala, Andrew, Porter, and I had one of our first visits to the Art Studio to draw a banana slug we had collected and then placed out on a tray. I wanted to know if the children's graphic representations would change if they had the specimen directly in front of them, not separated by a container's walls. This early representational experience didn't work out well because they were not yet comfortable seeing the banana slug outside the plastic container. Keala held her stomach when the banana slug slid on her paper, and she even stopped painting when the banana slug slithered closer to her. All I heard was muttering hesitancy from the children.

Later, one day in March, Porter, Keala, and Andrew asked to go the Art Studio so that they could investigate and create the snail, caterpillar, worm, spider, or banana slug with clay. Andrew took it upon himself to be the banana slug carrier as he toted the container to the Art Studio. Once I opened the Art Studio door, all of children helped themselves to the materials, eager to get started with their work. Keala took out the marker and paper and put it in front of her. She chose to draw the banana slug that was on the tray. Keala felt more at ease with the banana slug over these last few weeks. In fact, now she preferred to draw them after she had time to touch them and when they were placed in front of her (see Figure 11.4).

The children's drawings of the banana slugs also became more representational when they took more ownership of the banana slug, when they were able to come face to face with them. I also encouraged the children to make several sketches of the slugs, which resulted in an artistic series that shows their increasing observational and drawing skills. For example, Keala's depictions of the banana slug showed

Figure 11.4 Keala drawing the slug.

steady progress in that she looked at the banana slug as she drew. She felt very relaxed with the banana slugs in front of her. For example, one day in March, she picked up all the baby banana slugs and placed them on her tray. She announced that the last two pictures drawn were baby ones and that the eyes were looking at her (see Figure 11.5). As I reviewed the children's drawings of the banana slug, I realized that the students even noticed the banana slug's slime trails and became adept at drawing these trails (see Figure 11.6).

REPRESENTATION THROUGH CLAY

In using clay to represent the slugs, my goal was not for the children to create a scientifically accurate rendering of the banana slug, but to construct the clay as they observe the slugs, to internalize how the clay fits together, which features are important, and how the parts relate to the whole (Danoff-Burg, 2002). And all of the children approached the clay work and play in different ways. Over the course of a few months, the children made multiple representations of banana slugs through the use of clay. I saw some notable changes in how Andrew molds his banana slug (see Figure 11.7). Andrew's clay representations did not really take on the form of a banana slug until he had been working at

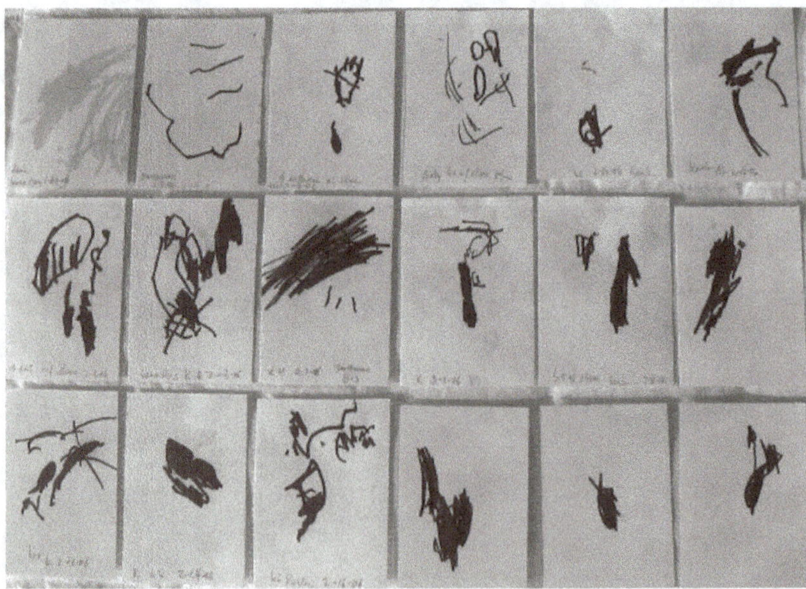

Figure 11.5 Keala's banana slug drawing series.

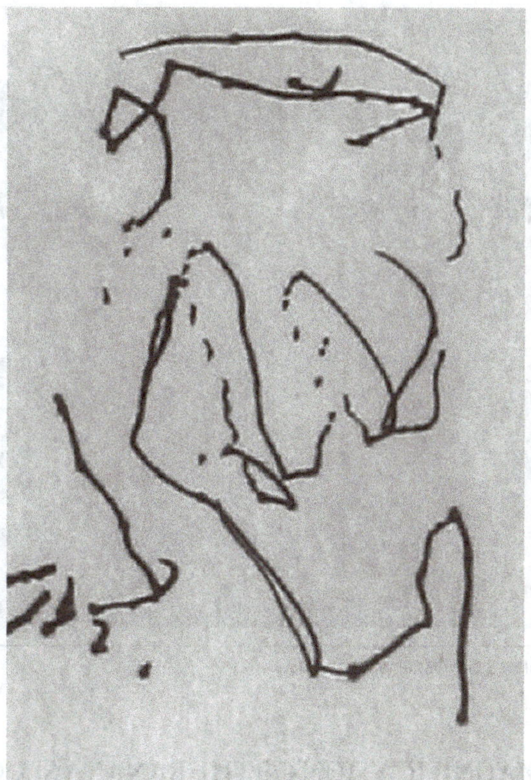

Figure 11.6 Porter's slug slime trail drawing.

the task for almost two months. Now Andrew could take the time and effort to examine the banana slug because he felt at ease with it. When he was able to carry it, and stroke it, his replicas began to take shape.

Keala's representation took shape when she picked up many baby banana slugs on the Ecology Trail. She repeatedly made many small clay representations of banana slugs. Each time she finished making them, she would state that those were babies. Porter had the initial shape of the banana slug, but like Keala and Andrew, the representations did not take definite form until February, after a month and a half of studying them. Porter was the only student who would not touch the banana slug, although he studied it up close if someone else held it.

The children's work and play with the clay became an effective three-dimensional complement to their two-dimensional drawings of the slugs. Taken together, the drawings and clay representations were artistic ways to revisit and reflect (Chalufour & Worth, 2003) on the slugs we had found on our nature walks.

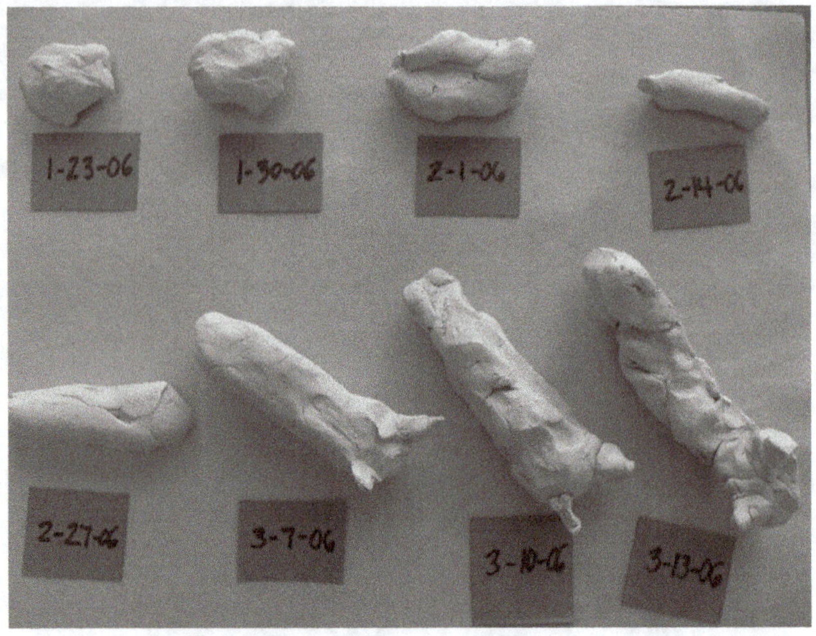

Figure 11.7 Andrew's clay banana slug series.

MAGNIFICATION OF THE BANANA SLUG

I continued to experiment with tools for the children to see the banana slugs in new ways and from different perspectives. I offered the children the chance to view the specimens on the overhead projector, which offered a new avenue for observation and discussion.

Banana Slug a Hundred Times Bigger

Keala took the banana slug container from the table to the overhead projector. This was something the children had never done before as most of our investigation took place on the table. Porter followed her and watched as she removed the lid. Keala dipped her hand, gently removed all baby banana slugs, and placed them on the overhead projector (Figure 11.8). As she laid them on the lighted surface all three heads simultaneously turned to the screen on the wall. Her passion with baby banana slugs had been ignited when she found some along the Ecology Trail. She only took the small ones and a single snail out of the container and left the big ones for Andrew to remove. As she looked at the screen, she commented on how similar the snail and her baby banana slugs looked. She rushed over to the screen and pointed

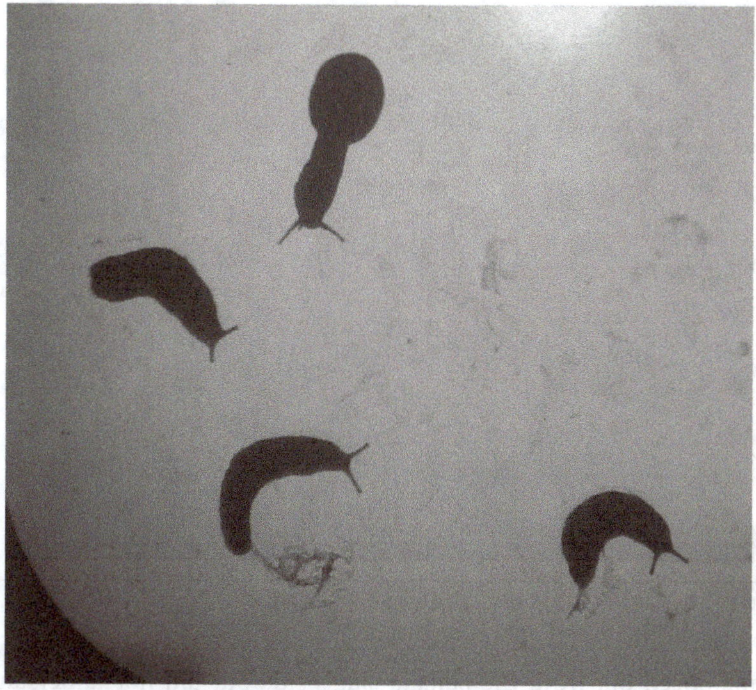

Figure 11.8 Keala's banana slugs magnified.

the features that resembled each other. "Look, the snail's head is the same as the babies," she called out. "Which one is the snail?" I asked. She pointed to it. "How do you know?" I questioned. "That ball is the shell," she replied.

After the initial surprise of the banana slugs' magnification, Andrew noticed the banana slugs' eyes that jutted out from the tops of their heads. He walked over to the screen, touched a banana slug's eyes, and looked perplexed about why its eyes did not retract like it had so many times before (see Figure 11.9). Andrew was fascinated with the banana slug's eyes and each time he "held" one on the screen he would gently tap them. He repeatedly poked and touched the shadow, hoping to elicit a response from the banana slug. He went back to the overhead projector when he saw that his actions on the screen were fruitless.

Porter, who had as of this date yet to touch the banana slugs, stood behind the overhead projector and watched Keala and Andrew manipulate them. Each time he saw his peers move them; he looked at the screen to check the results. The layer of slime projected on the screen prompted him to look for the hole on the banana slug. He knew

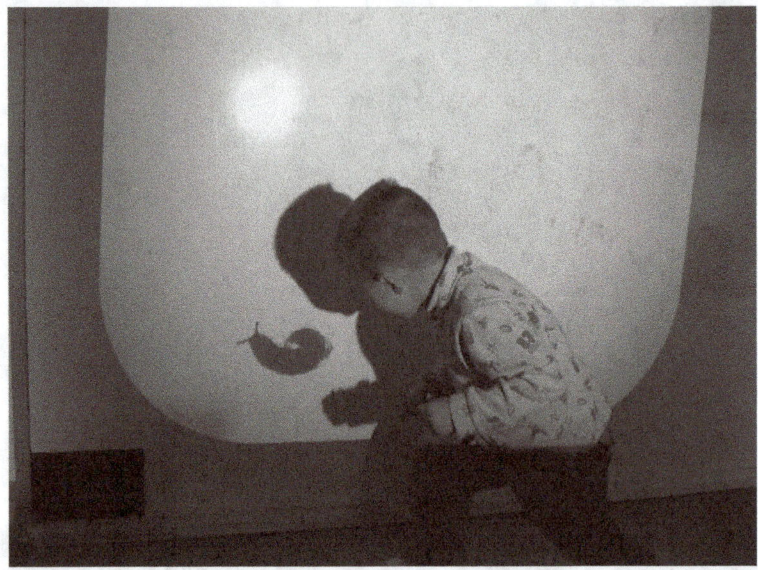

Figure 11.9 Andrew's fascination with the banana slug's eyes.

slime oozed out from the banana slug's side but did not understand why the hole was not visible on the screen. "Where's the hole?" he asked. Keala pointed to the banana slug on the overhead projector. "No, over there," Porter pointed to the screen. Andrew repeated, "Here, here," simultaneously pointing to the hole on the banana slug itself. Porter assumed the banana slug that lay on top of the overhead projector should also cast a three-dimensional image.

Each of the children had their own agenda for wanting to manipulate the creatures on the projector. Keala wanted to keep the baby slugs together while Andrew insisted on lining them up in a row. Porter pointed to the ones who slithered off the glass plate. As soon as the children moved the banana slugs to the spot they wanted, they would quickly check back to the screen to see how the projected image had changed. The children stayed with this newfound activity for over half an hour.

In our child-centered science curriculum, the children benefit from long activity periods that allow for independent planning and execution (Williams et al., 1987). The children took the initiative to examine specimens when they used the overhead projector as a new way to look at the specimens. Since toddlers learn primarily through their senses and through motoric manipulation, they needed the chance to touch, probe, and play to find out how things work (Williams et al., 1987).

SHARING OUR NATURE DISCOVERIES

As our nature study, and our exploration of banana slugs and other creatures continued, the children became more like real scientists as they shared their discoveries and specimens with others. Since there is an important social–emotional elements to nature learning, each child went about this sharing in a different way. For instance, when we first started collecting specimens, sharing was not an easy task for Andrew. If anyone tried to get a glimpse of what was inside a container he held, he would run away with it or get upset at the child. He hoarded specimens other children found and on Fridays when he knew the teachers had to release them back to the trails, he begged his mother to take the banana slugs home.

I observed his behavior during the first month of specimen collection and simply concluded that his passion for living creatures was intense – too intense to let others in sometimes. However, as weeks turned into months, he began to mature and would share some specimens with peers. The turning point for him to allow others into his world of science happened when Susie placed a slug on his hand. Up until that point, Andrew had never touched any of the specimens he collected. Once he realized the slugs did not hurt when they touched him, he was then able to hold one. It was then that I discovered that he probably needed to keep everyone at bay because he would not be able to retrieve a specimen if it was taken away.

It wasn't until our second month of collecting specimens that Andrew shared the creatures with peers, parents, and teachers. Andrew beamed as he stepped out to the toddler yard with a container full of specimens in his hands. One day when the older preschool children passed our yard to enter theirs, Jennifer, a preschool teacher, approached Andrew. Andrew gathered some slugs and worms and was about to put them inside the container. She asked, "What do you have there?" He replied, "A nanna A nanna." He picked up a slug, reached for her hand, and tried to put it on her hand. The actions he took mirrored Susie's when she encouraged him to touch the specimen. When Jennifer told him she only wanted to see it, she replaced her hands with Terence's so Andrew shared the slug with him instead. "What is it?" Jennifer asked. Terence joined Andrew and answered, "Slug, you find it there." Andrew took her hand and led her to the flower planters. He tipped one over and showed her the beetles crawling and the crickets jumping. "That's where you found your slugs?" Jennifer asked.

Terence took his slug and held it directly in front of her face. "That's slime," he pointed out. Jennifer questioned, "Slime?" "Yeah, so it could move," answered Terence. Andrew and Terence shared where the specimen could be found and what the slime was used for. Although Jennifer was not ready to touch the slug, Terence engaged her in a brief lesson.

Meanwhile, Andrew walked over to the fence and tried to get Gail, another teacher's, attention. Andrew held up the container so that she could look inside. He picked up another slug for her to hold. He wanted to share his discoveries with other teachers on the yard because he had finally overcome his fear of holding creatures. His level of confidence in collecting specimens made him a leader in the toddler room. When other children found something of interest, they called on Andrew to place it in the container. The reciprocity between the other children and Andrew grew as they invited each other to join in their exploration. Looking for spiders and other creatures became a regular routine for the toddlers, and I sensed that they could hone their investigative skills in any indoor or outdoor environment. They became less interested in the toys and more in finding spiders along the window screens. The toddlers continued to forge their own curriculum as they probed crevices with twigs, flipped things over, and studied the container of specimens.

THE ART OF SCIENTIFIC DISCUSSION

The activities of walking, drawing, sculpting, and magnification eventually come together for toddlers, and the integration of these activities promotes nature sharing and discussion between peers.

For example, Porter, Andrew, and Keala shared a conversation while they sculpted their clay slugs that shows their emerging scientific knowledge from our walks and other activities.

Mabel: What does a banana slug like to eat?

Porter: Worms.

Keala: No, birds like to eat worms. Remember they were out on the yard when it was raining.

Porter: Uh huh.

Keala: Slugs likes to eat grass and leaves. Snails has eyes, see. They don't have antennae.

Mabel: Snails don't have antennae? Then do banana slugs have antennae?

Porter: Banana slugs have eyes, no antennae!

Keala: Uh huh, banana slugs have eyes and antennae. You see the eyes over here and the antennae over here.

Porter: No, that holds the eyes up.
Mabel: You think those things are to hold the eyes up?
Porter: Uh huh, banana slugs don't have antennae. Oh it's going to bite me.
Mabel: Does a banana slug bite?
Keala: No. A bee stings me on my feet.
Mabel: Does a banana slug sting?
Keala: No, it doesn't have wings. It only has slime. A bee has a stinger. Look at the slime. (Pointing to the dried up slime along the top lid of the container)
Mabel: What does the banana slug use the slime for?
Porter: For the teeth.
Keala: (looking at the banana slugs) For the bottom, right there.
Mabel: For the bottom?
Keala: Yeah.
Mabel: Bottom of what?
Keala: So it could move.

In this conversation Keala shared her knowledge of the banana slugs with her peers and me. She reminded Porter that birds eat worms and banana slugs do not. She points out banana slugs have eyes and antennae. Porter corrects her and states that banana slugs do in fact have eyes, but not antennae. He theorizes that the rods above the banana slugs' head are what hold the eyes up. Keala settles the dispute about how banana slugs can not bite because they do not have wings. She assumes that anything with wings can sting people.

Although Porter thinks slime is used for the banana slug's teeth, Keala shares that the slime is used for their mobility. This kind of conversation, in part guided by my questions and probes, allow Porter and Keala to organize their thoughts and motivate them to ask questions. Through these kinds of scientific conversations, toddlers come to new understandings, which are more reasonable, though still not entirely accurate, than their old ones. As I document children's discussions over time, I can see how their observations become more focused, their vocabulary are used more skillfully to communicate their ideas, and how they share what they think is real and what they hear from peers enhances their discoveries.

CLOSING THOUGHTS – WHAT WE LEARNED

Over my years of teaching, I have noticed that many young children come to school with limited direct experiences with natural environments. Toddlers especially may have little understanding and great fears about what may happen to them in their encounters with nature. Young children tend to bond with what is familiar and comfortable. If they are to develop a sense of connectedness with the natural world, they must be given frequent opportunities to experience the outdoors – time to get to know it as a place of wonder, comfort, and joy as well as a place of danger. To know the beauty and warmth of the sun, they need gradual exposure to the world of nature, such as by having the chance to stand outdoors on a sunny day. Getting to know and care about nature and developing a sense of kinship with it requires positive experiences with the natural world during the early years of life.

In the past when we took the children for a nature walk, our main purpose was for the children to exercise their legs and expend their energy. Going on walks meant that the children had the opportunity to be away from the school atmosphere, take in beautiful surroundings, and be familiar with the natural environment. But rarely did the children want to stop and investigate the specimens that greeted us along the trail because we breezed through the walks.

After some reflection and discussion with my co-teachers, I wanted to see the toddlers' real interests when they walked outdoors. What caught their attention? What and where did they want to explore? How much did they comprehend when we started to introduce specimens from the trails? Was this going to affect them in their overall development and understanding of nature studies? The first step we took was to simply slow down when we walked. How did we achieve this? We had the children sit down at the base of the trail and asked what they might see as we hike along the trail. We made observations of the children and documented their behavior when we introduced live creatures. The children are now more focused on what is on the ground, and they have honed their investigative skills. Our goals for walks have changed and we now go on walks with a purpose – to collect specimens, bring them back to school, and delve deeper into our developmentally appropriate scientific investigations. And their observational skills also transfer to our school yard as the children continue to search the toddler yard for other specimens to examine.

Socially and interpersonally, the toddlers have more skills and motivation to collaborate, cooperate, and exchange knowledge with each other (Gandini & Edwards, 2001). Their collaborating with a partner strengthens their process of analysis and interpretation. As we listen in and document this verbal and nonverbal sharing, the children are more likely to invite us into their scientific world. Finally, children's scientific knowledge unfolds if the nature experiences are not only repeated, but also extended. The fact that they concentrated for several months on their clay sculptures and progressive drawings shows that if they are interested in some aspect of nature, they will represent and reflect on their learning in new ways. The inquiry tools that I used – making careful written notes, audiotaping children's conversations, and taking constant photographs – all increased my powers of observation and helped me learn how capable and sophisticated toddlers can be in their science exploration and nature learning.

REFERENCES

Chalufour, I., & Worth, K. (2003). *Discovering nature with young children.* Newton, Massachusetts: Education Development Center, Inc.

Danoff-Burg, J. A. (2002). Be a bee and other approaches to introducing young children to entymology. *Young Children, 57*(5), 42–46.

Edwards, C., Gandini, L., & Forman, G. (Eds.). (1998). *The hundred languages of children: Advanced reflections on Reggio Emilia approach to early childhood education.* Greenwich, CT: Ablex.

Flavell, J. H., Miller, P. H., & Miller, S. A. (2001). *Cognitive development* 4th ed. Upper Saddle River, NJ: Prentice Hall.

Gandini, L., & Edwards, C. P. (2001). *Bambini: The Italian approach to infant/toddler care.* New York: Teacher College Press.

Kupetz, B., & Twiest, M. (2000). Nature, literature, and young children: A natural combination. *Young Children, 55*(1), 59–63.

Sisson, E. A. (1982). *Nature with children of all ages.* New York: Prentice Press Hall.

Williams, R, Rockwell, R., & Sherwood, E. (1987). *Mudpies to magnets.* Mt. Rainier, MD: Gryphon House, Inc.

Worth, K., & Grollman, S. (2003). *Worms, shadows, and whirlpools.* Newton, MA: Education Development Center, Inc.

12

FROM FEAR TO FREEDOM

Risk and Learning in a Forest School

Heather B. Taylor

Box 12.1 Key Science and Nature Elements

- Learning science through exploration and discovery in forest schools
- Life cycles, seasons, ecosystems, and microclimates
- Animal habitats
- Decomposition and plant growth
- Content knowledge and understanding that emerges from long-term, repeated exposure to a large, child-accessible, natural areas
- Tool use and risk-taking in nature

Box 12.2 Key Inquiry Elements

- Use of a cycle of inquiry system
- Use of photographs, videos, and notes to reflect and write about each day's nature activities
- Children taking their own photographs for documentation and reflection
- Recording children's conversations via written notes, audio-taping, and videotaping

- Collecting and examining found objects and artifacts
- Children and Heather consult field guides and other nature resources for information and inquiry collaboration

It took me quite a long time to learn that nature itself is the curriculum. Children act just as wildly on a windy day in a forest school as in a traditional classroom, but at the Forest School where I recently taught for three years, they really felt and experienced what wind meant: ruffled hair, lightweight items blowing away, and cold hands when it's wet. My background in biology has served me well, as has my 16 years of working with young children as an indoor, garden, and forest school teacher. Eleven of these years have been solely outdoors. When a hummingbird flies nearby or a dead rat is found, the children come running and shouting my name. They know I will share in their sense of wonder and answer their questions honestly, along with providing titbits of information for those who show interest, helping them gain knowledge and a source of comparison for future experiences.

In this role, I view myself as an elder, one who shares a sense of trust and wonder with the children. I agree with Gita Jayewardene, in Chapter 4, who writes of the importance of "nature elders" who foster children's interests and who may be called upon to show the way for others who may have strong emotional reactions when confronted with the unfamiliar, such as snails in an urban environment. Children come to know who these elders are and share in their excitement and wonder. These elders tend to be those who can help others learn to mitigate risk through knowledge of the environment and the ability to define risk versus hazard (MacEachren, 2013). Some consider the relationship between the adults and children as one of the most important aspects of a forest school (Maynard, 2007), which places a high value on incorporating a true respect for the child and developing relationships based on mutual trust (Forest School Canada, 2014; Warden, 2010). Children's freedom to move about their environments is rooted in the physical, economic, and sociocultural worlds their families reside in (Kyttä, 2004; Louv, 2008). I support children's freedom and the ways in which nature serves as an innate teacher in my role as an Outdoor Educator.

MY EXPERIENCES WITH NATURE

I came to this work with a background in biological interests and outdoor recreation. Having grown up in California in the 1970s,

I spent the largest part of my free time outside the house. My childhood friends and I were mostly in our own yards, running or biking through the streets and on the levees or going to local parks, swimming pools, and open school yards. In public school, there was plenty of free time during recess and lunch and we were left to our own devices on the yard, playing however we wished on the playgrounds, fields, or under the trees. My skills as a natural scientist were developed by collecting insects, fish, polliwogs, and rocks, climbing trees, digging in dirt, sliding down hills, and splashing in waterways, along with all the time in the world. A rusty coffee can was a place to store random treasures on my bedroom shelf. My family embraced the sciences and I was allowed to keep small animals for a week before returning them to their natural homes.

My love for outdoor play continued into my teens. At age 13, we moved to a California State Park where my mother had gotten a job. My sister and I could play in the walnut orchard behind our house. We often rerouted the small creek, walked our dogs wherever we liked, and rode our BMX bikes all throughout the park on weekdays when park visitation was low. I ran on trails throughout Northern California as a member of my high school's cross country team. This is all to say that my sister, friends, and I felt a sense of freedom throughout our childhoods. Adult attention was largely absent and we were trusted to be safe and to come home when we noticed that it was dark enough out that cars were turning on their headlights.

My love for science continued through and beyond my college years, as I worked as a biology lab aide often focused on the care of animals. Later, I took on positions that were more administrative, but for me that was too far removed from what I considered to be dirty, fun, and rewarding work of directly working with animals.

My childhood story is similar to that of other natural historians. Harry Greene (2013), John Muir (1912), and Jane Goodall (Goodall & Hudson, 2014) spent their childhoods on the land and in nature without constant adult supervision, which connected them with life cycles and seasons, and created pathways to become naturalists and teachers. My current work is conducted in busy, urban environments where parents are fearful of leaving children alone. I have a strong desire to allow children to tap into similar experiences, and to find a balance between fostering their personal paths of experimentation and learning while also being the adult charged with their upbringing while they're away from their families.

Teaching was my second career. I taught in a private preschool classroom and continued my education. In my teaching role at Duck's

Nest Preschool, there was an emphasis on providing a beautiful environment because it was recognized that the environment was also a teacher. Early in my tenure there, I attended a workshop where I first learned about forest kindergartens from Robin Moore (Moore, Cosco, Kepez, & Demir, 2008). He talked about a forest school at a public park in Munich where children played in the snow all day and peed on trees. As I sought more ways to connect children with the outdoors, I became the Duck's Nest Preschool Garden Teacher when the school took over a vacant lot on the next block. Each of the school's five classrooms would visit the garden once a week.

On occasion, I became exposed to a sense of fear from some parents and visitors in the school garden. After some concerns about climbing height, the teachers were turned into climbing monitors. Capable children were denied their desires, and lesser-abled children did not have such lofty heights as aspiration. The sense of disappointment for children and teachers was palpable.

Around the time I was beginning this first outdoor program, Richard Louv (2008) wrote *Last child in the woods*, lamenting the loss of the childhood freedom I and others had experienced and the current lack of nature connection. At some point adults had lost their confidence, feeling as though children needed to be closely watched, kept in structured activities, and not allowed to be bored or have the run of public spaces (Kyttä, 2004; Louv, 2008). Forest school spaces are inherently more risky than the traditional classroom. Teachers carry emergency contact information, charged cell phones, emergency plans, and first aid kits to enhance safety. We come to know that as "they learn to self-regulate: as children experience more risky activities and terrain, they learn to determine for themselves whether something feels safe or not, rather than look externally to adults to decide this for them" (Forest School Canada, 2014). I agree with Bernard Spiegal (2017) that children:

> want and need to take risks. They do this "naturally" in the sense that, left to their own devices, they seek out and create encounters that carry degrees of risk or uncertainty. This process of risk-taking necessarily entails exploration, discovery, and learning about oneself, one's capabilities, and the wider world. To take a risk is to assert one's autonomy and power of agency. It is to learn by doing that actions have consequences. It is an aspect of moral education. Play and risk-taking are creative acts.

As I gained experience in outdoor teaching, the science curriculum I'd developed floated away and I set up areas similar to those found in a classroom – reading, art, and music, along with a tool table. Far later, I came to realize that these typical classroom areas, these *things*, were distracting the children from what was really important: nature connection and social interaction. Children were not in need of being taught in traditional curricular areas; they needed to learn with their whole selves. This was a far different set of values and experiences than that taught in the child development classes I'd taken. Soon enough, I removed the curriculum-based areas of the outdoor classroom and eventually left this original educational setting to teach at the forest school. There, I was able to put more effort into trusting the environment as teacher. Each day I came to school with an idea or project in mind, such as "making leaf necklaces" or "finding out how many petals are on the flowers." I quickly discovered that these were not activities in which the children were interested. I kept the ideas in mind in case a quick redirection in play was necessary, but I never did end up using those ideas and it became apparent that my own curricular ideas were never better than what the children had in mind. It helped me to develop the ways of teaching I was coming to discover on my own: the environment and the children themselves do the educating. A branch breaking off a tree, muddy hillsides to climb, blackberries warmed by the sun, ready to pick and eat, a favorite toy or book a child wanted to share, all represent examples of the curriculum that was ever-changing, unplanned, and ultimately meaningful. I was a facilitator. This new job and these new methods were a risk in my career and I realized that various levels of fear, small and large feelings, both real and imagined, existed within all of us. To be a successful forest school educator I would need to learn to address those feelings. Methods I used included deep breathing, moving in closer, reflecting with the group, colleagues, or just myself, and writing.

MY INVESTIGATIONS INTO OUTDOOR SCHOOLS AND INQUIRY

I decided early in my career as a teacher to document what the children and I were doing. When I worked indoors, I included examples of children's artwork, classroom displays, and note cards with quotes on them, all of which I stored in binders. This became more difficult when I began working outdoors, as the practical methods of storing and displaying things were more challenging. My methods now include editing daily notes, photographs, and reflections so that, by the end of each week, I have formed a solid story that represents a tale of the time my students and I had together. I provide documentation of each week's activities in the form of emails, including photographs, that I send to children's families and coworkers. The remainder of the photographs and videos are organized on a hard drive. I review these as the programs are still in progress, again at the end, and later whenever I want to see how much my teaching methods and physical spaces had changed over time. These photographs, emails, and binders are the records I hold of my history as a teacher.

As I conducted the research for this project, I worked at a forest school serving an ethnically and financially diverse community in the San Francisco Bay Area. Programs included a mixed age preschool and kindergarten, a weekly program for families, and summer camps for children over the age of three years. In this chapter, I discuss specific data collected over two weeks of camp in 2017. My groups of children were ages five through eight, attending Monday through Friday. With the exception of morning meeting/snack time and lunch time, the bulk of the days were spent as free play.

My project was guided by a set of questions focused on nature education, fear, and freedom: Could I step back and allow the children to discover and choose their own interests? Would the children form cohesive groups that worked together? Would they choose adventures that might be perceived as dangerous? Why do I regularly experience a sense of fear as my students do something new or out of character for themselves? Could I push through my feelings and perceptions of fear as well as that of others?

I adopted Broderick and Hong's (2011) cycle of inquiry system to provide a framework for my investigations. The first step is in recording observations of the children. In doing so, I took photographs with my iPhone throughout each day to document individual and group play. I also took notes with pen and paper and on the iPhone, which were then incorporated into weekly emails. The children and I occasionally used the iPhone for videography as well. I designed my weekly roster form to include a writing area at the bottom for taking notes and writing about each day's highlights to share with families. The second step is developing hypotheses, which I did by editing photos daily and uploading them onto a Mac computer. Looking at the photographs, videos, and notes allowed me to reflect and write about each day's activities.

This daily review facilitated the planning of research questions, which is the third step of the cycle of inquiry and helps guide a direction for activities. As each week went on, I began the fourth step of the process, which is planning the interventions to guide the children's thinking. I thought of some ideas and included them in items for discussion in our class' morning meetings. The last step in the process involves setting up and facilitating play, which is comprised of the children and I planning ideas of possible activities as themes emerge and solidify. The children in my groups are very much involved in this entire process, and present their own ideas readily when they arrived in camp at the beginning of each day and at our morning meetings.

As part of the data analysis, I read books written by naturalists such as *Tracks and shadows: Field biology as art* (Greene, 2013), *Seeds of hope: Wisdom and wonder from the world of plants* (Goodall and Hudson, 2014), and *The story of my boyhood and youth* (Muir, 1912). I also read the works of other scientists such as *Free to learn: Why unleashing the instinct to play will make our children happier, more self-reliant, and better students for life* (Gray, 2013) and journalists (e.g., *Last child in the woods* (Louv, 2008)). I was able to communicate with some of these resources via email and social media. Their suggestions helped me gain focus for the research and my teaching.

In the sections below, I take a narrative approach in describing and reflecting on my data. In particular, I highlight two stories, "Barnyard Animals" and "Trout."

In the first story, "Barnyard Animals," I present a series of events that caused me worry as I practiced giving up control of my group's activities within a large public space. I wondered how I could move past my feelings of unease. In the second story, "Trout," the group of students took on a cooking project involving fire. I had a desire for the children to do what they wanted, but also needed to find ways to mitigate risks to bodily injury. Both adventures involved children's decision making and planning, built upon child-led conversations that started earlier in the week, and are unusual for groups of young children. At various times the children, families, and myself felt a sense of fear as we watched others with more confidence pushing boundaries, then subsequently pushed our own boundaries outward. Following are examples of these adventures.

"BARNYARD ANIMALS" – A STORY OF INDEPENDENCE

"Heather, come look at this!" – Violet

Our camps were within a vast, popular urban park that was familiar to many local children. One particular group of children enrolled for a week adored animals, often collecting banana slugs in a deep canyon, bringing them out to crawl in obstacle courses they created, then put them back where they were found when they were done. They expressed interest in hiking to see the farm animals they knew were nearby. Often their families were arriving later in the morning, so after the children planned all week, the families all arrived early for the hike on Friday at the children's bidding. They figured that an early start to the day would allow them to maximize their time at the farm. We started out so early that it wasn't even snack time until we were well on our way on the trail. They first led the way across the street, down a trail past the blackberry bushes, and across to a favorite climbing tree, called Mr. Nobody. Since I was the only one familiar with the next part of the trail, I guided them further along and across a parking lot. The children began to get tired, hungry, and thirsty, so we decided to stop at a quiet, shady place that appealed to us all for a break to climb, drink water, and eat snacks (see Figure 12.1).

At that point we were close enough to the farm for surroundings to look familiar to the children again, so the group then led the way to the farm animals. School buses were arriving as the parking lot was filling up and I began to feel nervous about the numbers of people coming. The rest of our camp time together had been peaceful overall, and I was unsure about how we might get mixed up within large groups of people. I verbalized this sense of apprehension and stated that we should probably stick together. The children shared their thoughts and we decided together that once we arrived at the farm area that we would find a meeting place in case any of us became separated. This little farm area in the Regional Park is less than one acre. There is a small barn where a few animals live which can be touched and fed over a divider, and just behind

Figure 12.1 Trailside snacking.

the barn is a gentle fenced slope where goats and sheep live. There are also some shade trees, a restroom, and a few benches.

Once we got situated, we found that designating a meeting place was very easy to do, as there was an unused bench area off to the side. As the children were becoming hot and thirsty again, we all took our backpacks off and drank some water. I suggested to the children that it seemed like a safe place out of other people's way and that we could leave our belongings and find one another if we should become separated. They all agreed.

While most were excited to see the cows and wander inside the barn, Leah became very fearful and agitated at the thought of having to pass by the cows and couldn't pry herself away from the bench. I nervously wondered whether I could leave her on the bench alone and whether she would be okay, as I wanted to go inside the barn, too. I thought other families and caregivers present might question her or me. I decided that verbalizing our plan could help mitigate these worries, and explained that I was going to go inside the barn and that I would come back to check on her. When I peeked through the doors I saw she was sitting, looking around, and did not appear upset. On the other side of the barn I could watch her from above the fences as I also watched the group near me. Everyone was doing whatever they needed to do to feel comfortable (see Figure 12.2).

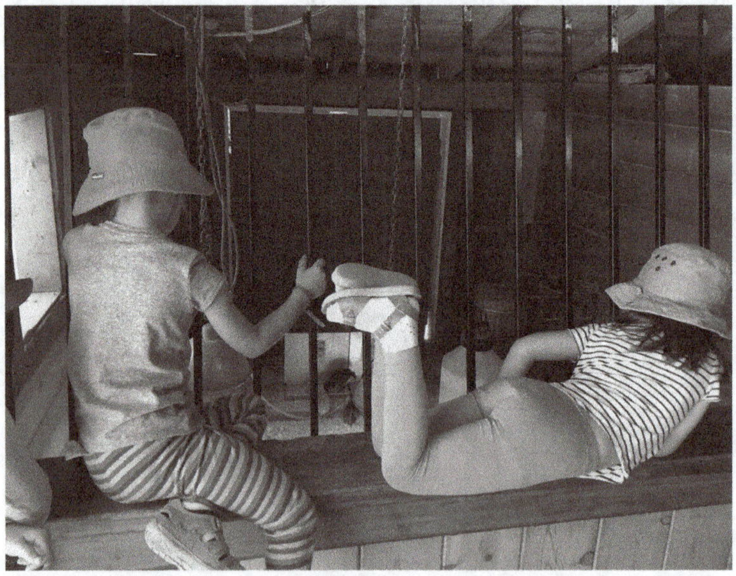

Figure 12.2 Inside the barn.

My group was ready to move along to see goats. Violet and Desi came with me to check on Leah while others went on ahead. I explained to her that the other children wanted to see the goats, that they were around the corner, and that I wouldn't be able to see her from there. I encouraged her to come see the goats with us and she agreed.

The children who had come back with me wanted to stay in the shade for a while and I pondered whether they would they be okay, too, and whether other people might question the children being left without an adult caregiver within view. The children had big smiles on their faces and I thought they wanted to try being by themselves also. As with Leah before, I explained where I would be. As Leah and I were about to round the corner, Violet and Desi noticed me look back at them, "Teacher Heather, we're going to the bathroom!" I gave them a thumbs up, trusting that all would be fine even though I felt hesitant about them going to the bathroom on their own. Leah and I went back up the hill. She remained close by my side as we observed families feeding the goats. After a time, I told them that I was going to check on the other two. When I peered around the corner, I noticed that they were quietly sitting next to their backpacks, looking content. I left them to their solitude without their knowing that I had looked after them. When Erik expressed an interest in moving further up the hill to see sheep, I told him that I'd let Violet and Desi know, thinking they may want to join him.

Leah began looking nervous again; I could tell she was torn between wanting to see the sheep and staying by my side. I told her I would send the other girls up and that she should go on ahead. To my surprise and delight, she did! I was sure it was the work we had done to establish relationships with one another that helped her along. She had come to trust me and to become friends with Erik. This was a big move for her and her level of confidence. I went and told the other children about the sheep and we walked up the hill together. Once there, I explained that I'd go back down the hill, out of sight, to be by the backpacks, also desiring other farm visitors to know that these backpacks were, indeed, attended. I left the children up the hill and practiced deep breathing when I felt nervous. My normal role as the nature elder was less in need on this day, with this group. When I looked, I saw that the children were having fun watching the sheep. The next time I checked, I noticed they were talking with a family so I decided to go nearer. One of the children in my group and the family's child were thrilled that they not only were wearing the same mismatched socks, but had even worn them on the same feet! All was well.

Once I discovered that everyone was all smiles, I decided to try leaving them alone again, with this family we had just met knowing about it, and left them with the camera from my phone so they could take their own photos. I told them that I was going to set the timer on my phone for ten minutes and then opened the camera, asking if they'd be able to take turns until I got back from checking at the bench again. They agreed and I went down the hill, around the corner. I later saw them giggling in the pathway. When the ten minutes had passed, they ran down to me, giggling and laughing, wild with tales from their adventure. Their story: They wanted to take pictures and then went to take a video, which they accidentally made into a "slo-mo." When they watched the video, they thought there was a cow mooing in the background, but it was Erik saying, "I'm dying!," so slowly! They loved their time alone, getting to do their own thing. I think we all felt proud with their newly gained independence (see Figures 12.3 and 12.4).

On our hike back we stopped for lunch at another shady location. The family who had interacted with us at the farm found us and struck up a conversation. The mother said I seemed relaxed and that the children had more freedom than others. She stated that she wanted the same thing for her own daughter. I was relieved that she sought us out and that her opinion of our group and activities was so positive.

Figure 12.3 Children's photographs.

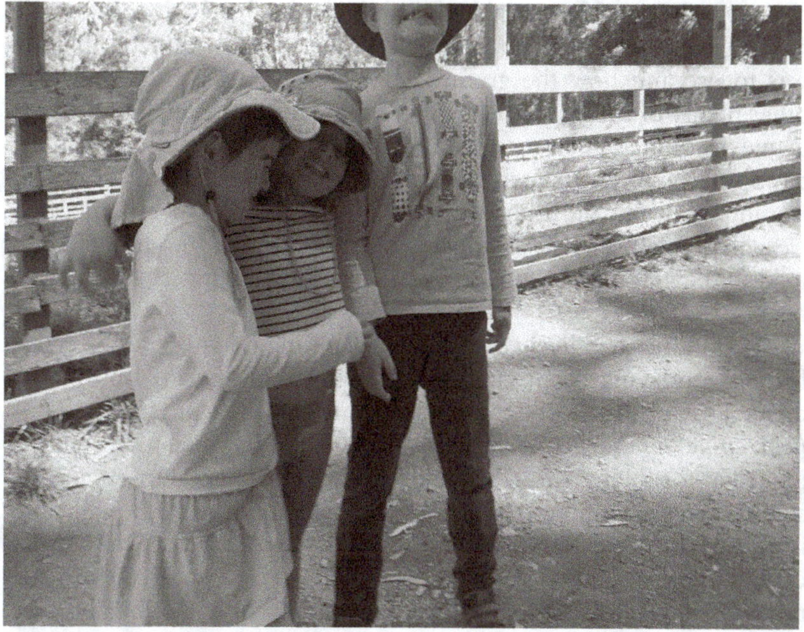

Figure 12.4 Children's photographs.

"TROUT" – A STORY OF ACTIVE LEARNING AND COMMUNAL RISK-TAKING

I felt emboldened by the previous week's campers. The following week's group happened to be enamored with fish. Nate had recently been visiting family on the East Coast and had caught an eel. He remembered from last summer a sign by the creek in our park with a picture of a trout on it. Early in the week, the group decided upon a fishing trip and hoped we could catch a fish. In preparation for our excursion, many in the group experimented with fire making in a barbeque pit at our site.

I had recently purchased a fire starting steel. Many children were able to make sparks and contributed to tinder, kindling, and wood piles. Anyone who engaged in working with the fire steel did so at the barbeque pit, and I also had them take off their hats and jackets, as I was initially fearful they would ignite. As we all worked to learn how to use the fire steel, the children regulated themselves in terms of space given to someone trying to start the fire and taking turns. I wanted to see if they would persist in using the tool even though it was difficult. While most of us only got a brief spark, two children got a small flame to appear, but no one was able to start a lasting fire. I felt comfortable moving farther away once I was able to see just how difficult the tool was to use and how the group kept themselves safe by giving each other plenty of space and behaving calmly around the area of the barbeque. I became much more confident in the group's safety. The next day Kev brought one match from his home. This was his third summer in camp with me and I knew him and his grandmother well. Because we all had established a relationship of trust, his grandmother told him to keep the match in his pocket until we were ready for its use. Indeed, he did.

The children had lively discussions, planning on going to the creek, fishing, returning to our campsite, cooking, and figuring out how to divide a trout so that all could have some. I had a copy of *The Laws field guide to the Sierra Nevada* (Laws, 2007), which the children looked at for themselves. The children reviewed illustrations and were sure it would be rainbow trout that we fished for. The site we hiked to is a resource protection area, so those at the creek needed to be very careful to remain quiet, stay on rocks, and take care not to disturb any mud. If they were careless, either accidentally or intentionally, they would have to move away from the immediate area. Nate brought his homemade fishing pole from home, which consisted of a bamboo pole, string, and a Lego tied to the end. Everyone took turns with it but otherwise held sticks carefully over the water, held their hands together to catch fish, or used hats as nets. Kev improved his chances of catching a fish by connecting a blackberry bramble to the Lego as a hook and attaching a worm when it was his turn to use the fishing pole (see Figures 12.5 and 12.6).

As the elder of the group, I practiced encouragement in getting to our goal of seeking fish. When all were quiet and peaceful, trout appeared! Dozens of small fry, about 1.5 inches long. Amazing! I wondered aloud whether if we caught one that we would be able to divide it to eat. Leah noted, "Larger ones have more meat." After more than an hour, without trout in hand, it was time to head to a picnic site to eat lunch and pick blackberries. Afterward, we returned to our normal gathering site. As it neared time for families to pick their children up, Kev expressed an interest in starting a fire with his match. Based on our relationship built over the three summers, his trustworthy nature, and his previous experience with campfires, I knew he could safely succeed in building a fire. The children gathered up their collection of tinder, kindling, and dead branches, while Kev set them up carefully in the fire pit, as designated areas are the only safe places to have fires. We all rejoiced as Kev was able to get a fire going with that one match.

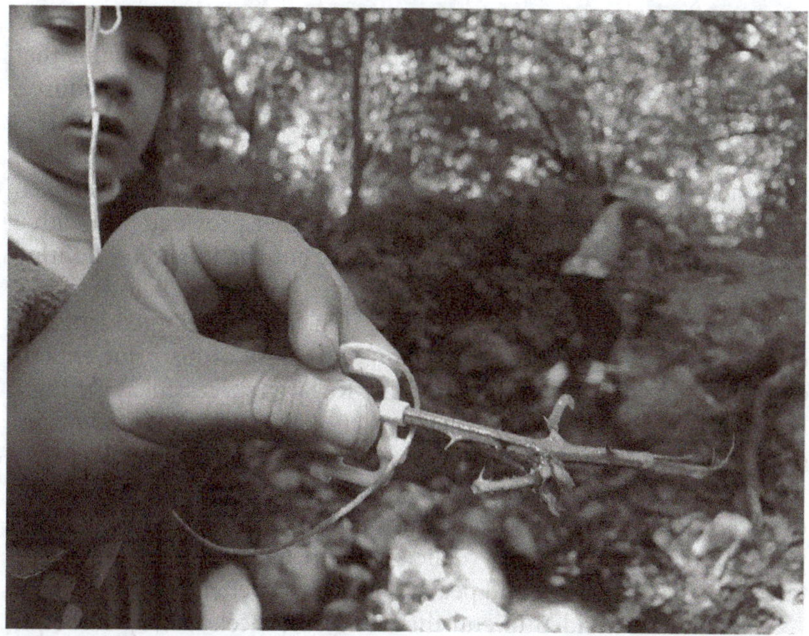

Figure 12.5 Homemade fish hook.

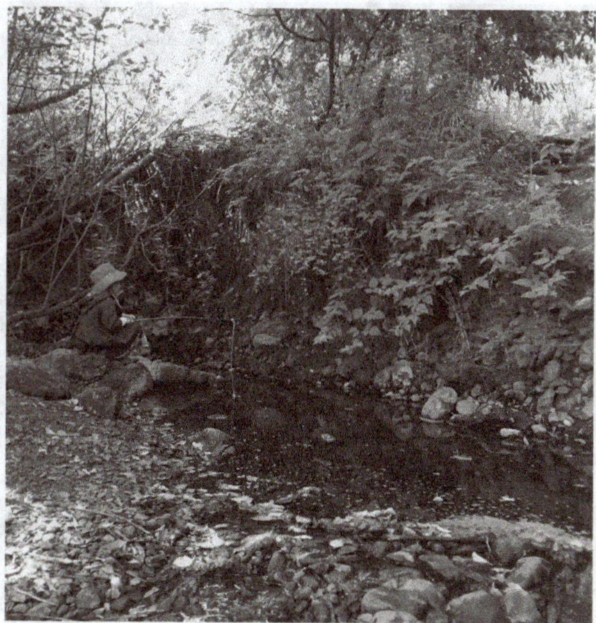

Figure 12.6 Fishing.

When we were done, we doused the flames with excessive amounts of water from the bathroom, making sure we did not leave remains that even felt warm to the touch, since California is susceptible to wildfires. Everyone decided to barbeque the next day (see Figure 12.7).

Fire starting proved fascinating enough that all the children talked with their families about it. Nate asked his father to pack him a chicken skewer, which he kept on ice. Kev's grandmother provided him with a packet of matches. Everyone who felt ready got chances to try lighting them. Those who had been scared observed for longer before trying, while others decided not to try at all and instead contributed by gathering dead brush to keep the fire going. Because of his prior experiences in camp and with his family, only Kev was successful at getting a lasting flame. We contributed the chicken skewer and other food from our lunches. Since fire is so hot, everyone knew innately how close they felt safe getting to the fire pit, or how long a stick to use to place items on the grill, or who to ask to do such a thing for them. A happy surprise was learning just how delicious barbequed fruit is! The apple tasted just like apple pie, and peaches were even better.

The children decided to end the week with a celebratory barbeque potluck, which was entirely planned and prepared by the children.

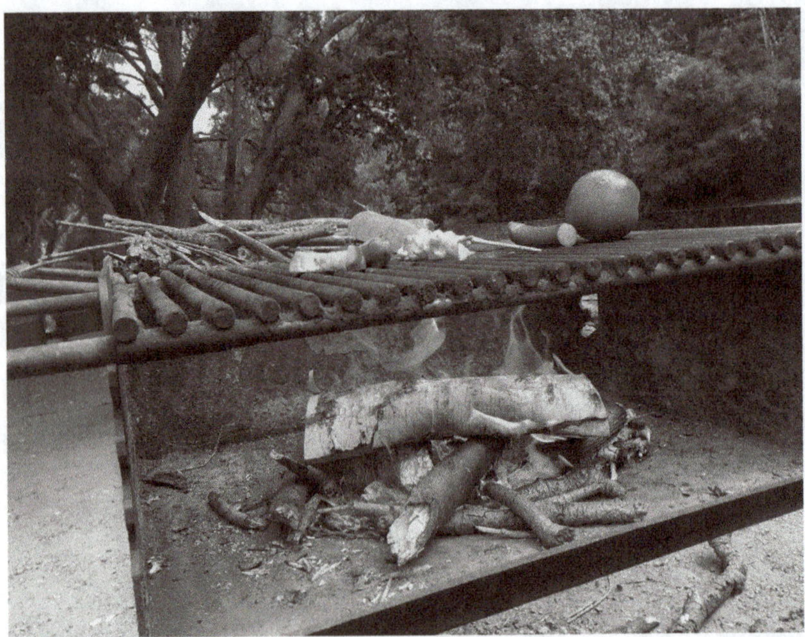

Figure 12.7 Shared food on a child-created fire.

They had been doing such a great job of communicating with their families that I decided not to interfere by laying out and communicating the plans myself. Once again, my job as an elder was less in need with this group.

Having told his grandmother about our plans, Kev asked to arrive early for our week-ending festivities to get the fire started. Everyone had asked their families to help them prepare food to bring to camp. Our meal included a trout, hot dogs and sausages, and all the sides and fixings. With eight-year-old Kev taking on the role of the group leader and organizer, the children cooked it all to perfection! My only contribution was putting foil down on the grill since the fish had started to break apart. Kev even removed its bones when it was done and plucked the meat off the skeleton, placing the tasty chunks on a platter so everyone could access it more easily. Nate tried the fish's eyeballs, which had turned white. Kev said that he regularly eats fish heads, including the eyeballs, and thought they were good. In this case, though, Nate's face turned from delight to disgust as he tasted and felt the new texture in his mouth. Despite this, he hung in there and ate both of the eyeballs, reporting on the sensations to his curious friends, since none of the rest of us had eaten them before (see Figure 12.8).

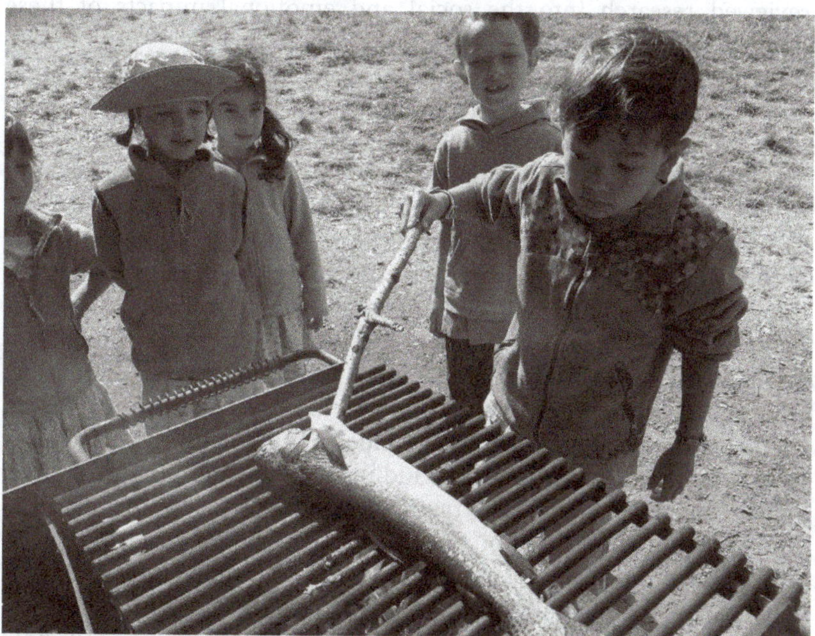

Figure 12.8 Young chefs.

After these experiences, I finally felt fully confident in moving away from planned curriculum and embraced the opportunity and discovery that child-directed learning provided. I could not have planned richer activities during those weeks. I applaud the children's creativity and openness and appreciate their families' support and encouragement. As they excitedly told the stories of what they had done and shared leftover food with their families at the end of the day, the sense of joy and freedom was palpable in their voices and on their faces.

CLOSING AND LOOKING TO THE FUTURE

These informal teaching methods led me to truly understand one aspect of teaching outdoors that cannot be understated: the necessity for the teacher to have absolute agency in planning and curriculum (Lytle, 2012). The very nature of free time is organic and flowing and an educator needs to have enough awareness, knowledge, and flexibility for what's needed at any given moment. Being dedicated to working toward what's best for everyone in the group is a common thread for outdoor educators (MacEachren, 2013). In terms of children's development there are many reports of forest schools' physical benefits (Fjørtoft, 2001). However, there is a need for long-term, peer-reviewed research into the social and emotional impacts of these schools.

At the beginning of my research, I wondered what the individuals and groups of children would be interested in, whether they would form social groupings, and if they may choose to be involved in activities that had a potential for danger. I verbalized my worries and worked to build relationships with the children so that we could learn to trust one another. In conducting this work with feelings of fear, both my own and my students', we boosted our courage in trying new things and got practice with activities that made us feel uncomfortable. I gained confidence in both my own skills and believing in the skills of the children I was teaching. I am more sure now that children know what is best for themselves and may look for a system of support from friends and educators, their nature elders. In the end, these activities were celebrated by all of us, including families and strangers alike, which further justified these types of explorations. By documenting and reflecting upon these processes and my own growth, I have been able to learn more about myself. I feel like I can move forward as an equal partner with children.

I used an inquiry-based approach because I was curious about how I could work through the strong feelings of myself and others in an open, unstructured environment. By my providing the physical and emotional spaces, the groups led me along with them to memorable, independent experiences. By reviewing the literature, I discovered that my work was far more connected to others than I realized, and I learned that other forest schools and their pedagogies are aligned with my own practices (Forest School Canada, 2014; Fritz & Sobel, 2016; Warden, 2010). I now feel more connected with my classes and with the wider community. I would like my stories to be inspirational to others interested in offering more decision making and risky opportunities for those in their care, to trust that the right kinds of learning are taking place, feel encouraged to tackle similar challenges and feelings, and conduct research as well.

Children exhibiting similar feelings tried new things, too. It is my hope that all children can have similar adventures, that they can be trusted to be further away from direct adult attention. The experiences are held in minds and hearts. The expressions on the faces of children, their families, and the public as they recognize when new skills are being tried, learned, and embodied is nothing short of magical. It's the feeling of freedom.

REFERENCES

Broderick, J. T., & Hong, S. B. (2011). Introducing the cycle of inquiry system: A reflective inquiry practice for early childhood teacher development. *Early Childhood Research and Practice, 13*(2), 2.

Fjørtoft, I. (2001). The natural environment as a playground for children: The impact of outdoor play activities in pre-primary school children. *Early Childhood Education Journal, 29*(2), 111–117.

Forest School Canada. (2014). *Forest and nature school in Canada: A head, heart, hands approach to outdoor learning*, ed. C. Den Hoed. Canada: Forest School Canada.

Fritz, R. W., & Sobel, D. (2016). The challenge of transplanting the European forest kindergarten to North America. In D. Sobel (ed.), *Nature preschools and forest kindergartens: The handbook for outdoor learning*. Saint Paul, MN: Redleaf Press.

Goodall, J., & Hudson, G. (2014). *Seeds of hope: Wisdom and wonder from the world of plants*. New York: Grand Central Publishing.

Gray, P. (2013). *Free to learn: Why unleashing the instinct to play will make our children happier, more self-reliant, and better students for life*. New York: Basic Books.

Greene, H. W. (2013). *Tracks and shadows: Field biology as art*. Berkeley and Los Angeles, CA: University of California Press.

Jayewardene, G. (2013). Overcoming our fears: Embarking on a nature journey. In Meier, D. R., & Sisk-Hilton, S. (eds.), *Nature education with young children: Integrating inquiry and practice* (pp. 83–101). New York: Routledge.

Kyttä, M. (2004). The extent of children's independent mobility and the number of actualized affordances as criteria of a child-friendly environment. *Journal of Environmental Psychology, 24*(2), 179–198.

Laws, J. M. (2007). *The Laws field guide to the Sierra Nevada.* Berkeley, CA: Heyday.

Louv, R. (2008). *Last child in the woods.* Chapel Hill, NC: Algonquin Books.

Lytle, S. L. (2012). Some thoughts on teacher research in early childhood education. In Perry, G., Henderson, B., & Meier, D. R. (eds.), *Our inquiry, our practice: Undertaking, supporting, and learning from early childhood teacher research(ers)* (pp. 195–201). Washington, DC: NAEYC Books.

MacEachren, Z. (2013). The Canadian forest school movement. *LEARNing Landscapes, 7*(1), 219–233.

Maynard, T. (2007). Forest schools in Great Britain: An initial exploration. *Contemporary Issues in Early Childhood, 8*(4), 320–331.

Moore, R., Cosco, N., Kepez, O., & Demir, E. (2008). *My place by the bay: Prepared environments for early science learning, Bay Area Discovery Museum (BADM), Sausalito, California.* Final report to the National Science Foundation, Project #0125740.

Muir, J. (1912). *The story of my boyhood and youth.* Madison, WI: The University of Wisconsin Press.

Spiegal, B. (2017). Here we go again: No risk, no play. Retrieved from https://bernardspiegal.com/2017/12/17/no-risk-no-play/ on June 22, 2019.

Warden, C. (2010). *Nature kindergartens and forest schools: An exploration of naturalistic learning within nature kindergartens and forest schools.* Crieff, UK: Mindstretchers.

13

STUDYING NATURE

Jana Walsh

Box 13.1 Key Science and Nature Elements

- Studying trees' form and function and change over time through repeated sketching
- Exploring the interdependence of living things (insects, spiders, plants) in a garden environment
- Repeated experience and documentation in one place (school garden) to build depth of understanding and connection
- Drawing as a support for development of scientific concepts and language

Box 13.2 Key Inquiry Elements

- Nature journaling as a form of documentation and data collection
- Narrative inquiry as a tool to capture children's stories and experiences as they explore and build connections with the natural world
- Reducing direct teaching to allow children to explore and develop their own questions and ideas
- Examining children's experiences through analysis of photographs, teacher journals, and children's documentation

From Memory:

> "Fuchsias, rhododendrons, rose geraniums, poppies, and especially nasturtiums" with their surprisingly bright yellow and orange blooms and their hidden taste of sweet nectar (we were lucky we knew where to look), I can still hear my mother's richly timbered voice, daydreaming as she was forever telling us the names of local flowers and plants. As children we knew those names by heart because during our playtime in our backyard where she and Grandpa Newt gardened, and during family picnics in Golden Gate Park, we always heard my mother naming the plants we saw, and sharing her practical knowledge about caring for that specific plant. As we walked our neighborhood, we knew all the names of the local plants, even though we were ever only half-listening to my mother's stories. Today as I walk with my own children, I hear the resonance of my own deep voice, listing the same familiar names, "Pansies, snap-dragons, azaleas, and marigolds."

Since before I could remember, I loved nothing more than going outside into our backyard to play with my sister. Time spent exploring our garden was pure magic. We watched plants grow, told stories and dug in the dirt, forever discovering roly-poly bugs and enjoying a delicious, unprecedented sense of freedom and belonging. Time stood still. As a mother myself, I wanted to give my children that same liberating experience, so even though we didn't have a backyard, I took my children outside for a walk every day. Fresh air and a change of scenery rejuvenated our bodies and refreshed our spirits. My children are adults now, but we still enjoy walking together. So, for this exploration keep in mind that being outside in nature is necessary, calming and beneficial to us all.

BACKGROUND

I have taught kindergarten for 18 years, and I am passionate about nurturing my students and helping them learn through play. Returning to San Francisco State University for my Masters of Arts in Education after 15 years in the classroom reinvigorated my teaching practice. I was immediately drawn to narrative inquiry as a tool for teacher research, and I wanted to learn about garden journaling right alongside of my students. I hoped experiences in nature would provide my students with an authentic reason to write, because my education and my experience taught me that hands-on learning and free exploration is an excellent basis for learning and developing literacy. But I wondered, "How do I put this into practice?" This chapter explores the assumption that students learn better outdoors, and chronicles my teacher action research.

I was inspired to use nature journals with my students when I saw John Muir Laws speak in Berkeley. He described his life's work as an outdoorsman, artist, educator, and California naturalist. His passion is taking kids outside and teaching them to closely observe their natural world, a process he described as actually "falling in love with nature." He teaches students useful, specific drawing techniques that expand their scientific recording skills. But what struck me most was when he admitted as a student he was "a teacher's worst nightmare." He hated sitting still and he struggled with reading and writing. However, Laws (2016) said that outside he could sit observing for hours because his mind was engaged and curious, and his senses were pleased. Drawing and writing the brief descriptions and bullet points he entered in his nature journal was a short, doable, and even an enjoyable task.

A nature journal is one of the oldest reasons for writing and art. An empty book provides a place for the writer to record what she sees, hears, smells, and feels using a combination of illustration and words. Often the goal is scientific, for example to accurately capture details like date, time, temperature, size, color, line, and form. But the nature journal can also capture personal impressions, feelings, poetry, or impressionistic artwork. Nature journals provide a personal record of where one has been, and can also become an instructional tool (Laws & Breunig, 2010). Early childhood educators have used nature exploration as a source for learning and literacy since the invention of preschools.

I experienced the power of journaling in nature myself during Daniel Meier's Narrative Memoir class. Every week, we sat outside to write and reflect in our favorite nature spot. This forced me to step outside of my routine, be still, gaze at the magnolia tree in the small courtyard of my teacher's lounge, breathe in fresh air, and write for my own pleasure and purpose. The peaceful change of pace allowed me to become grounded and calm, finding my personal writing voice in the process. It felt like home.

In order to create this same nature journal experience with my students, I used the process of narrative inquiry. Narrative inquiry is a method for teachers to explore a research puzzle, something they wonder about in their teaching practice. Rather than asking a research question, which may imply a solution or an answer, "Narrative inquiry carries more of a sense of a search, a "re-search" and a searching again" (Clandinin, 2000, p. 124). Narrative inquiry asks teachers to explore our relationships and conversations with students, while acknowledging that we live rich lives outside of school as well. Data comes from field texts, such as oral stories, journals, interviews, artifacts, and photographs, which can help us better understand our classroom journey together as teacher and student in connection with each other (Clandinin, 2013; Edwards, Gandini, & Forman, 1993; Sisk-Hilton & Meier, 2017).

As I wondered what effect weekly writing time outdoors might have on my emergent writers, I asked:

- Will being outside help my students concentrate on writing for a longer time? (Sense of Place and Belonging)
- Will being in the garden elicit personal stories from my children? (Sense of Story)
- Will nature journaling help my students develop their literacy skills? (Authentic Literacy)

I collected the following data: student work samples, student dictation, my own reflective journal entries, and photographs of students writing outdoors. As I was thinking about "what" I wanted to capture in my data, I was excited to use narrative inquiry methods as a way to explore the personal stories of my students. Sisk-Hilton and Meier state,

> When we are seeking to understand students' and teachers' stories, we are slower to try and fix them. And sometimes this shift, from repairperson to storykeeper, can result in new ways of engaging with the standards as well as with our students. (Sisk-Hilton & Meier, 2017)

So, I allowed children time to experience nature, creating authentic writing opportunities grounded in that experience which would help children to build stamina, develop fine motor skills and literacy knowledge. In addition, I wanted to allow time to hear their stories. I wanted to make room for building relationships and experiencing joy.

NATURE JOURNAL PROJECT

I took my class outside, into our school garden, once a week for a 45-minute literacy block. Students brought paper, a black pen, and a clipboard. We began by studying trees, one of our science topics, and my lessons were inspired by the California Native Plant Society's curriculum. At the very start of each session I gave my students a "minilesson" in sketching. I modeled looking closely at a tree, and gave examples of breaking down the tree into bite-size bits like line, shape, and proportion. As I drew I often added a small story about myself, recapturing my own sense of wonder and calm from my earlier nature journaling experience. I worked alongside my students, and facilitated their sketching. I wanted to reduce how much I used my direct teaching to allow more of an open-ended, peaceful, natural experience with my students.

Originally, I only planned to teach nature journals for two months, but it was so powerful that I continued to use nature as a springboard for literacy for the rest of the year. I shifted my teaching focus to explore flowers, vegetables, insects, birds, and even the clouds. We took field trips to the local shoreline and the botanical gardens, bringing our paper and pencils to sketch in real time. I learned to reflect in my journal, listen to students' stories, take dictation, photograph lessons, and to look closely at student work. As a teacher, I was amazed by the possibilities that unfolded using these narrative inquiry tools to capture and reflect on our outdoor experience. For both teacher and students, outside there was a synergy that allowed more pleasure, understanding and deeper connections. To illustrate some of my "aha" moments and expand on the themes that came out of my research, I will focus on just a few early spring days that we spent out in our school garden exploring trees.

A SENSE OF PLACE AND BELONGING

Simply moving our work outdoors during the school day was interesting and exciting to the class right from the beginning. On our first day they asked, "When is it time to go outside, Mrs. Walsh?" As students settled into working around a tree, I could see that they were concentrating because they took more time drawing and they added elaborate details. This echoed the research that simply being outside may help a child relax and think more clearly (Torquati, Gabriel, Jones-Branch, & Leeper-Miller, 2010).

Inspired by Shagoury and Power (2012), I focused my attention on the experience by note-taking. My teacher journal helped me remember the experience with detail and depth. My entry from this day read:

> Students spread themselves out all over, but they're not bothering each other! Outside there is room for each child to assume a comfortable position, I see their bodies are relaxed and content. This is so COOL! There's hardly any noise, it's quiet. Everyone's working. Usually in the garden children get a little too active and playful.

> Usually I'm talking in my "teacher voice" reminding them of the rules, "Do this!" or, "Don't do that!" Not today. Today is peaceful. Matthew told me about the apple trees in his grandmother's backyard, and Teresa said she helps her mother in the garden growing tomatoes. Ahh! There's a lot to say about the garden. Overall, the kids drew with detail, and stayed on topic. Today feels different.

The other way I shifted my focus was by intentionally including photographs during the nature journaling time. These garden photographs became powerful tools, allowing me to focus on and think about what happens during the school day, even in a single hour. It was fun and challenging to capture what was happening by zooming in or zooming out on the action. Each camera angle showed something slightly different: the overall class activity or the quiet wonder of one child. Photographs of Mark, Figure 13.1, and Gabby, Figure 13.2,

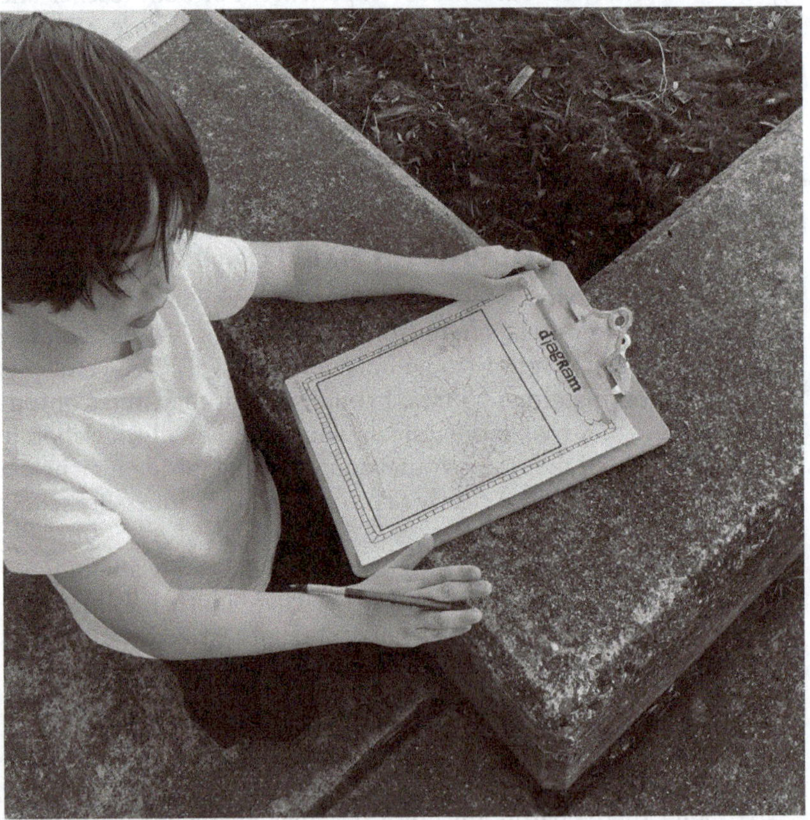

Figure 13.1 Mark sketching comfortably in the garden.

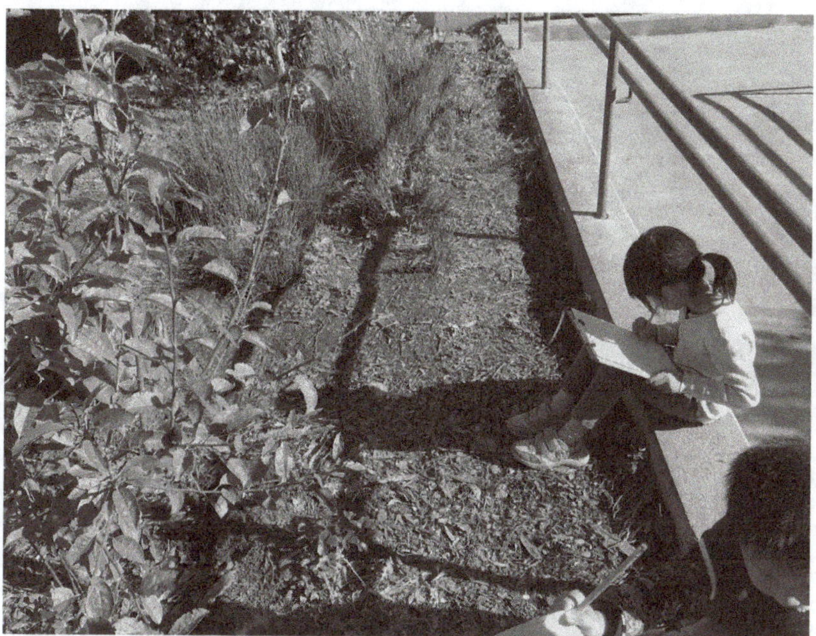

Figure 13.2 Gabby sketching comfortably in the garden.

captured the mood of calm stillness as the students sketched, clearly absorbed. Looking at my photographs later helps me to remember with clarity and emotion what happened that day, *what we were doing*. As students and teacher together, we were discovering our world, marking our place in it, and creating our sense of belonging.

This brought to mind John Muir Laws talking about kids being able to "fall in love with nature." Falling in love takes time, and I noticed that in the garden my students didn't become bored, restless, or ask when they could "be done," as they have so often when faced with more predictable tasks inside the classroom. Outdoors, students worked with focus and concentration, and their nature work was elaborate. They explored their environment, and became scientists, teaching each other. These changes speak to the power of stepping outdoors, experiencing the difference in our bodies and our minds. The photographs of Maddy, Figure 13.3, and Emma, Figure 13.4, in the garden capture the sense of peaceful curiosity and affection that research tells us to expect outdoors.

Place-based education emphasizes grounding a student's knowledge in practical, hands-on experience to ensure that knowledge is not simply an abstraction. Studying one's place allows one to reconnect

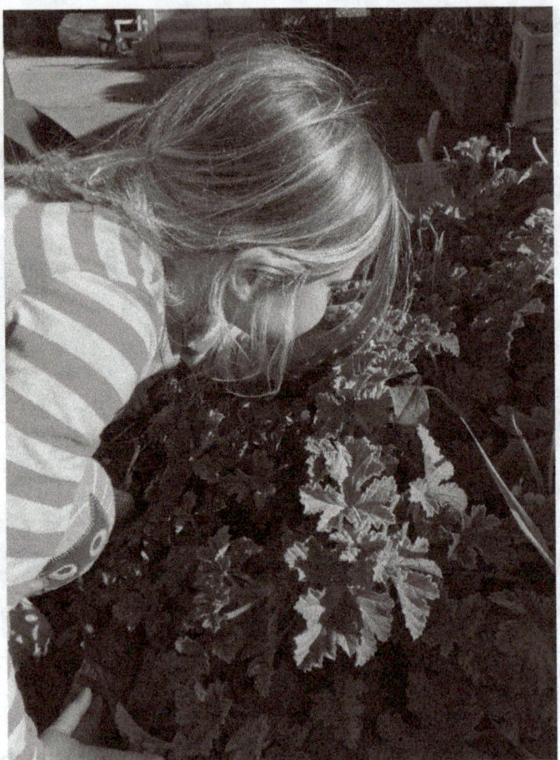

Figure 13.3 Maddy smelling a flower in the garden.

and build a sense of belonging to and caring for both a community and a physical place, creating sense of home. Orr (2013) describes this process as becoming a good inhabitant, which requires knowledge of place, observation, care, and rootedness. Quiet time in our garden helps my students build memories around this school-place in a more intimate way, allowing them to develop a deeper sense of belonging and caring. This work reinforces the values of my school community, which hopes that students feel at home on campus and they begin to practice stewardship here.

Working in the garden also provided me with an opportunity to ease up on my direct teaching practice, instead letting the students' creative process unfold in a more natural way. I wrote in my journal, listened to the kindergarteners talk, and answered questions. Time spent outdoors reminded me more of free time than of a lesson. Being in the garden also allowed me to let go of the classroom-based notion that students "sit still," so instead I allowed the students to move about,

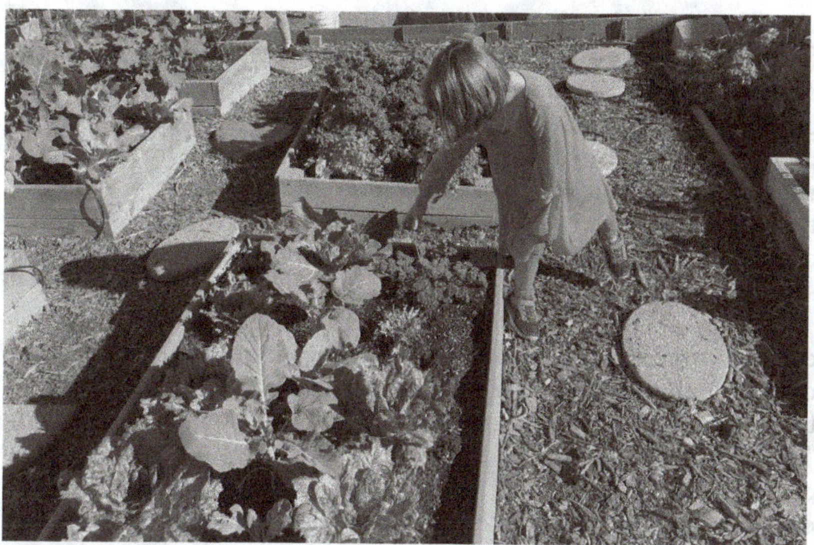

Figure 13.4 Emma touching a plant in the garden.

seeking their own space and body positions. I think the physical flexibility of outdoor work, as opposed to the rigidity of in-classroom seating arrangements, largely accounted for my students' ability to stay focused on their journals.

SENSE OF STORY

Children make sense of their world through stories. Five-year-old students are more capable in speech than in writing, so teachers must pay attention and listen closely to uncover the richness of their students' real and imagined lives. Listening to and transcribing the organic stories that arise while children play can help a teacher gain insight into a child's thinking and identity, and it proves to the child that what they are saying has value (Paley, 2012). When a child has ample time to develop and narrate his experience with a proficient and interested adult, it allows the child's thinking to become more complex, his ideas to become more well-formed and his memory more enriched and deeply engrained (Edwards, Gandini, & Forman, 1993; Engel, 1995; Vygotsky, 1978).

Sisk-Hilton (Meier & Sisk-Hilton, 2013) describes a preschool field trip to the beach, when a lost bucket became a sandy mess, and a complex science experiment for the children. Teachers provoked their interest, asking questions like, "I wonder …?" and "what would happen if …?," noticing that these young children had not yet learned to wait for teachers to provide correct answers. In fact, it may be best to allow children's scientific understanding to develop from their extended play. Sisk-Hilton states, "Young children move in and out between pretend adventures with fairies and examination of the tree stumps in which they might live. We need not prevent this mixing of imagination and direct observation" (Meier & Sisk-Hilton, 2013, p. 22) because children take up big ideas when they play. Play situated in natural spaces allows children to build their understanding of our world.

The garden was a natural springboard for all of our stories; this combined beautifully with the narrative inquiry techniques of dictation, photography, and teacher journaling to draw my attention to the students' stories. Listening closely changed how I thought about "all that talking." I tried to circulate between students' ongoing conversations, and listening when a child wanted to talk to me. Students told each other and me stories about something they saw in the garden, or about an imaginary scene taking place in the garden, or asked me questions. Through the narrative inquiry teaching practice, I had time to listen.

One of the stories I listened to was told to me by a 5-year-old student named Sally. Sally's story illustrates that written work in kindergarten is only one piece of a larger story. Paper provides a place to record, a place to remember. While Sally's picture, Figure 13.5, appears fairly simple, she has a lot to say: "The apples growed [*sic*] on the small tree. Some flowers were in the tree; they had a little bit of stuff in there. That is the little spider. He was crawling around." Speaking to Sally and uncovering the hidden depth in her drawing taught me that it is important to ask children to elaborate, honoring their sense of story.

I was lucky enough to catch a photograph, Figure 13.6, of the moment that Sally spotted the spider. It helps me remember the real, time-consuming work that goes into composing; before a storyteller even begins, they have to observe, develop, and inhabit their story. In the photo Sally and two friends are discussing the little apple growing on the tree and tracking the movements of the spider. Sally, in the yellow shirt, is making meaning from this experience. I remember she was trying to get everyone to agree about where the spider lived. Sally was imagining the life of the spider, and co-constructing that spider's story with her peers. Just like in the "sandy beach" story, Sally's spider story illustrates how children learn through both imagination and scientific thinking to build an understanding of their world. These girls spent a long time studying that tree, and showed many classmates that spider. It became their tree and they were the experts that day.

20
The apples growed on the Small tree.
Some flowers were in the tree, they had a little bit of stuff in there.
That is the little spider he was crawling around.
Day 5

Figure 13.5 Sally's drawing of the apple tree, with dictation.

Another little girl, Elly, an early English language learner has been quiet, shy, and careful about speaking at school. Shown in Figure 13.7, she drew an amazing tree, colored it beautifully, and actually spoke up to me when I asked her about her picture. As Elly pointed to her drawing she said, "Flower. Leaf. Trunk. Butterfly." That was the most sophisticated language I've heard her use all year. I think that having both the garden experience and the picture in front of her gave Elly a concrete reference for her language and something important to say. She wanted to tell this story, and by the look in her eyes I knew she had a story just as rich as Sally's. Even though Elly didn't have sufficient English, I could sense her passion and intention. Valuing her story, I gave her warm encouragement, repeated her story, and asked her questions, "Did you see a butterfly?" "Was there only a little blossom?" I believe sharing Elly's apple tree story helped us deepen our

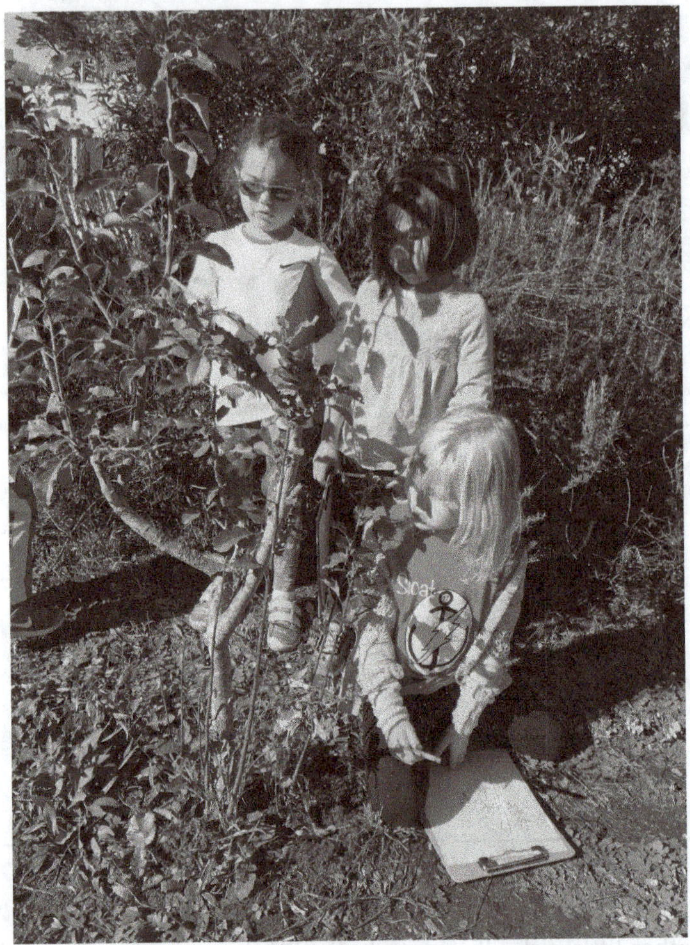

Figure 13.6 Three girls looking at the apple tree and discussing the spider.

relationship. She looked so proud of herself, excited to share with me what she knew about apple trees. I think she was courageous for speaking up, and I feel grateful for her trust.

These stories illustrate what research tells us, that when teachers shift their attention to listen to children's stories, they become more attuned to the relationships inside and out of the classroom, as listening to children's stories deepens our personal connection and understanding of our students, as well as ourselves as teachers (Sisk-Hilton & Meier, 2016). Clandinin (2013) suggests that the field of inquiry start with the ongoing conversations between teachers and students, as "conversations create a space for the stories of both participants and

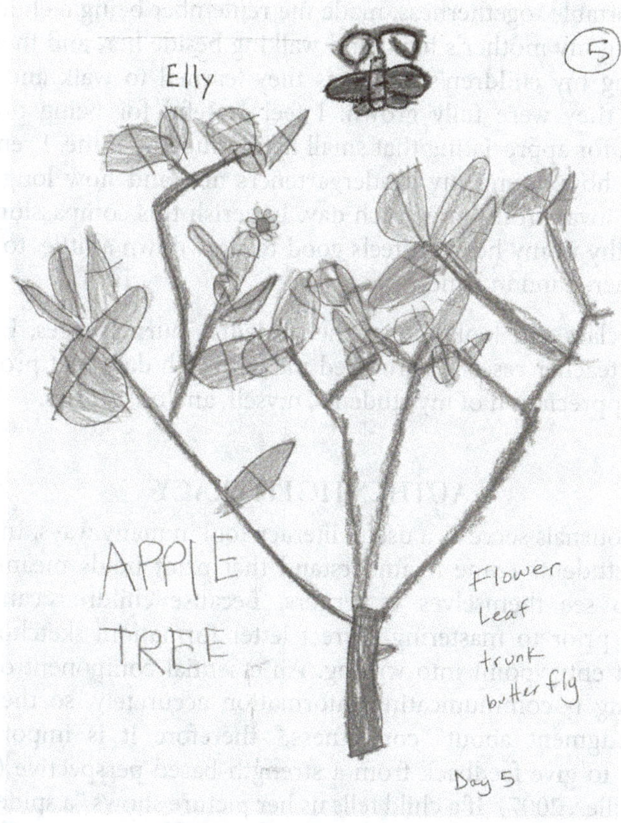

Figure 13.7 Elly's drawing of an apple tree, with dictation.

researchers to be composed and heard" (p. 45) and that when we situate ourselves as living alongside of our students we become part of the stories we, and they, tell. I see this connectedness in my journal entry from that day:

> This day was amazing. There was so much talking and storytelling and discovery, apples were actually growing on the small tree, and children were especially fascinated by of all the little insects crawling around. There were ants, spiders, butterflies and bees. They were talking to each other a mile a minute and I was trying to listen, trying to enjoy the experience. It was a beautiful day.
>
> Jacqueline came up beside me and slipped her small hand into mine. We simply held hands, as she walked beside me quietly. Something about her openness and her trust, our

> comfortable togetherness, made me remember being a child and holding my mother's hand and walking beside her, and then me holding my children's hands as they learned to walk and later when they were fully grown. I feel grateful for being present today, for appreciating that small hand touching mine. I remembered how young my kindergarteners are, and how long they spend away from home each day. I cherish this compassion and empathy in my heart. It feels good to slow down a little, to walk together, hand in hand.

Back in class as I looked over the students' journal pages, I realized that my teacher research provided me with rich data that provoked a deeper appreciation of my students, myself, and our stories.

AUTHENTIC LITERACY

Nature journals serve as a useful literacy tool in many ways. In kindergarten, students come to understand that print holds meaning, and begin to see themselves as writers. Because children can master drawing prior to mastering correct letter formation, sketching is an excellent entry point into writing. An essential component of nature journaling is communicating information accurately, so there is no value judgment about "correctness," therefore it is important for teachers to give feedback from a strength-based perspective (Hobart, 2005; Miller, 2007). If a child tells us her picture shows "a spider on the short apple tree" and she has drawn that with lines and circles, this is an excellent journal entry because she has recorded her story, knows that her print holds meaning, and has a sense of authorship. I compliment her, appreciating her good observation skills and rich detail. As teachers, we build on the positive. If students feel encouraged, they will keep working. This repeated practice, combined with seeing mentor and peer examples, and further discussion will help the child move to more sophisticated drawing and writing naturally (Laws & Breunig, 2010) (see Figure 13.8).

The experience of nature journaling provided my students with opportunities to practice reading and writing for pleasure and purpose, and to see themselves as writers. For the purpose of describing five and six year olds who don't "write" in the traditional sense, I define "writer" as someone who has a story to tell, and composes that story on paper using a combination of drawing, writing, and dictation. In their nature journals, my students used literacy the way writers do in the real world. Writing in the garden meant my children could explore

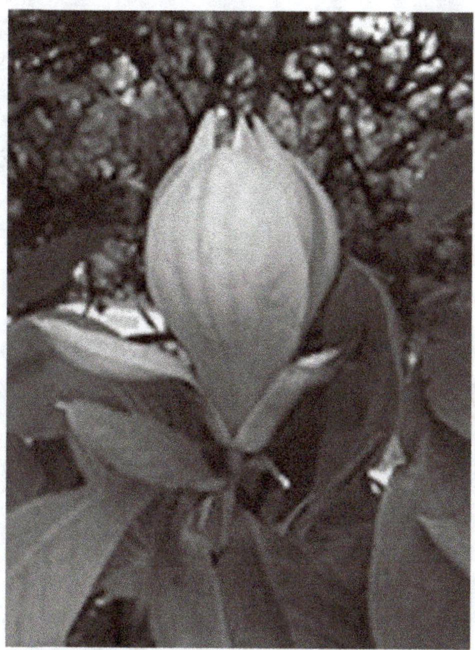

Figure 13.8 Magnolia blossom, an inspiration for sketching.

and observe first, so that this direct experience provided a meaningful inspiration for their writing. They created detailed sketching, told rich stories, and did some writing. They were motivated to draw in a way that impressed me, and this garden experience was more engaging than our regular indoor writing time.

These drawings from Mark, Figure 13.9, and Emma, Figure 13.10, illustrate how my students found their nature experience to be meaningful inspiration for their compositions. That day we went into the courtyard to see the magnolia tree. For the mini-lesson, I modeled how to label the parts of the tree and asked the children to try to do the same, as I was spelling aloud the words, "tree, leaves, blossoms and trunk." Their sketches of the magnolia tree were full of wonderful lush pink petals. Although each drawing is distinct in style, they both capture the blooming tree that day, and include the petals scattered on the ground. Each child had a unique approach to labeling their drawing. Mark wrote his words in and among the branches, while Emma wrote the words more like an orderly list. I appreciate that they had the freedom to fill their paper as they wished, and that both papers achieved the goal of conveying meaning.

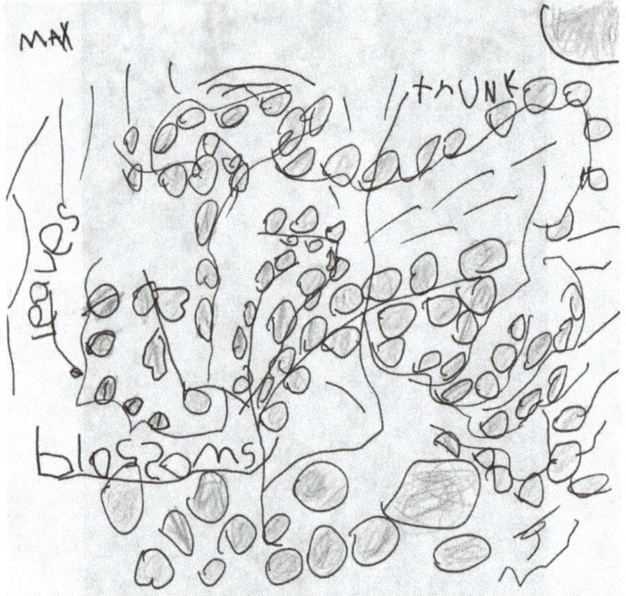

Today we saw a Magnolia Tree after the rain. It had big white and pink blossoms and green leaves. There were a lot of petals on the ground.

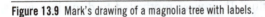

Figure 13.9 Mark's drawing of a magnolia tree with labels.

In my journal I noticed how Mark was sketching in the courtyard:

> Seeing the magnolia tree was sweet, after the rain, with all its petals fallen around on the ground. The children wanted so much to touch the petals, play with them, and collect them. The pinkish-white, soft petals were still wet. I let the children hold the petals until we had to leave the courtyard. It was a shame to leave, such a beautiful day and finally no rain. Ah, spring! Mark was holding his pencil up to the tree, then drawing, then looking up again, as if to measure the tree, just like a painter might. He has so totally recorded the fullness of the tree. His paper is bursting with blossoms and he has made it so dreamy-looking. He's such an imaginative little guy. I'm going to miss his smile and sly jokes next year. Teaching is bittersweet! We are always learning about new children, embracing them, and then letting them go.

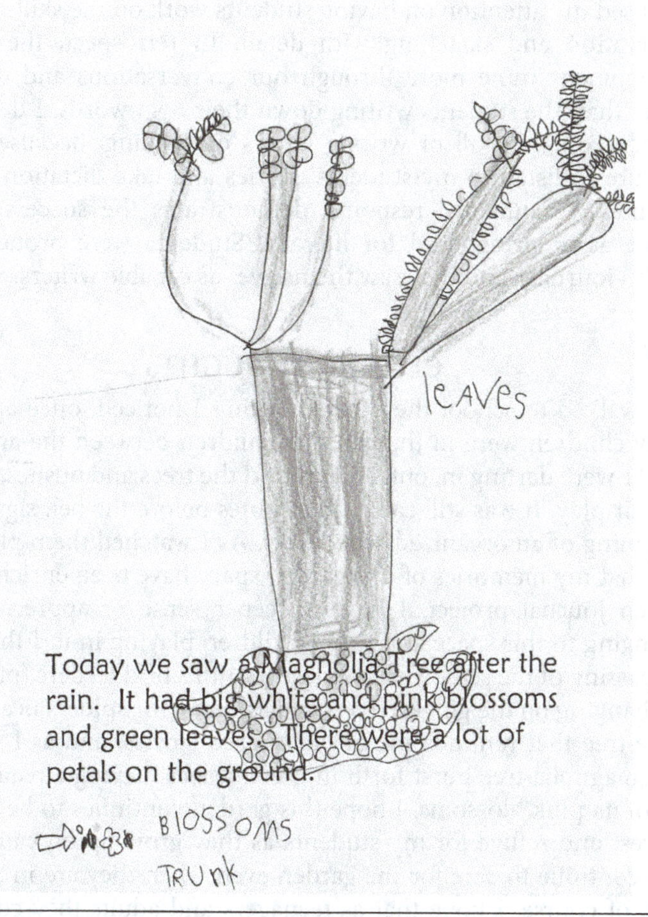
leaves
Today we saw a Magnolia Tree after the rain. It had big white and pink blossoms and green leaves. There were a lot of petals on the ground.
BLOSSOMS
TRUNK

Figure 13.10 Emma's drawing of a magnolia tree with labels.

Emma's paper speaks volumes. She has also recorded so much detail, she must have been very attentive and excited to record what she saw, her tree has beautiful proportions, a strong trunk, and countless leaves and blossoms. She said, "I saw the trunk was a little bit fat, and the leaves were small, the branches were long and thin. The blossoms were pink." Even though it is easy to appreciate Emma's artistry, it is important to remember that all of these pictures contain a wealth of information about the tree.

At the end of each lesson, my students were always excited to show me their journal pages. As the year went on and each student filled up his nature journal, I also noticed that they enjoyed rereading their previous pages, remembering their stories. Looking back, I realize that

I focused my attention on having students work on the skills of careful observation and sketching with detail. In retrospect, the language development came more through our conversations and dictations, rather than the students writing down their own words. I decided not to focus on the skill of writing letters or spelling, because it was a pleasure to listen to my students' stories and take dictation this time around. My students' response demonstrates the success of using nature as a springboard for literacy. Students were proud of their garden journals, and they saw themselves as capable writers.

CLOSING THOUGHTS

As I walked to school the other morning I noticed, once again, how many children were in the garden. Children between the ages of five and 11 were darting in, out, and around the trees and bushes, absorbed in their play. It was still early, 20 minutes before the bell signaling the beginning of an organized school day. As I watched them play, I realized that my memories of this garden space have been enriched by my garden journal project. I have a deeper sense of appreciation and belonging to this space and to the children playing in it. I think about the passing of the season as I see last-month's bird feeders (pine cones) still hanging on the gingko trees, and as I scan for spiders near the little apple tree that reminds me of our shared stories, and as I watch the lone magnolia tree burst forth in green leaves, having already lost the last of its pink blossoms. I hope this garden continues to be a place of interest and refuge for my students as they grow up on campus, that they continue to care for the garden even when they are in 5th grade. And, of course, I hope that as teenagers and adults they continue to step outside and enjoy nature as a source of inspiration.

I enjoyed the entire nature journal project. I was rejuvenated by expanding my teaching repertoire and this regular practice helped me build new muscle memory. I took my class outside to write, I routinely wrote in my teacher journal, I took photographs weekly, and I took dictation from my students. Each of these practices produced interesting results, but the synthesis created a dynamic and exciting learning environment for all of us. This project helped me learn more about my students and what they found interesting. When I listened more closely to their stories, it helped me know each student a little bit better and hold them more dearly in my mind and in my heart. I look forward to continuing my narrative inquiry journey in the future, and I would encourage all teachers to try some of these practices in their classroom.

This project also brought me full circle, in the sense that it helped me remember who I was when I was my students' age. Working in the garden helped me think about how I can more closely align my everyday teaching practices with my deepest wishes. Grounding this project in local nature provided the students and me with inspiration and joy. Stepping outside with the students, I felt revived. When I look at this portfolio of work, I can see how these narrative inquiry teaching practices helped me demonstrate how I valued my students, how I kept them at the center of my attention and of my teaching. This work reminded me of the Reggio Emilia preschool teachers who keep diaries of their children, which help make visible the heart of their practice, by giving the child the awareness that he is the "subject of love" (Edwards & Rinaldi, 2009).

Experimenting with narrative inquiry and nature journaling has also broadened my identity as a teacher. I appreciated this academic opportunity to study and reflect on my teaching experience with nature journals, and now I feel more at home as a teacher–researcher. It has been a fabulous journey redefining my identity in my classroom and in my teaching community. I'm excited to start a new project next year, I wonder where it will take me.

REFERENCES

Clandinin, D. J. (2000). *Narrative inquiry: Experience and story in qualitative research*. San Francisco, CA: Jossey-Bass Publishers.

Clandinin, D. J. (2013). *Engaging in narrative inquiry*. Walnut Creek, CA: Left Coast Press.

Edwards, C. P., Gandini, L., & Forman, G. E. (1993). *The hundred languages of children: The Reggio Emilia approach to early childhood education*. Norwood, NJ: Ablex PubCorp.

Edwards, C. P., & Rinaldi, C. (2009). *The diary of Laura: Perspectives on a Reggio Emilia Diary*. St. Paul, MN: Redleaf Press.

Engel, S. L. (1995). *The stories children tell: Making sense of the narratives of childhood*. New York: Freeman.

Hobart, A. (2005). Sketching in nature. *Science Teacher, 72*(1), 30–33.

Laws, J. M. (2016, September). *The art and science of keeping a nature journal*. Teacher workshop presented at the Lawrence Hall of Science, Berkeley, CA.

Laws, J. M., & Breunig, E. (2010). Opening the world through nature journaling: Integrating art, science & language arts. California Native Plant Society. Retrieved from www.cnps.org/cnps/education/curriculum/owtj_dl/cnps_curriculum-otwtnj.pdf on June 12, 2019.

Meier, D. R., & Sisk-Hilton, S. (eds.). (2013). *Nature education with young children: Integrating inquiry and practice*. New York: Routledge.

Miller, D. L. (2007). The seeds of learning: Young children develop important skills through their gardening activities at a midwestern early education program. *Applied Environmental Education and Communication*, *6*(1), 49–66.

Orr, D. (2013). Place and pedagogy. *NAMTA Journal*, *38*(1), 183–188.

Paley, V. (2012). Teacher research – it can be done: Getting started. *Voices of Practitioners*, *7*(1), 3–6.

Shagoury, R., & Power, B. M. (2012). *Living the questions: A guide for teacher-researchers*. Portsmouth, NH: Stenhouse.

Sisk-Hilton, S., & Meier, D. R. (2016). *Narrative inquiry in early childhood and elementary school: Learning to teach, teaching well*. New York: Routledge.

Torquati, J., Gabriel, M. M., Jones-Branch, J., & Leeper-Miller, J. (2010). A natural way to nurture children's development and learning. *Young Children*, *65*(6), 98–104.

Vygotsky, L. S. (1978). *Mind in society: The development of higher psychological processes*. Cambridge, MA: Harvard University Press.

EPILOGUE

As this book was going to press, several news outlets reported on a study in which researchers seemingly quantified the ideal amount of time people should spend in nature (Sheik, 2019; White, Alcock, Grellier, Wheeler, Hartig, Warber, & Fleming, 2019). As I (Stephanie) read the key finding, that 120 minutes per week maximized benefits of nature for humans, I imagined that fitness trackers would soon be upgraded to count minutes in nature on top of steps, pulse, and hours of sleep and that whole new industries might spring up to monetize reaching this target number. And despite my own commitment to nature education and to finding nature small and big in daily life, I also thought, oh great, another way to fail as a parent and teacher. If we begin counting minutes in nature as the measure of success, we will always know when we have failed to provide enough, but how will we know what good has happened in the 30 minutes spent climbing a neighborhood tree and building fairy houses?

What bothered me in this round of "more nature" headlines was the simplistic quantification of something that is important in part because it cannot be easily reduced to a single number or strategy or outcome. Children's experiences in nature are often powerful, but this power is not easily measured. Becoming both skilled and brave enough to fish and to light a fire surely impacted Heather B. Taylor's students (see Chapter 12), and overcoming fear and building skills does in fact take time and repeated experiences in a place. Observing a tree over the course of a year, as Jana Walsh describes in Chapter 13, allows children to attune themselves to subtle changes and interdependence of living organisms that may not become obvious in a single experience. To learn in and through nature, time certainly matters. But time spent is the roughest of measures for the potential of children's coming to know and learn in nature.

Rather than counting up to a total to be checked off, the stories of learning in this book explore what happens to children in and through time in nature. Sometimes the world seems to slow down, and children whose attention spans in other contexts are fleeting can spend hours puzzling over how to represent a forest they are coming to know on a paper map. The complexity of natural settings invites children to come back over and over, to build their understanding and connection to place a little at a time. Minutes spent do matter, not for the minutes themselves but for how children are able to use expansive time to build meaning.

So if minutes are not the best measure of the value of nature-based education, how do we account for what is gained when teachers support children to experience and learn in nature? The educators in this book point the way, offering rich documentation that continually circles back to time in the form of repeated experience, slowing down to notice, returning to ideas over and over. Time is represented in children's drawings that grow more detailed and accurate as young scientists and artists return to an object or creature of interest, with each visit noticing something new, choosing a new detail to represent and wonder about. Time is expressed through ongoing outings to urban forests, where children sometimes run with abandon, sometimes build a home for real or imagined creatures, and sometimes sit quietly and notice, building comfort and connection with a place that becomes their own through time and experience. Time is required in conversations that grow over days and weeks, immersing children in ideas about how they feel about and respond to color, what it means to care for living things, how to reconcile culturally bound ideas of "good" and "bad" with a growing understanding that nature moves and changes on a different plane than human morality (see Chapter 6 for Patricia Sullivan's discussion).

Just as many of the educators in this book facilitated nature experiences for their students in small, available spaces more than in large stretches of harder to access wilderness, so too they found small moments of time as well as large expanses to support children's explorations. New experiences may be exciting, but they also arouse caution and sometimes fear, as Gita Jayewardene (see Chapter 4) found in her students' exploration of wood lice and other small creatures. Time and attention allows curiosity and understanding to grow, and sometimes brief experiences build a base for longer and more complex future explorations.

This book is a compilation of teachers' careful documentation of time. Their willingness to not only notice and engage but also to document how young children learn in, with, and through nature allows us a series of windows into children's lives. Photos, teacher journal entries, dictation of children's thoughts and ideas, records of conversations, and children's own art and artifacts allow us a glimpse into children's lives and how they make meaning of the natural world. This gift of children's and teachers' stories offers, I think, powerful evidence of both why and how to prioritize experience in the natural world as a cornerstone of early childhood education. Not because we are counting minutes, but because attention to place and inquiry into children's interactions in and with nature builds connections that persist beyond a particular time.

REFERENCES

Sheikh, Knvul (2019, June 13). How much nature is enough? 120 minutes a week, doctors say. *New York Times*. Retrieved from www.nytimes.com/2019/06/13/health/nature-outdoors-health.html on September 21, 2019.

White, M. P., Alcock, I., Grellier, J., Wheeler, B. W., Hartig, T., Warber, S. L., & Fleming, L. E. (2019). Spending at least 120 minutes a week in nature is associated with good health and wellbeing. *Scientific Reports*, *9*(1), 7730.

INDEX

Page numbers in *italics* denote figures.